DRIVEN TO MURDER

Shepherd: Okay, I'm sitting here and I'm watching you, Cody. I mean, you've got tears in your eyes and I need to know why. You were talking earlier, and you said that if you lie, it will always come back to bite you in the butt. That you get it worse. Is that what you said?

Posey: Yes.

Shepherd: All right, Cody. You need to tell me what happened.

(Around this point, Cody Posey said, "I might as well tell you the truth," and there was a whole shift in his demeanor and the things he said.)

Posey: I got tired of Dad hitting me. Yelling and screaming at me all the time. He hit me and I couldn't take it anymore.

Shepherd: So what did you do, Cody?

Posey: I tried getting rid of them.

Shepherd: How?

Posey: Get him off this planet, cuz I'd be better here without him.

Shepherd: So what did you do, Cody?

Posey: I shot him.

Also by Robert Scott

Killer Dad

Dangerous Attraction

Deadfall

Like Father Like Son

Married to Murder

Monster Slayer

Rope Burns

Savage

Unholy Sacrifice

saw a light in Cody's eyes. Cody told me, 'Don't worry, Mr. Mitchell. I won't disappoint anybody.'

"The public doesn't think Cody is a threat, and the people I trust are the people of Lincoln and Chaves Counties, who don't think Cody is a threat. This was a situational incident. When Cody graduates from college, I hope he will invite me to his graduation. I have great confidence in him. I expect him to do great things. It's a new age for the children of New Mexico."

Sandra Grisham, Verlin Posey and his family, Pat and Leona Basham, walked out of the courtroom without a word to reporters. They were obviously crushed by Judge Counts's decision. As Cody was led from the courtroom by a bailiff, cheers and applause finally rang out, and shouts of "We love you, Cody!" filled the courtroom from his supporters, until other bailiffs made them simmer down. As he had done throughout the trial, Judge Counts remained quiet and dignified at the bench, finishing up paperwork, and uttering not another word when he walked into his chambers.

Gary Mitchell, Corliss Clees, Jake and Sandy Schmid, Slim Britton, former juror Norman Patterson, and hosts of others gathered on the courthouse steps, however, for a press conference. The constant among all of them were the smiles of joy and relief on their faces. There was a thrill of celebration in the air on the courthouse steps. Cars cruising up and down the street honked their horns in support, their occupants just having learned the outcome by word of mouth, which spread through the city of Alamogordo like wildfire. For Cody and his supporters, it was if a blanket of gloom had suddenly been lifted.

In front of a bank of microphones, the man of the hour was Gary Mitchell, who had seen Cody through his darkest hours since July 5, 2004. Mitchell said, "I didn't sleep last night at all. Cody was apprehensive before the decision. To thousands of people, Judge Counts is certainly a hero for what he did. It was a great reflection of justice. I felt all along that he had to follow the laws and he believed Cody is amenable to treatment. He followed the law. He didn't have to. To me, that's courageous. When the decision was read, finally you prison as an adult. By factor six, however, the tide began to change.

Sixth factor was prior history. Judge Counts found that Cody had no prior history of violence or trouble with the law, and this was in favor that he could receive treatment.

Seventh factor was safety of the public. Counts said, "Sequoyah is a secure facility available to children. This weighs in favor of treatment. It was a situational nature of violence."

Eighth—any other factor. "No other factors weigh in."

Judge Counts said in a solemn voice, "The court finds that the weight of evidence received leads to the conclusion that the respondent, Cody Posey, at the time of the offenses, suffered from post-traumatic stress disorder and depression. Since respondent's detention, respondent has continued to suffer from PTSD.

"I have considered all the factors in this case—the state has failed to meet its burden that Cody Posey is to be sentenced as an adult. The court has no discretion to find an adult sentence. The court finds that there is a possibility of treatment for Cody Posey. Therefore, the court commits Cody Posey to the state's Child, Youth and Families Division until the age of twenty-one."

There was a huge sigh of relief on the side of the gallery that was pro-Cody, and stunned disbelief for those who wanted a harsh sentence for him. No shouting and cheering, because everyone knew that Judge Counts would not allow emotional outbursts in his courtroom. One image, however, became indelibly etched on everyone's memory of that moment, and photographer Ellis Neel, of the *Alamogordo Daily News,* captured it in a photo. Corliss Clees raised her hands in the air in silent exultation, with a huge smile on her face. The caption below the photo would read: HALLELUJAH!

sonal whims or the tide of public opinion is the basis of my decision today.

"I have sworn to apply the law of the state of New Mexico," he said. "I find that Cody Posey was fourteen years old on July 5, 2004, and the juvenile code controls the law in this case. Under the law, a youthful offender may receive an adult sentence."

Judge Counts spoke of the issues before him now: Was Cody Posey amenable to treatment? Was there a place in New Mexico that could treat Cody, and if he was released, would Cody be a threat to the community? There were eight key factors that Judge Counts had to take into account when formulating a sentence, and each factor could be an aggravating circumstance, mitigating circumstance, or neutral.

Number one was "seriousness of the crime." Judge Counts said, "There is no offense more serious than first-degree murder." He found the circumstances to be aggravating against Cody.

Number two was premeditation—Judge Counts also found circumstances to be aggravating against Cody.

Number three was the use of a firearm. Cody had used a firearm to kill his victims—aggravating.

The fourth factor was against a person or property. Obviously, it was against persons—aggravating.

Fifth—dealt with socialization and maturity of the perpetrator. It was neutral, since Judge Counts found that Cody was intelligent and mature for a fourteen-year-old, but he also lacked "street smarts" and was socially immature.

By the sheer numbers alone now, things did not look good for Cody Posey. There had not been one factor in his favor, and it seemed that when the numbers of factors were tallied up, Cody would be sentenced to life in

Chapter 23

Light at the End of the Tunnel

At 9:00 A.M., on February 23, 2006, into a courtroom packed with family members, friends, reporters, and citizens of the area, Judge Counts entered from his chambers and walked to his chair behind a podium at the front of the court. He looked tired and careworn, as if he had spent a long night wrestling with the momentous decision he had to make. There was absolute silence in the courtroom as Judge Counts slowly put on his glasses and began to speak.

As a preamble to the decision, Judge Counts said that many in the public believed that judges made their decisions of sentencing on their personal beliefs, but that was not the case. "I've heard comments since beginning this case, 'I wouldn't want your job.' I take that to mean that the decisions I have to make are an exercise in unrestrained discretion without any guidance from the law. The law of the state of New Mexico and not my per-

your Honor to sentence Cody Posey as a child today—
a man I welcome into my home and at my table."

After everyone had spoken, and as the gallery began
to clear, one person there said to another about Judge
Counts, "I wouldn't want to be in his shoes right now."
In fact, they were very big shoes to fill. What he thought
and what he decided upon would not only affect Cody
Posey, but members of his extended family and the
whole state of New Mexico and how they viewed the juvenile judicial system within their state.

DRIVEN TO MURDER

ROBERT SCOTT

PINNACLE BOOKS
Kensington Publishing Corp.
http://www.kensingtonbooks.com

PINNACLE BOOKS are published by

Kensington Publishing Corp.
850 Third Avenue
New York, NY 10022

All Kensington Titles, Imprints, and Distributed Lines are available at special quantity discounts for bulk purchases for sales promotions, premiums, fund-raising, and educational or institutional use. Special book excerpts or customized printings can also be created to fit specific needs. For details, write or phone the office of the Kensington special sales manager: Kensington Publishing Corp., 850 Third Avenue, New York, NY 10022, attn: Special Sales Department, Phone: 1-800-221-2647.

Pinnacle and the P logo Reg. U.S. Pat. & TM Off.

ISBN-13: 978-0-7860-1819-2
ISBN-10: 0-7860-1819-4

First Printing: January 2008

10 9 8 7 6 5 4 3 2 1

Printed in the United States of America

Acknowledgments

I'd like to thank the staff at the Otero County Courthouse and Lincoln County Courthouse for their cooperation on this book. Also, to the people of Alamogordo, New Mexico. Special thanks go to my editor at Kensington Publishing Corporation, Michaela Hamilton.

Chapter 1

Sam's Ranch

As a journalist, Sam Donaldson had been all over the world, covering its hot spots and the halls of power in Washington, D.C. He always had a nostalgia for his roots, however, having grown up in the ranch lands of New Mexico. In his later years Donaldson bought three working ranches around Roswell, New Mexico, that ran hundreds of head of cattle and over a thousand sheep. The ranches were generally known by their local names— Slaughter Ranch, Pajarito Ranch, and the main ranch complex known as Chavez Canyon Ranch. Sam's ranch headquarters was located at Chavez Canyon Ranch.

The Chavez Canyon Ranch, located near the small town of Hondo, New Mexico, was reached by a road that ran about a mile and a quarter to the property from Highway 380. In the summer of 2001, Donaldson needed a new ranch manager and he heard from others in the area that Verlin Posey was a good manager on another ranch. Sam contacted Verlin, who mulled over the idea of switching from the ranch where he was working, but in the end decided not to make the change. Instead, Verlin told his brother, Delbert Paul Posey, about the job, and Delbert, better known as Paul, applied for the position. Donaldson interviewed Paul and one other man.

Wanting to make sure about the choices, Donaldson and his wife looked over the two men's résumés and phoned Royce Griggs, manager of the Diamond A Ranch in the Hondo Valley. The Diamond A was owned by longtime friend Robert Anderson, and then later by the ex-president Gerald Ford. The Donaldsons trusted Griggs's opinion, and Griggs had known the Posey family for many years. In fact, the Poseys had lived on the Diamond A Ranch for a period of time. Griggs said that the Posey boys, Verlin and Paul, were "very honest and straightforward. You can rely on them."

With that information, Sam Donaldson hired Paul Posey and his family, which included wife Tryone, son Cody, and stepdaughter Marilea, to come and live on the ranch and manage it. Donaldson was very satisfied by the way they got right to work on the property and tried to improve conditions there.

Donaldson said later, "Paul began to organize the herd. One of our problems was our cows were not on schedule. Paul began to do the kind of maintenance that was necessary—fixing fences, checking the waters, replacing underground pumps, and looking after some of our wells. He did the things necessary to get the ranch back in good operation."

To Donaldson, the Posey family seemed polite, respectful, and very industrious. He would recall later, "Tryone was very hardworking. She did things for us that we didn't ask her to do around our small compound, where we lived across from the manager's house. She was always bright and bubbly. We liked her.

"As for Marilea, she was a sparkler. She was very effervescent. The family would often come out as a family unit when we were in the barnyard or the horse corral, and Marilea was just fine."

Regarding Cody, Donaldson later said that he was somewhat withdrawn, but many teenage boys acted that way. For the most part, however, Cody was polite and hardworking, like the rest of the Posey family.

On Friday, July 2, 2004, Tryone spoke with Sam Donaldson and told him that she and Marilea were going to her mother's place. Tryone's mom was going to be having a yard sale on the Fourth of July, and Tryone and Marilea wanted to attend. In a previous yard sale, some customers had taken items right off the grounds without paying for them. Tryone and Marilea were going to help keep an eye on things and make sure that didn't happen again.

The next day Donaldson saw Paul and Cody up at one of three guest houses on the property, replacing a board on a wooden porch. Donaldson said hello to both of them and briefly spoke with Paul. As far as Donaldson could see, everything looked fine.

Sunday, the Fourth of July, rolled around, and Donaldson phoned over to the manager's house to remind Paul that he and his wife were going to Santa Fe for the day. Cody answered the phone and Donaldson told him, "Cody, would you please tell your dad, and remind him, my wife and I are going to Santa Fe and we'll be back probably tomorrow, late in the afternoon." Cody assured Donaldson he would tell his dad.

Donaldson and his wife, Jan, met Jan's parents in Santa Fe, and it was a special occasion. Jan had been born on the Fourth of July, so they all had a birthday dinner for her and celebrated in town. The next day all four of them returned to Chavez Canyon Ranch and arrived on the property late in the afternoon.

Donaldson recalled, "After supper we went over to the horse corral, just to see the horses, and it was getting almost dark. The light was on in the manager's house. The ranch truck that Paul used as his vehicle was there, but I noticed that the Poseys' personal truck was missing. Paul did not come out. Normally, anytime we were in the barnyard, if he saw we were there, he would come out and say hello. But he didn't and I didn't think anything of it. We saw the horses and went back home."

The next morning, July 6, 2004, Sam, Jan, and her parents planned on going to the Capitan Mountains for a picnic. Donaldson related, "I was expecting mail from my office, by FedEx, and I noticed that the FedEx truck had gone to the ranch headquarters. On the way to the picnic, we went over there to see if there was a FedEx package for me. I walked up onto the porch, and I was looking at the screen door, and there was a FedEx package there. I went and looked at it, and it had my name on it, so I got it, walked back, and got in the truck, and we left for the mountains."

The Donaldson party picnicked in the Capitan Mountains for the day and returned to the ranch about 4:00 P.M. Sam stopped the vehicle at the main house, and became concerned by this time because he still had not seen anything of Paul or the rest of the Posey family. This was very unusual, and Sam said to the others, "We've got to find out what's going on here!"

Donaldson phoned over to the manager's house, but only received a recorded message. He then climbed into a truck, along with the others, and drove down to the manager's residence. Sam parked the truck and all four of them started up toward the manager's house. There were two entrances to the place, both leading down from a wooden porch. In the morning, when looking for the FedEx package, Sam had approached the house from one entrance, but now he approached from the other side. As he walked up toward the residence, he immediately saw things that he later described as "very disturbing."

"I saw a large reddish swath, which I identified clearly as blood. I'd covered the war in Vietnam, and I'd seen a lot there. At the house I saw a cap and I saw glasses. The glasses were crumpled on the stoop. At that point I said to the rest of my family, 'Stay here. Don't come up!'

"I opened the screen door and walked into the kitchen, and immediately saw the red swath, that was on the porch, was also on the kitchen floor." He noticed a great quantity of congealed blood by the alcove near the washer/dryer. Going from room to room, Donaldson checked to see if any of the Posey family members were there—dead or alive. He saw no one.

Donaldson recalled, "I didn't use the phone in the manager's house, because if there were fingerprints on the phone, I didn't want mine on there. I didn't touch anything. I came out and said to my family, 'There's a big problem here. We've got to go over and call the authorities.'

"We went over to the main house across the arroyo, and I knew Ken Cramer, who is a deputy sheriff at the Lincoln County Sheriff's Office. I knew his number. He had investigated a robbery two years previously. Before we had hired Paul, we'd been robbed at our house of two paintings and an odd collection of things. So I called the sheriff's office at that time, and Ken Cramer came out to investigate. None of the goods were ever recovered."

Donaldson couldn't get through to Ken Cramer now, but he did contact the main sheriff's office. Donaldson identified himself and said, "I can't find my ranch manager, but I found a great deal of congealed blood at my manager's house and I want to report it."

Sam Donaldson and the three others waited for sheriff's officers to arrive. Donaldson didn't know what had happened at the Posey family residence, but he knew it had to have been very bad. Someone didn't lose that much blood without there being dire consequences. And one more thing was very disturbing—if there was that much blood, where were the bodies? On the evening of July 6, 2004, there were a lot more questions than answers on Sam Donaldson's ranch.

Chapter 2

Slaughter Ranch

Sergeant Robert Shepherd, of the Lincoln County Sheriff's Office, was on duty on July 6, 2004, when he received a call from dispatch telling him to proceed to the Chavez Canyon Ranch. Shepherd was assigned to the Major Crimes Unit and had more than six hundred hours of advanced training in burglary, sexual assaults, and homicide. Sergeant Shepherd met Sam Donaldson at the entrance gate, and Donaldson told him that he hadn't seen his ranch manager in a while and there was blood at the manager's residence.

Both men proceeded up to the manager's house, and as Shepherd approached the place, he noticed a green coffee mug lying upside down in the dirt. There were only three steps leading up to a porch area, and across the porch there was an apparent blood trail. Sergeant Shepherd told Donaldson to stay where he was, and proceeded to cross the porch up to the front door. The storm door was closed, but near the bottom of the main door, a large pool of congealed blood had collected in the area. Moving inside, Shepherd noticed another large pool of blood in the kitchen area near the refrigerator.

At that point Shepherd backed out of the house and went up to the Donaldsons' main residence, where he phoned the sheriff's office and requested the crime team of Sergeant Kramer and Sergeant Baines. He also told the office to notify the New Mexico State Police (NMSP) mobile crime lab team, as well as the sheriff and undersheriff of Lincoln County. It still wasn't evident what had occurred at the Posey residence, but things didn't look good.

Returning to the outside of the Poseys' home, Sergeant Shepherd noticed a pair of glasses in the area, but he let them stay where they were rather than picking them up. He also spotted a blood-soaked, rolled-up carpet. On the south end of the porch at the bottom step, there was a small pool of blood that had collected. Not far away, two large, wide tire tracks had left their imprint on the ground, and there were two scrape marks between the tire tracks.

Searching for equipment that could have left such tracks, Sergeant Shepherd discovered several pieces of equipment east of the barn, including a John Deere backhoe. As he looked more closely at the backhoe, he noticed there was an apparent blood spatter on the bucket. Shepherd followed the backhoe tracks, making sure not to step on them, and found an area on the ground where someone had tried digging with the bucket. After a few scrapes at the dirt, the person had given up, but there was a small pool of blood there. Searching farther, he noticed that the backhoe tracks led down to a manure pile. Shepherd could tell where the front bucket had dug and removed some material from the pile.

He circled around the manure pile, to a small ravine,

wanting to look at the back side of the pile. Once again he made sure not to step on any tire tracks. At that point Shepherd smelled an odor of something that was obviously dead. Further inspection uncovered an aging deer carcass in a nearby ravine, but the odor he was smelling was too new and strong for that. Sergeant Shepherd moved closer to the manure pile and saw several groups of flies hovering around one particular area. They landed on a spot where the odor was the strongest.

Shepherd found a two-foot-long stick and started scraping some of the manure away from the pile. He didn't have to remove much when he discovered a blood-soaked shirt within the manure pile and there appeared to be a person's arm within the shirt.

Not wanting to disturb what might turn out to be a body dump site, Sergeant Shepherd backed out of the area and circled around to the residence. He began taping off the area around the house until Sergeant Kramer and Sergeant Baines arrived.

When those officers did arrive, they all huddled together for a briefing. A short time later, Sergeant Hardy and Agent Norman Rhodes, of the NMSP, arrived on scene as well.

Criminal Investigator Rhodes was skilled at processing crime scenes, identifying evidence, and packaging it for further study. He often processed crime scenes for other agencies, and he had special training in photographing scenes and bloodstain pattern analysis, as well as crime scene reconstruction. By the year 2004 he had been to more than two hundred crime scenes, mostly in the southern part of New Mexico.

Rhodes was assigned as crime scene manager, after a briefing with Robert Shepherd. Rhodes gave tasks to the other officers present, concerning who would draw a diagram, who would videotape, and who would do other tasks. Eventually five investigators made up the team.

One officer went up to the Donaldson residence, while the other officers stayed behind at the ranch manager's residence and started their search for other bodies that might be in the house. The team members didn't find any more bodies in the Posey ranch house, and they didn't touch anything, awaiting a search warrant before they began that procedure. The crime scene was taped off for the night.

It wasn't until six the next morning, July 7, that the team finally had a search warrant in hand and were back on the property. By that time the area was really filling up with investigators, including a crime team from Las Cruces, New Mexico. After another briefing, a few investigators, including Sergeant Kramer, went inside the residence.

Early on it was decided there were two main locations of the crime scene—the ranch manager's residence and the manure pile. Rhodes and some team members did a walk-through of the residence, starting on the north side steps. They noticed a coffee cup that was lying upside down near the steps and a spent shell casing nearby. There were two trails of blood on the porch area. Also in the area was a brown-colored throw rug with eyeglasses that lay on top of it. One of the lenses was missing from the eyeglasses. There was a large red stain on another throw rug that lay near the first one.

Proceeding inside the house, they discovered a red stain spatter on the south wall of the kitchen area. Rhodes could surmise some directionality of the blood spatter and it seemed to indicate a southward direction from possible arterial spray. Two nails on the wooden outside deck rose above the surface and hair and fiber were wrapped around them.

In the kitchen area, the missing lens from the eye-glasses was found, and a crack ran through the lens. The glasses and lens were collected, and Investigator Rhodes termed this initial walk-through a "raw scene."

Inside the living room they saw a sofa, and upon it there was a dark apparent blood-soaked section. On the couch there was a pillow and a book near it. There was a discoloration on the pillow, red in color, and there were also hairs, fiber, and human tissue on the pillow. In the living room were blood spatters on the west wall and south wall. It appeared that a body had been dragged from the living room through the kitchen and then out across the porch. Blood smears followed this general path.

The investigators checked the other rooms, and on top of a computer desk, there was an open notebook with a note written on it. The note read, *Sorry coppers, needed the kid to do the dirty work.* Just what that meant was not immediately clear.

In one bedroom there was a pair of work gloves that appeared to be stained with blood. The master bedroom was checked, but nothing of evidentiary value was found there. About this time an office of medical investigators (OMI) team arrived from Albuquerque, as did Investigator Melissa Armstrong.

The investigators did a walk-through of the house with Dr. Colmar, of the OMI team. They noted the apparent areas of blood and certain amount of disarray in the house. Then it was time to dig through the manure pile and recover the body, or bodies. As the investigators began their search, they noticed the arm of one victim and the upper torso of another in the manure pile. As manure was stripped away, the investigators reported, "The victims were dumped there in an erratic commingling." In all, there were three bodies within the manure pile—on the top was Paul Posey, in the middle Marilea Schmid, and on the bottom, Tryone Posey. Their limbs were intertwined in a blanket. Marilea's left cowboy boot had been removed, but it was thrown onto her body. A driver's license in the wallet of his jeans identified him as Paul Posey. The bodies were removed and placed in body bags and sealed with evidence tags. They were sealed to ensure that no one tampered with the bodies from the time the investigators put them in the body bags until an autopsy was performed in Albuquerque, which was almost two hundred miles away.

Dr. Jeffrey Nine did the actual autopsy on the bodies of the victims. He was a medical doctor who specialized in pathology and investigated suspicious deaths. Dr. Nine held teaching positions at a university and also a medical school. Because of his training, he often testified as an expert witness at homicide trials.

Dr. Nine began his first autopsy on the body of Tryone Posey. Her body had arrived at the medical examiner's (ME) office, delivered by a transport company and brought to a storage facility in Albuquerque. Dr. Nine began the autopsy by examining the clothing and items found with Tryone. She wore a blue shirt, blue jeans, braided belt, and brown boots. Her shirt had been pulled up over her breasts. Other items that arrived with her body were a white metal ring with stones, and eyeglasses with one lens missing.

In his external exam Dr. Nine observed some decomposition and two gunshot wounds to her head. There was early stages of decomposition, where tissue had softened and there was discoloration as well. It was hard for him to tell what she had looked like when alive because of the decomp and gunshot wounds. Dr. Nine made some incisions, removed internal organs, and then removed her skullcap and brain. This was to see if he could track the gunshot wounds and see what structures had been damaged by the path of the bullets.

One bullet had entered Tryone's forehead near the right eye and caused a fracture at the back of the skull where it lodged. The second gunshot wound was on the right side of the head in the temple, and there were pellets from snake shot, or handgun pellet ammunition, in that area. Because of decomposition, Dr. Nine couldn't tell the true path of the gunshot wound within her head. The size of the entry wound near the eyebrow, however, was determined to be about a half inch in dimension. The right temple wound was about two and a quarter inches in size, and he removed thirty-four small pellets from the wounded area. When he removed the bullet from the back of the skull, it was all in one piece.

Dr. Nine couldn't tell in what order the wounds had been inflicted, but he determined the wound to the temple area, caused by the snake shot, was not a fatal wound. A person who had been shot in that manner could still talk and move around. The gunshot wound that had entered near the eyebrow would have been fatal. Dr. Nine listed the cause of death for Tryone Posey as "gunshot wound of the head—homicide."

Dr. Nine's next autopsy was upon the body of Paul Posey. Paul's body was in a similar state of decomposition as that of Tryone. He wore a blue-and-white button-down shirt, jeans with a ripped back pocket, hearing aids, and had nine keys on a key ring.

Paul had a single gunshot wound to his head near the right eye. The bullet had entered near the eyebrow area and lodged on the left side of his brain. Dr. Nine recovered the bullet from Paul's brain, and it matched that of the one he had found in Tryone's brain. Because of decomposition, Dr. Nine couldn't follow the exact path the bullet had taken.

When he tried to determine the range at which the gun had been fired, it was very hard to tell, but he judged that it had been fired at "intermediate range." There was possible gunshot residue on the bone, which would have meant close range, but because of the decomp, it was hard to tell. Dr. Nine listed the cause of death for Paul Posey as "gunshot wound to head—homicide."

The last body Dr. Nine examined was that of Marilea Schmid. She had been wearing a bluish green shirt, bra, denim jeans, and tan cowboy boots. There were tears on her shirt in the right shoulder and armpit area. These tears were from an inch to nine inches in length. Later it would be determined that these tears might have been caused by a raised nail on the porch of the Posey residence. When Marilea's body was dragged across that area, her shirt might have snagged on the nail and become torn in the process.

There were two gunshot wounds to Marilea's head. One bullet had entered the front of the head at the right eye and exited the back of the head. The other had entered at the left jaw area and lodged there. The wound in the jaw area was not fatal, and Marilea still could have moved around. The wound to the eye went through the brain and exited the middle of the back area of the head. It would have been fatal. Dr. Nine listed cause of death for Marilea as "gunshot wounds to head—homicide."

* * *

While the investigation at the ranch was proceeding on July 7, 2004, a Mr. Kennedy, from the Hondo Country Store, called the sheriff's office and a message went out to Sergeant Shepherd that Kennedy wanted to talk to someone about the Posey situation. Kennedy was a relative of Marilea Schmid Posey. When Shepherd and Armstrong got there, they spoke with Kennedy, who said that Paul Posey's son, Cody, was out at a friend's house in the small town of San Patricio. The name of the friends were Leo and Gilbert Salcido.

It was a few miles from the Chavez Canyon Ranch to San Patricio along the Ruidoso River. It was just a small village of farmers and ranchers. San Patricio had been a key locale during the days of "Billy the Kid," and he had often sought refuge there among the Hispanic people of the area. They all got along well with Billy, and often shielded him from the law. It remained to be seen if a modern-day equivalent was in the works concerning the Posey case.

When Armstrong and Shepherd approached the Salcido house, Cody was apparently inside. The officers identified themselves and said they would like to talk to Cody alone. Several kids came out of the house, and there were already people outside.

In a short while, Cody Posey came out of the Salcido residence and walked up to the squad car, where Shepherd and Armstrong were. Even at this point it was uncertain as to what Cody was—a suspect or a victim. To be on the safe side, Shepherd read Cody his Miranda rights, and Cody said that he understood them.

As Cody and the officers stood in the driveway, they asked him about where he went to school, and he answered Capitan High School. They asked him what grade he was in, and Cody told them he was a freshman.

Asked how long he had been at the Salcido residence, Cody answered that he'd been there for two days.

The officers wondered why Cody had been there for so long, and asked if he was having problems at home. Cody said that he was at the Salcidos' because he and his father had an argument on the morning of July 5, and his dad had told him to grab some things and leave until things cooled off.

The officers wanted to know what the argument was about and Cody answered that it had been over his dad's displeasure about the way he'd been cleaning the horse corral that morning. His dad had told him he wasn't doing it fast enough, and Cody admitted that he'd mouthed off to his father and said, "I'm doing a better job than you could, because you never do it!"

The argument hadn't ended there, according to Cody. Both he and his dad had gone back into the house, where the same argument flared up once again. Getting more and more angry, his dad had finally thrown a set of truck keys at him and told him to clear out.

Cody was asked if he had a driver's license, and he admitted that he didn't, but he had driven the truck before around the ranch. Asked if his dad had hit him that morning, Cody answered that he hadn't.

"Why are you shaking?" one of the officers asked.

"Because you're cops!" Cody answered.

"Have the police ever been to your house?"

"No."

After a while, Cody's nervous behavior quit. He settled down, and all three of them talked about the Poseys' pickup truck that was now on the east side of the Salcido residence. Once again the officers asked if his dad let him drive it, and Cody said that once in a while he was allowed to drive the truck down to the store in Hondo. The officers took a closer look at the pickup and there were new scratches all up and down the driver's side and the driver's handle had been knocked off. Asked for an explanation about this, Cody said that on the way to the Salcidos', he'd run off the road and hit a fence.

Once again the officers returned to asking about how Paul treated Cody. Investigator Armstrong asked if there was any physical violence on Paul's part, and Cody answered, "That morning (July fifth), Dad said, 'If it wasn't against the law, I'd knock your head off! You need to leave now!'" Then Cody added that there had been arguments in the past, and his dad would usually leave first. There was no further talk about being hit by his dad, at least in the past few weeks, but Cody did admit that two years previously his father had become so angry at him, he'd knocked him out of a chair at home and given him a black eye.

The officers weren't giving Cody any information at this point about the fate of his family. They asked him if his parents knew where he was, and Cody answered that he'd called home, but nobody had answered the phone.

Armstrong took some photos of Cody at the Salcido residence, and it was noted that Cody had some burn marks on his left shoulder. Asked how he got them, Cody answered that he had been welding at the ranch, stood up, leaned against hot metal, and gotten burned. On closer inspection the officers thought that the burn marks looked old and probably hadn't happened within the last few days.

The officers started asking Cody once again how he got along with his family. Cody said that he got along okay with his dad and stepmom, Tryone, and that he loved his stepsister, Marilea. The officers wondered if

Cody had packed any clothes since he had been staying so long at the Salcido residence. Cody said that he hadn't. In fact, Cody said that he'd borrowed some clothing at the Salcido place.

The conversation with Cody went on at the Salcido residence for about an hour and a half. All of it was audiotaped, but the sound quality on the microcassette was poor at best. The officers weren't quite sure what to do with Cody at this point, and they phoned Lincoln County district attorney (DA) Scot Key. It was still unclear: Was Cody Posey the sole surviving victim of a family tragedy, or was he somehow involved?

Investigator Armstrong and Sergeant Shepherd went back to the Chavez Canyon Ranch to confer with the other investigators there, but returned a short time later to the Salcido place. When they returned, Cody and several of his friends were walking down the road, and the officers told Cody he needed to return to the Salcido house. Cody got into the front seat of the squad car and was driven back to the Salcidos' residence.

Once back there, the officers asked if Cody would come with them to be interviewed and videotaped, since the microcassette recording had been so poor in quality. They said he could take an adult with him. Cody agreed and decided to bring Faustimo Salcido along. Faustimo was the father of Cody's friends, Leo and Gilbert Salcido. All four made their way to Ruidoso, a resort community in the Sacramento Mountains, which had an office of the Child, Youth and Family Department. (CYFD). Within the CYFD office was something called the "safe room." It was a room where victims of abuse were often taken to tell their stories in a safe environment. There was a camera and an audio-recording device within the safe room, along with table, couch, and chairs. There was also a two-way mirror, where Faustimo Salcido could watch the proceedings.

As the interview began, the investigators asked Cody his full name, date of birth, and who else lived with him in the house on Chavez Canyon Ranch. Cody said that he was born on October 9, 1989, was now fourteen years old, and that his dad, stepmom, and stepsister lived with him. Asked what kind of grades he got at school, he answered A's and B's. Cody told them that he'd originally gone to Hondo High School, but his parents made him transfer to Capitan High in 2003. Cody said the reason for the change was that they didn't think he cared about doing his homework at Hondo, and they were concerned about his relationship with a fourteen-year-old girl named Brenda Lucero. Cody referred to her as his girl-friend, and he was not pleased about the change to Capitan High.

Getting back to the immediate time of the last few days, Cody said that he'd been gone for two days from his home. He'd arrived at the Salcido residence about noon on July 5 and had driven the truck from the ranch. Asked if he'd been drinking, he answered no. Once again the officers noted that he didn't have a driver's license, but Cody answered that he'd been driving vehicles on the ranch since he was eight years old.

Asked about the argument on the morning of July 5, Cody went over it once again and described the work clothes he'd been wearing at the time. Cody said that he'd changed into other clothes later on, and Cody described his normal workday as getting up around 5:00 A.M. and taking care of four horses and fourteen cows before going to school. He'd feed the horses first, and then tend to the cows. His sister, Marilea, also helped out with the chores.

Cody said that he hadn't eaten much breakfast on the morning of July 5, had gone out to the horse corral, and the argument had started around 6:00 A.M. It had taken place out near the horses and then continued once he was back in the kitchen. It was at that point that he said that his father had thrown a set of keys at him and told him to clear out. Cody described the house in general, and the kitchen more specifically. As time went on, the investigators started zeroing in more on the crimes and Cody's possible involvement in them.

Shepherd:	Okay, I'm sitting here and I'm watching you, Cody. I mean, you've got tears in your eyes and I need to know why. You were talking earlier, and you said that if you lie, it will always come back to bite you in the butt. That you get it worse. Is that what you said?
Posey:	Yes.
Shepherd:	All right, Cody. You need to tell me what happened.
	(Around this point, Cody Posey said, "I might as well tell you the truth," and there was a whole shift in his demeanor and the things he said.)
Posey:	I got tired of Dad hitting me. Yelling and screaming at me all the time. He hit me and I couldn't take it anymore.
Shepherd:	So what did you do, Cody?
Posey:	I tried getting rid of them.
Shepherd:	How?

Posey: Get him off this planet, cuz I'd be better here without him.

Shepherd: So what did you do, Cody?

Posey: I shot him.

Shepherd: With what?

Posey: .38 Special.

Shepherd: Where's the gun? Where did you shoot him?

Posey: In the head.

Shepherd: Where was he standing?

Posey: He was walking through the door.

Shepherd: Out on the porch?

Posey: Kitchen door.

Shepherd: From outside the house, into the house?

Posey: Yeah.

Shepherd: Where did you get the gun, Cody?

Posey: Marilea had it in her saddlebag for shooting snakes.

Armstrong: What? Marilea had it?

Posey: In her saddlebag.

Shepherd: So when he was yelling at you to come in the house, where did you go?

Posey: Yeah, he already hit me before that. He slapped me. He was like, "You're doing it wrong. Here, come in the house while I put up the tools."

Shepherd: Okay, so you went in and got the gun out of the saddlebag. Where's the gun at right now?

Posey: In the river.

Armstrong: In the river?

Shepherd: Up here?

Posey: Yeah. Not that far away.

Shepherd: Okay, so you shot your dad going in the house?

Posey: Um-hmm.

Shepherd: Was he outside the door?

Posey: Yeah, he was walking in.

Shepherd: And you shot him, where?

Posey: In the head.

Shepherd: Where?

Posey: Oh, I was next to the refrigerator. I got in the house before he did. Cuz he was out there looking at his truck or something.

Shepherd: So you shot him. And where in the head did you shoot him?

Posey: I don't remember.

Armstrong: Do you need a tissue or anything?
(No audible response.)

Armstrong: Take your time.

Shepherd: So you shot him and he fell.
(No response.)

Shepherd: What about your stepmom?

Posey: I shot her too. She hit me and stuff.

Shepherd: Where was she when you shot her?

Posey: On the couch.

Shepherd: What about Marilea?

Posey: She was right behind my dad.

Shepherd: What did you do to her?

Posey: Shot her too, so she wouldn't go tell or nothing.

Armstrong: Then what happened, Cody?

Posey: I stole the truck and left with it. I had to get out of there.

Armstrong: Where were they?

Posey: I put them in the backhoe and tried to bury them. It didn't work too well.

Armstrong: It didn't work too well?

Posey: They're out there next to the sand pile I told you about.

Shepherd: Where did you throw the gun?

Posey: At the farm.

(Another ranch, called the hay ranch, that was several miles away.)

The officers wanted to know if Cody got blood all over himself when he shot his family, and he said that he had. He told them that he changed his clothes and washed up at the house. He had first tried digging a hole to bury the bodies in the ground, but it was too hard. Then down near the ravine and the manure pile, he'd nearly flipped the backhoe.

The questioning went back to the argument that had caused the chain of lethal events, and Cody told them about circumstances earlier that had triggered the shootings. He started talking about an incident that had happened the night before, on July 4. Cody said that his father had called him into the master bedroom, and when he arrived there, his dad was dressed only in underwear, and his stepmom lay on the bed, completely naked.

Armstrong: She was what? What were you saying?

Posey: I don't know. My dad and Tryone would like—wouldn't have sex, or something like that, and they were trying to do something to me. She grabbed my head and put it on her breast. And he is the reason I got those burns. He had a hot torch thing, like a welding rod, and he told me he'd burn me if I didn't do it.

Armstrong: The day before [the murders]? Sunday? (Cody nodded his head yes.)

Armstrong: Okay, and then what? They were going to have sex or something?

Posey: No, they were wanting me to do her or something. . . .

Armstrong: They wanted you to have sex with your stepmom?

Posey: Yeah. She was like, well, "We're not related. We're not blood. Come and do it." And I didn't, because I thought it was wrong. And so, he had like a welding rod and a torch there. That's how I got those burns.

Armstrong: Had you had sex with her before?

Posey: No.

Armstrong: Where did this take place?

Posey: In his bedroom. In their bedroom.

Armstrong: Where'd he get the torch from?

Posey: He had a little bitty torch that he uses to melt pipe and stuff.

Shepherd: Fix water leaks and stuff?

Posey: Yeah.

The questioning went on for many hours, until the investigators asked Cody if he was hungry, and he said that he was. They all went to a fast-food place in Ruidoso to get something to eat. Cody had chicken nuggets, tater tots, and a soft drink. After that, Cody and the officers

went to Sam Donaldson's hay ranch, and Cody pointed
out the area in the river where he had thrown the pistol.
Since it was too dark at the time, there was no attempt at
recovering the pistol that evening.

The next day a New Mexico dive team went into the
river and eventually retrieved the gun. Around the same
time a new search warrant was issued for the Posey residence, and investigators searched for the welding torch
and rod that Cody had mentioned. They didn't find a
torch or rod in the bedroom, nor in the house. They did,
however, recover a saddlebag off a saddle that was in the
barn. A holster was on the floor of the barn.

The pistol was a crucial bit of evidence, and eventually forensic scientist Katarina Babcock took a look at
it under strict lab conditions. Babcock was a specialist
in firearm identification and had a bachelor's degree in
criminology from the University of New Mexico. She
was later accepted to the Alcohol, Tobacco and Firearms
(ATF) Academy in Rockville, Maryland. This was quite
an accomplishment—only ten students per year from
around the nation were admitted to the academy. During
her training she went to nineteen firearms manufactur-
ers around the United States, and also to ammunition
plants. She wrote fifty-four papers while there, plus two
larger published works for the academy.

Once out in the field, Babcock started working cases
with noted firearms expert Larry Warheim and eventually testified as an expert in fifteen court cases. Generally, she looked at two basic areas in a firearm—one of
these being class characteristics imparted by the manufacturer. Before a firearm is ever sold, a manufacturer
decides how many lands and grooves there would be in
a barrel. These "spirals" have a twist in the barrel of the
weapon and cause the bullet to be more accurate when

fired than from a smoothbore gun. Beyond the manufacturer's characteristics, every firearm itself has unique
characteristics. There are always small markings imparted into the barrel, as every tool during manufactur-
ing creates a slightly different alteration. One thing
remains a constant however—a bullet fired from a gun
at one time, and ten years later, could be identified as
being fired from the same gun.

In the case concerning the deaths of Paul, Tryone, and
Marilea, Babcock test-fired four times the pistol that
Cody had indicated he'd thrown into the river. This was
to gain a consistency of results. The firearm was test-
fired into a water tank, and the bullets and casings were
collected. These results were then compared to bullets
and casings from the Chavez Canyon Ranch crime
scene.

In the Posey case the pistol was a five-shot revolver
.38 Taurus brand number 85. There were only five
chambers in the cylinder, rather than the more common
six. Each cartridge had to be loaded manually into the
cylinder. The pistol was also what was known as a
single-action pistol, which meant that the person firing
the gun had to pull the hammer back before the trigger
was pulled. At that point the hammer would fall and fire
the gun.

When Babcock tested the weapon that Cody Posey indicated that he had used to kill his dad, stepmom, and
stepsister, she removed it from a can of oil, where it had
been placed to inhibit rusting. All five chambers of the
pistol were loaded, and she unloaded them, one at a
time. Two of the cartridges were live ammo, while three
others had been fired already. The ammo was all .38
Special ammo. To make sure the three casings in the gun

had actually been fired from that gun, she tested them against the bullets recovered from the bodies.

A bullet recovered from the body of Paul Posey was listed as OMI—1. It was a damaged bullet, and Babcock determined that it had the same class as the test-fired bullets from the .38. Microscopically, however, she couldn't determine if it had been fired from that exact gun.

OMI—2 came from the body of Marilea, but it was just two pieces of lead. There was no rifling on it, and it was of no evidentiary value. OMI—3 came from the body of Tryone, and it also was a damaged bullet. Once again Babcock couldn't say for sure it came from the pistol in question.

OMI—4 came from the body of Tryone as well, and unlike the other bullets, this was a scattering of lead pellets and a small plastic wadding. It was a shot shell, not unlike those fired from a shotgun. Babcock weighed all of the pellets and examined them under a stereo microscope. She got an average weight of the pellets, looked up literature regarding the weight of the pellets, and the book indicated that it was #9 shot. Number 9 shot was normally used for snake shot. This kind of shot could be fired from the Taurus revolver.

On the request of Assistant District Attorney (ADA) Sandra Grisham, the investigators made a video of the area from the corral to the barn and up to the house on the Donaldson Ranch. In slow motion it showed the corral, front part of the barn, the foreman's residence, up across the porch, through the kitchen and living room. The vehicles were also searched and videotaped, including the pickup Cody had driven to the Salcido residence.

Also, at the Donaldson ranch, investigators searched

the corral area and barn as well. They collected some items from a saddlebag that included fence pliers, a hoof pick, and two cartridge holders. There was .38-caliber bird shot shells in the saddlebag, or snake shot. There were also regular .38 cartridges.

Inside the house the investigators seized computers from Cody's room, Marilea's room, and the ranch office. Marilea's and Cody's computers were not connected to the Internet, and they could not access Wi-Fi abilities from that area. The ranch computer was connected to the Internet, however, and in time some very disturbing evidence would be found on the ranch computer's hard drive. It contained pornographic material that related to father/daughter incest and mother/son incest. Some of the material was very graphic. The question was: Who within the Posey household had viewed those incest sites?

On July 8, 2004, ADA Sandra Grisham listed Cody Posey as "a delinquent child who poses a substantial risk of harm to others, and he poses a substantial risk of harm to himself." There was no doubt that whatever Cody Posey had done, and why he had done it, there would soon be a case going through the court system. Originally the case went to the Honorable Karen L. Parsons, but she excused herself from the proceedings. Cody Posey's fate from that point on would lie within the Honorable James Waylon Counts's courtroom.

Cody already had a local attorney as his lawyer, Gary Mitchell, who practiced law in Ruidoso. Mitchell made a motion of appointment to name Corliss Clees, Cody's maternal aunt, as his guardian, and Judge Counts so stipulated. Judge Counts also signed an order that Cody should be held as a delinquent child, because he posed a danger to others and himself. Cody was not going to be out of confinement for a long time.

On July 9, 2004, there was a detention hearing, and Cody was present with Gary Mitchell. During the hearing Cody remained silent as Sandra Grisham presented a case that there was good cause for an extension of time to seek adult sanctions against Cody Posey, even though he was still only fourteen years old. She also sought to hold a grand jury hearing on the matter, for a preliminary examination to determine whether probable cause existed. Then Cody was taken back to his new residence—the Bernalillo County Juvenile Detention Center (BCJDE).

News of the triple murders on Sam Donaldson's ranch exploded throughout the media, transforming the normally quiet small town of Hondo, New Mexico, into a beehive of activity. The reporters were everywhere, asking questions, especially about Sam Donaldson, and this time Donaldson was on the receiving end of a media frenzy that threatened to overwhelm the area. Reporters, cameramen, microphones, news vans, satellite trucks—they all converged on the hamlet of two hundred people like a flood. Donaldson made a brief statement to the gathered throng: "Jan and I are so very, very sorry about the loss of these fine people."

Later Donaldson elaborated a little more on the situation in an interview with Albuquerque's KOB-TV. Donaldson described Cody Posey as "withdrawn, like any typical teenager." He described Paul Posey and Tryone and their children as a happy, well-adjusted family.

Donaldson also did an interview for *Good Morning America,* in which he called the Poseys "an all-American ranch family. Paul was a little hard on his son, but that's the way you raise young men. I never saw Paul raise his voice or his hand in anger to his son. But he clearly expected a lot of him."

A very unclear situation soon developed with inaccurate information being put forth, such as Cody burying the bodies in a shallow grave, rather than a manure pile. By the next day, however, more accurate information was being dispensed, including the fact that Cody said that an argument with his father had been the flash point. An AP article reported some abuse from Cody's father, and "this time [the slap] was across the face for not cleaning horse stalls fast enough, and the teenager said he had had enough."

The reports went on to describe Cody taking the pistol from Marilea's saddlebag in the barn and returning to the house. "His first target was Tryone. He shot her twice in the head, and when his father raced toward the house, Cody shot him in the head." The AP report added, "Cody confessed to then shooting his stepsister in the head. The affidavit said the teen shot the girl a second time because she was still moving."

District Attorney Scot Key was in the spotlight, and he told reporters, "We've never seen a triple murder and the circumstances of a juvenile committing a crime against family members hasn't been experienced here."

Faustimo Salcido was being interviewed as well, and he told reporters that Cody had come to his house on Monday and stayed over all through Tuesday and into Wednesday. Cody had played basketball with his sons, Gilbert and Leo Salcido, played in the river, and shot off fireworks. Not once did Cody mention anything about his family. Mr. Salcido told reporters, "He told me these were the happiest two days he'd had in his life. He thanked me for letting him stay."

Mr. Salcido began telling something else as well. He said that a pattern of abuse by Paul upon his son Cody was well-known to his sons and others in the close-knit community. "There was a lot of people who wanted to whip his dad because of the way he treated Cody in public."

Faustimo Salcido's sons backed him up in this contention. Gilbert told reporters, "One time he (Cody) had a big ol' black eye. Cody said, 'I got hit in softball.' We were all saying, 'A softball couldn't do that!' He finally told us his dad had punched him." Gilbert and Leo added that they saw Cody show up at school many times with black eyes, bruises, and scrapes. They, along with others, were sure that Cody had received them as abuse from his father.

Sheriff Tom Sullivan was asked by reporters about this alleged abuse, and whether Lincoln County deputies had ever investigated such abuse. Sullivan answered, "I can say we did not. However, if a teacher had reported it, we would have done something about it. If there had been abuse and it had been duly reported, this whole thing could have been avoided."

Already lines were being drawn—those who believed Cody Posey had been horribly abused by his father and stepmom as well, and those who believed he was making the whole abuse issue up, to save his skin. Corliss Clees, Cody's maternal aunt, weighed in and told reporters, "Something caused Cody to snap, because that's not who he is."

The question in the long run was not who fourteen-year-old Cody Posey was—the main question was why had he done what he did. In the weeks and years after the morning of July 5, 2004, many, many facts about his life would come to light. But always these "facts" were reflected through a prism of whoever the beholder was. Cody Posey became a lightning rod for issues far beyond his control. Cody, and what he had done, became the battleground for issues of child abuse, accountability, how children are psychoanalyzed, and the very judicial system itself.

Chapter 3

Young Cody

Paul Posey was eighteen years old when he married nineteen-year-old Carla June Clees in Roswell, New Mexico. Paul was home on leave at the time from basic training in the U.S. Army. Both Paul and Carla moved to New York State, where Paul served in the army, and Cody Austin Posey was born to them on October 9, 1989. (Carla had a daughter named Cheyenne by a previous relationship, but Cody was Paul and Carla's first child together.)

The marriage between Paul and Carla was rocky at best, and there always seemed to be some kind of argument going on. Not unlike Cody, however, Paul Posey had his admirers and detractors. Some would say he loved Cody and always tried to do the best for him. Others said Paul was abusive to Cody from a very early age. One of these was Sherry Gensler, a cousin of Cody's mother.

Gensler recalled, "During Cody's potty-training years, Paul picked him up because he had peed in his

Wrangler jeans. Paul lifted him off the ground and spanked him. Cody wasn't even two yet."

Jim Forrester was acquainted with the Posey family, and he would later recall an incident when Cody was about two years old. Forrester and a friend were over at the Posey residence when Paul became angry at Cody for some reason. According to Forrester, Paul picked up Cody and threw him across the room onto a couch. Cody was screaming and crying and soiled his pants. Forrester and the other man had to restrain Paul from inflicting further abuse upon Cody.

The marriage between Paul and Carla was filled with verbal arguments. Some also contended later that he abused her as he did Cody. There is also documented evidence that Carla had problems with alcohol and drugs during this period. In January 1992, Carla and Paul got a divorce.

Paul, however, did not like living alone, and on April 3, 1993, Paul married Sandra Paul, and he, Sandra, and Cody moved to Roswell, New Mexico. Roswell services a large area of ranches in that portion of New Mexico. It was also famous, or infamous, as the spot where aliens had supposedly descended to Earth in the late 1940s, and the subject had been kept under wraps ever since by the United States government. At least that was what certain conspiracy theorists and outer space afficionados believed.

Aliens or not, the area around Roswell is filled with farms along the Pecos River and large ranches that raise cattle. It was also another area rich with Billy the Kid stories. He had been all over that country during the 1870s.

For the Posey family, which now included Paul, Sandy, and Cody, they lived in a little house on Eighth Street in Roswell, and then moved to nearby East Grand

Plains, which was more of a country setting. Sandy Posey worked for EGP Services, which dealt with fertilizer and agricultural products, while Paul worked for Leprino, a cheese factory. Sandy's shifts were 8:00 A.M. to 5:00 P.M., Monday through Thursday, while Paul originally worked the graveyard shift and then swing shifts. Sandra would recall later, "I was the primary parent for Cody. Cody's mom, Carla, did visit him once in a while. I had a pretty good relationship with her. As for Paul, he never had a whole lot to do with Cody. I would try to protect Cody when Paul's temper flared up. When he gave Cody a spanking, I would eventually step in and say, 'That's enough!'

"Paul had a quick temper. He would get so angry, and would be out of control. I was the dominant person in that house, and that's how I protected Cody. I'd step in when Paul got too rough. I was concerned that Paul really did not like Cody. I was afraid if I wasn't there, what he might do to him."

Cody later could not recall his very early years living with his natural mother, Carla, but he did remember living with Sandy and Paul at East Grand Plains. Cody recalled the ten acres of land and a garden area around the house. He also recalled that they raised dairy cattle and a few beef cattle. Every once in a while, his father would buy some horses and trade them later. It was halfway between a farm/ranch–style environment and a suburban home.

Cody began classes at a private Christian school called Abundant Life Christian School, where he attended classes from kindergarten to the third grade. Everything on that small bucolic acreage should have been wonderful for a young boy, but for some witnesses to the Posey family life, there were a lot darker things going on in East Grand Plains than just a country lifestyle.

Cheryl Paul was married to Sandra Posey's brother, and she recalled Cody from age three to nine years of age. She saw the Posey family about three times a week when they lived in East Grand Plains, and Cheryl said later, "The first time I met Cody, he was about three years old. He and Paul walked into my house and Cody was shy. I reached down and said hello to him, and he kinda turned toward Paul, because he was shy. Paul jerked his little cowboy hat off and popped him on the back of the head. Paul said, 'How do you treat people when you first meet them?' That bothered me he would do that to a child of that age.

"Another incident occurred when Cody was about five years old. It was around lunchtime and I went over to my sister-in-law's house. Cody was eating lunch, and if he didn't want to finish all the food that was in front of him, Paul would slap him in the mouth. I saw him bust Cody's lip one time. I was shocked. Sandy jumped up and grabbed a towel and was angry at Paul.

"Paul would never allow Cody to be a child. He never really allowed him to run and play like most kids. If Cody fell down and hurt himself, Paul would call him a 'sissy' or 'wimp' and stuff like that. He was not a very caring person when it came to Cody."

Cody loved Sandra, and called her his mom. She was the first real mom that Cody could remember. Sandy was good to Cody, and on more than one occasion, she protected Cody from Paul's anger.

One incident that Cody later would relate concerned a water trough. He said that a family relation had left hay for the horses, and Cody assumed the person had also watered them. Watering the horses was generally

Cody's job, and when his father found there was no water in the trough, he devised a punishment. Cody was to fill up the entire water trough, one small Dixie cup of water at a time. It was a hot day, and as Cody walked back and forth, filling up the trough with small cups of water, he felt like he might faint from the heat. When his dad left for work, Sandy came out and told Cody to fill up the trough with a hose. She said Paul wouldn't know the difference.

The first class that Cody could remember later on was when he was in second grade. He said, "We didn't get letter grades then. It was pluses and minuses on papers. And I got a series of minuses, so my dad got mad. He swatted me with a paddle."

Cody also recalled, "If I didn't eat all my food, I was punished by a slap to the face. Sometimes if I didn't finish food, it would sit there all night, and I'd have to eat the cold food before I could have anything hot to eat. More than once, food was dumped on my head if my dad didn't like the way I was eating."

Cody also said, "In East Grand Plains, I was wiggling a tooth around because it was loose. My dad came up and hit me in the jaw and said, 'There, now you'll stop playing with it.'

"He also used to smack me across the face with the wire end of a flyswatter when I did something he didn't like. It left an imprint on my face. I was little then, and I couldn't figure out later why I had marks like that on my face. I thought they might be some kind of disease, and they scared me."

Vicki Harrington remembered Cody from around this time period, because her son, Brandon, and Cody were friends at the Abundant Life Christian School. Cody and Brandon wanted to spend time together outside of school, and Vicki recalled that when Paul wasn't around, "Cody would hit the door running. He wanted to play and not sit still. Brandon came one time to see me and said, 'I'm tired. I need rest.' But Cody wanted to ride bikes, climb trees, run around. He was just a bottle of energy that exploded, but I never had problems with him. He was always respectful and polite. He was a good kid. We enjoyed having him around."

Sherry Gensler also spoke of how Cody acted when Paul wasn't around. "When he was with us, there would be just normal behavior for a kid. The kids would eat and play. When we would tell Cody it was time to go back home, within seconds his whole demeanor would change. He would be quiet and withdrawn. His head would go down. It would be just the opposite when we picked him up. He'd tell us about the week, what he'd done, and what he wanted to do. When he was with us, he'd wear sandals or flip-flops and shorts. When it was time to go home, it was back to jeans, long-sleeved shirts, and boots."

Cody was pulled out of Abundant Life Christian School during the fourth grade and started attending a public school called Brindell Elementary. If Cody didn't get good grades, the swats from his father only increased. One paddling was exceptionally violent, according to Cody. He said later, "My dad began hitting me with a board. It got harder and harder, so I tried to step away. He then brought the board up over his head and hit me on the small of my back. The board broke."

After this incident Cody went on a weekend visit to Carla's house. After Cody had played all day long, his mother told him to bathe. He didn't want to, but she insisted. When Cody took off his shirt and T-shirt, Carla saw why. Cody had bruises on his back and buttocks. Reluctantly he told her the reason they were there—according to Cody, his father had hit him with the board.

Carla was irate and took him to the hospital, where a full-body check was performed. Officer Sharon Barry would become involved with the incident. Officer Barry had been in law enforcement for over twenty years by the time Cody visited the hospital. When Barry was with the Otero County Sheriff's Office (OCSO), she got a message concerning a possible case of child abuse on a youth named Cody Posey. She didn't start the investigation, that was done by an officer named Mike Herrington, but eventually it was given to her. She interviewed Paul, Carla, and Cody individually, and Cody went to a hospital, where photos were taken. Just what the photos actually showed would become a point of debate later on. They seemed to show bruising on Cody's buttocks and perhaps the small of his back. There did not seem to be bruising farther up his back.

Things were about to change again in the Posey household. Paul was working at the Leprino plant near Roswell, and it was there that he met a woman named Tryone Schmid. Tryone was married to a man named Jacob Schmid, and they had a young daughter named Marilea. At some point around 1996, Paul and Tryone started having an affair. Before long, Paul left Sandra, and Tryone left Jacob, and they began living together. Sandy would recall of this period, "Paul came home from work one morning and said, 'I found someone else, and it's over.' It was just like that."

Paul and Tryone got married in 1997, and they took Cody and Marilea into their home. To make matters even more complicated in this family affair, Jacob

Schmid and Sandra Posey got together to commiserate about their situation, and ended up getting married. In essence, the two couples had swapped mates, though it was in the legal sense.

Jacob Schmid saw Cody on occasion because Sandy had visitation rights. At first, the Schmids got Cody and Marilea every weekend, but as time went on, this began to trickle off. Paul or Tryone kept coming up with one kind of excuse after another why the kids couldn't come over. They said the kids were sick or had some other kind of excuse. The Schmids began to see Marilea only about once a month, and Cody even less often.

Jacob said later, "I was concerned about Cody. He sometimes seemed nervous or downright scared. It wasn't a feeling I liked to see—a child that scared of something. He seemed scared to go home, but there wasn't anything we could do. Marilea never voiced anything, but there was trouble there. I was constantly defending myself against lies that Tryone told Marilea. Tryone told her that I had affairs during our marriage and that's what broke us up. It got to the point where Marilea didn't want to see me. But the fact was, I never had an affair on Tryone—she had one on me. I thought we had been happily married. I was fooled."

One thing Jacob wouldn't stand for was Paul spanking Marilea. He told Paul that he didn't spank her anymore, and that he'd better not find out that Paul was doing it. As far as Cody went, Jacob said, "We never had any discipline problems with him. He was a good kid. He never did anything wrong."

But that was not what Jan Calloway said; Tryone had been telling her things about Cody. Calloway related, "I used to wait for my son to come out every day from school. And Tryone would be there some days too. And we would talk. She was very ugly and verbal about Cody. She would call him names. Say he was 'stupid,' 'sorry,' or 'useless.' She'd say these things almost every time. At one point I was cleaning up after a party, and she came in and told me that she hated Cody and he wasn't going to get in between her and Paul."

This theme was also picked up by a friend, Lorrie Taylor. "Tryone called Cody 'worthless,' a 'horrible child.' 'He never listens. He's a problem. I can't wait until his mother comes and gets him. Under no circumstances is he going to come between me and Paul.' I was completely shocked. I took myself out of the room, because it made me so angry," Taylor recollected.

Sandy would recall an incident where "we had Cody over for a weekend, and he was scared and shook up because he had left a paper at school. He said, 'I'll really be in trouble when I get home!' On Sunday he wanted me to call his dad and see if he could stay one more night because he was afraid to go home. I went in on Monday to the school and talked to a counselor because I was concerned about Cody being abused by Paul." She even went so far as getting in touch with CYFD. Not long after this, the visitations from Cody and Marilea stopped. "Once Cody was taken to the other ranch, visitations became more difficult. I would try calling Cody, but Paul wouldn't let me speak with him."

Paul, Tryone, Cody, and Marilea—no two people ever saw these individuals the same way. The Posey family moved about thirty miles north of Roswell when Paul got a job as a manager on the 5 Mile Ranch, which was owned by the Corn brothers. David Corn recalled that Paul was a good employee, and he would see Cody on different occasions. David said he never saw any signs of abuse against Cody, and never heard his dad cuss at him or belittle him while he was around.

Verlin, Paul's brother, would also occasionally visit the family at the 5 Mile Ranch during this period. He recalled one trip when he and his boys and Cody and Paul went camping up at Boy Scout Mountain in the Capitan Mountains. Since Paul had learned rappeling in the army, he taught it to the boys, and Verlin said, "They got a kick out of it. He never forced them to do anything they didn't want to do. We camped overnight, got up and had breakfast, and sat around and visited. We did short hikes, some rappeling, and target shooting. The boys had some .22s. We roasted marshmallows in the evening. I left my oldest son, Clay, there with Cody and Paul for a few days because I had to get back to work. If I had suspected in any way that my brother was a child abuser, I would not have left Clay in Paul's custody.

"I believe Paul's relationship with Cody was a good relationship, but also a difficult one. I never heard Paul say that he hated Cody. I never heard him cuss at him. Things weren't always peaches and cream, but he wasn't an abuser. We even had Cody stay with us a while, and he never told us once that his dad hit him."

Yet, Cody would recall that things only got worse for him at the 5 Mile Ranch, not better. Cody had worked with livestock at the place in East Grand Plains, but not to the extent of the cowboy life out on the 5 Mile Ranch. There were aspects of the ranch that were new to him. Cody recalled that once he was riding a horse and the stirrups were too short. It hurt his legs, so he put his feet outside the stirrups. According to Cody, his dad came up and said, "Don't do that. This is what will happen to you!" His dad knocked him off his horse into some rocks and brush.

"Another time we were gathering cattle, and it was my first time doing this. We had to cull some old ones out of the herd. I got a rock and threw it at one cow, and my dad saw me. He picked up a rock about the size of a softball and threw it and hit me in the chest. He was only about ten feet away and it left a big bruise on me," Cody remembered.

"To wake me up in the morning, my dad often threw cold water in my face or even shocked me with a cattle prod. A hot shot feels like getting kicked with electricity. It hurts pretty bad. I almost always got cussed at when getting out of bed," he continued.

Just how differently people could view a single event in Cody's life was portrayed by an incident concerning branding and vaccinating of cattle on the 5 Mile Ranch. As Cody remembered it, "This was another first for me, and I was in what was called a 'crowding chute.' I was about nine or ten years old at the time. I was in there amongst cows that were bigger than me, and moving them in with a hot shot. Cows that big concerned me, and I got up on the fence with some other kids, but my dad told me to get back into the crowding pen. I told him I would get kicked in there by the cattle, but my dad pushed me off the fence, anyway. As soon as he did, I got kicked in the head and ribs by the cattle. As I was getting up, I got squashed against the fence. A young guy named B.A. Corn jumped in there to help me, and he ended up getting one of his fingers broken.

"There was also branding and vaccinating going on there. The vaccinations were done at a calf table. They'd have their head caught by a headgate and you'd pull a lever so they couldn't move their bodies around. I was doing vaccinating, where you'd lift up a lever and pull out a bar, but my dad didn't like the way I was doing it. He slammed the bar down on my arm and it lasted for three or four minutes. A two-inch gap was left on my arm for a long time."

David Corn would recall that day in a very different manner. He said later, "There was branding one spring, and it was a family operation. My kids showed up, Verlin brought his kids, and Paul and Cody were there. There were kids ranging in age from seven to sixteen. We used a 'flanking table' to brand the calves. Paul and me and my brothers were doing that. The older boys brought the calves up a chute to the table, and the youngest kids were on the fences. We were branding calves that were a month or two old, and they weighed about two hundred pounds.

"Cody and my daughter and Marilea were in the back of the pen most of the time. The older boys were feeding the calves into the chute. I was the only one using the bar at the flanking table. It went across the midpart of a calf, and I never saw Cody get his arm caught under a bar. That would be pretty hard to do, anyway. Also, we didn't use a hot shot when branding cattle, and I wasn't aware that my nephew B.A. Corn ever got any fingers broken while working the chute.

"I do recall Cody getting kicked by a calf. He was at the back end of the chute and he got kicked in the shin. It wasn't an issue that stopped the work. All the kids and adults got kicked by a calf on occasion."

Verlin Posey weighed in on the issue of branding cattle on the Corn Ranch as well. He said, "'Neighboring' is a term when ranches will exchange work. Friends will help friends do ranch work. There is no outlay of cash that way. I did some 'neighboring' on the Five Mile

Ranch owned by the Corn brothers. I brought Coy and Clay along with me and I didn't see anything unusual at the pens or chutes.

"At other times I didn't see Cody on a horse on that ranch, because there were spoiled cattle there and bad ground. Lots of mesquite and holes. It's not somethin' you're gonna be let loose in that kind of country, unless you've had a lot of experience on horseback in keeping up with a crew and silly cattle."

Yet, Cody recalled that life was becoming hell on the 5 Mile Ranch. He said later, "I got hit in the face two or three times a week. I lost count. I'd get hit in the face with an open hand, a back hand, fist, rods from the shades, boards, ropes—in the face and all parts of the body. I was kicked as well in the groin, stomach, butt, and legs."

According to Cody, it got so bad that he eventually told his stepmom Sandy about it on one of his visits to her. He especially told her about all the verbal abuse that Tryone was heaping upon him. Sandy wasn't standing for any of this, and she contacted CYFD.

Art Ortega had obtained his core training in Albuquerque, where he learned interviewing skills. He was called in on the Cody Posey case in 1999 when he received a referral at his office about a possible case of emotional abuse against a child. Ortega drove to the 5 Mile Ranch unannounced, and Paul, Tryone, Marilea, and Cody were all there. Paul met Ortega by the gate.

Ortega explained who he was and why he was there. He said he needed to speak with Cody alone, and Paul stuck his head in the door of the house and called for Cody. Cody came to the door, and Ortega had Cody come with him to the corner of the yard, away from the others.

Ortega said later, "We usually try to make the child feel comfortable. Since the Poseys were standing outside, I posed Cody so that his back was to them. I proceeded to ask him a few questions about how things were around the house. Cody was very polite. I asked him about name-calling, because the referral said that his stepmother was calling him names. He said, yeah she was, but then he added, 'It's only when I'm bad.' I said, 'Do they use anything?' (Meaning force.) He said, 'If I'm bad, I have to stay in my room or double up on my chores around the house.' He didn't indicate that he was in any danger at the time. I didn't see any signs of bruising or black eyes. He didn't indicate any kind of physical abuse going on.

"I went up and started interviewing Mr. and Mrs. Posey. I spoke with Mrs. Posey first and asked her if she had been calling him names. The report said they were calling him 'faggot' and 'pussy boy.' I asked her, and she said, 'I might have called him "stupid," but I never called him any of those names.' She did say some kids probably called him 'faggot' at school because of the way he danced and fooled around."

Ortega asked Paul Posey the same things, and he said he'd never called his son "faggot" or "pussy boy." He also said he never called him "stupid." In fact, Paul said, Cody's grades were dropping and he told him he needed to get in gear because he *wasn't* stupid.

"I went back a day or two later, and since school was out, there was nobody at school I could speak with. But I tracked down the school counselor and asked about Cody. He said that when Cody first started there, he was kind of a shy kid, but then he had blossomed and done pretty well. He wasn't too worried about Cody. He did mention that Cody had told him he had been called 'stupid,'" Ortega recalled.

After talking with various people, Ortega discussed the issue with his supervisor to determine if the case needed any more input, and did a safety assessment to see if services were needed. In the case of the Posey family, it was determined that Cody wasn't in danger and no further services were required. As Ortega said later, "There was no disclosure from the child that abuse was going on."

Yet, it was always difficult to get a read on Cody, to determine if he was being abused or not, and abused children will not always tell a stranger if they are being abused. In Cody's case a new incident was just around the corner. Cody claimed later that he was talking to his dad in a hallway of the ranch house, and must have said something that his dad didn't like. Suddenly Paul punched him in the mouth and Cody fell backward and his head hit the wall. The impact made a hole in the wall, and as his punishment for having created the hole, Cody was forced to putty the hole by himself. He said that he got a can of drywall plaster and patched it up. According to Cody, it took nearly a whole can to do the job.

The Posey family was on the move once again by 1999, this time to a ranch in Weed, New Mexico, near Cloudcroft. The ranch was called the Cross D Ranch, and it was owned by John Yates. If Cody thought things were going to be easier for him at the Cross D Ranch, however, he was in for a rude surprise.

Chapter 4

The Fatal Road

The Weed area is actually more scenic than the name implies. It's bordered by the Lincoln National Forest, and the National Solar Observatory is not far away on 9,200-foot Sacramento Peak. Cloudcroft, the largest town in the area, is a summer and winter resort, with good skiing at the Ski Cloudcroft area. Along the Sunspot Scenic Byway, there are several pullouts where the dunes of White Sands glimmer far below like an enormous mirage.

One new element about Cody's time at the Cross D Ranch was the fact that his biological mother, Carla, had cleaned up her act and was starting to see Cody a lot more often. Not happy about living with his dad, Tryone, and Marilea, Cody wanted to move back in with his mother. Cody kept after his dad with a constant barrage of requests to go back and live with his mom. By this point Carla had met a young man, William Brust Jr., who was in the U.S. Navy. They were married in

Roswell, New Mexico, in February 2000. William met Cody and liked him. He seemed like a nice kid to Brust.

Carla, who had been in the navy years before, wanted to rejoin the service as well, but because of medical reasons, she couldn't. Cody became more and more persistent in his efforts to move in with Carla and William, and finally Paul became fed up with this and took a very drastic step. He decided to create a document that disinherited Cody.

The document was called a Modification Agreement, and Delbert Paul Posey was the petitioner, and Carla June Brust (Clees) the respondent. There were several stipulations within the agreement.

1. *Paul gave up all parental rights to Cody.*
2. *Paul was no longer morally or financially responsible for any debts incurred by Cody.*
3. *Cody forfeited all rights to any of Paul's estate, and was being formally disowned by Paul.*
4. *No contact was to be made by Cody, Carla, or Paul in the future.*
5. *All past debts of child support were going to be canceled in full.*
6. *Carla was to receive all clothing, prescription medicine, and paperwork pertaining to Cody.*
7. *Cody had the right to change his last name from Posey if he wished to do so.*
8. *Paul was not liable for any future child support.*

In addition to this, there was another agreement written on April 14, 2000, with several more stipulations.

1. *Cody was to remain in Paul's custody until the legal documents took effect.*

2. *Cody was going to be returned to Carla by 6:30 P.M. on Sunday, April 16.*
3. *None of the terms were to be changed.*
4. *If Carla couldn't afford to file, Paul could afford to by June of that year.*

This document was signed by both Carla and Paul, but the original modification agreement didn't seem to have any signatures upon it.

Cody did move back with his mother and her new husband, William Brust. He would say of it later, "It was the greatest time of my life. I loved being with her and my family, the Cleeses. My aunt Corliss was great. They didn't treat me like my dad did. They treated me like a son. I wasn't yelled at, screamed at, kicked, and punched. I got to do things I wanted to do. I was given more privileges. They said nice things to me. I believe that they loved me."

William had been on a tour of duty in Hawaii when he got a call from Carla that Paul had agreed to give her custody of Cody. Cody was able to celebrate his tenth birthday with his mom in Roswell. William later was stationed at Woodby Island, in the Puget Sound area of Washington State, and Carla was all for a move there. William remembered, "When we were moving to Washington, Cody was originally not too happy with it, because he'd miss his friends. But later he seemed agreeable with it, and he and I got along very well. He called me 'Dad' half the time. He was a good kid."

The plan was that it would take them three days to drive from Roswell to Washington State. William, Carla, and Cody loaded up William's Ford F-150 extended-cab pickup and headed for their destination in July 2000. On the way there an error in navigation, which seemed so minor at the time, would have tragic consequences later. They missed the turnoff that headed for the most direct route to Seattle via Salt Lake City. Instead of turning around, and correcting the mistake, they decided to go up to Interstate 40 through Wyoming, and then across Montana and Idaho to Washington State.

As the interstate heads north across the plains of Wyoming near Sheridan, it undulates gently over the low hills and plains, seeming to stretch to the horizon. Cody recalled later, "Near Sheridan, I told my family maybe we should stop and take a rest, but they wanted to move on. Mom crawled into the back, where I'd been, and I moved up front to the passenger seat. I wanted to talk to my new stepdad and she wanted to rest."

William also recalled Cody coming forward in the cab. "He wanted to sit with me and talk. We'd driven a long way, and I'm not sure if I fell asleep or not. The police up that way say it's something they see a lot. They call it 'highway hypnosis.' It's an acute form of tunnel vision, where you tend to lock up on the road. It's almost like a self-induced hypnosis."

Cody became aware too late that William seemed to be mesmerized by the road, and the pickup truck was starting to drift. Cody yelled for William to watch out.

William recalled, "I barely remember Cody yelling my name, because we were drifting off the road. The passenger tire actually hit the dirt."

William's overcorrection only made matters worse. The pickup flipped over several times, going at least seventy miles an hour. He and Cody were buckled up with seat belts. Carla was not.

"When the truck came to a still position, I crawled out

of the truck window and began searching for Mom," Cody remembered.

William recalled, "When I first got out, I was in shock. I didn't know what was going on at first. I told Cody to climb out. We didn't know at that point that Carla had been ejected. I told Cody to move away from the vehicle because I could smell gas. When I didn't spot Carla, I stood up and started calling her name. When I did, Cody started calling out for his mom. He was actually the one who spotted her first and pointed her out to me."

"We both ran over to where she was lying. She was lying faceup. Her body was in convulsions. I've been told those were her death throes. She had broken her neck when she was ejected from the vehicle. We both were there until a driver pulled up. The woman driver said she was a nurse and pulled us away. She said she would look after Carla. Another passerby had to physically pull us away.

"I don't even remember law enforcement at the scene until I was loaded into an ambulance. All I remember was a man grabbed my shoulders and a female grabbed Cody at the same time and pulled us about thirty feet away. The whole time Cody kept calling out, 'Mom! Mom!'

"I was told in the ambulance by one of the people in there that they had told Cody that his mom was dead." Either that did not happen, or Cody was in such a state of shock that he didn't remember it. Cody would recall, "They took me away as I was trying to help Mom. And they put me in the back of an ambulance. I asked many times if she was okay, and the doctors said she would be fine. I got stitches on my arm from a cut going through the window. Before I went to bed that night, a doctor told me that she had died on impact. A police officer was there with the doctor."

"After Carla was killed, Cody and I returned to Roswell. Carla had always wanted a funeral service there, and her ashes were to be scattered in New Mexico. We returned to New Mexico to prepare for the funeral services and so that Cody could stay with his aunt Corliss," William remembered.

The funeral services would be something Cody would remember all too well in years to come. Doyle Baker was a cousin of Cody's, and he attended the funeral for Carla, along with other family members. Doyle was talking to Cody at the funeral before the service, turned around, and saw Paul Posey come into the church. (Others would say that Paul never did come into the church sanctuary, where he could be seen.) Whatever the circumstances, Cody realized his father was there, and a panicked look spread across his face. "Once he found out his dad was at the church, trying to get him back, he was a whole different person. It was the biggest change I've seen in a person. Just a split moment of time," Baker recalled.

Cody's friend Courtney Taylor also saw the dramatic change in Cody when he realized that Paul was there. She said later, "When his father came to the church, I looked at him and he was devastated. He was crying. It was like a horror movie. He said he would rather live on the streets than go back and live with his father."

Lorrie Taylor, a friend, also attested to the way Cody felt. "He was extremely upset. He said, 'I will never go back with my dad! And they can't make me!' He started off mad, then crying."

Another person later spoke of how Cody reacted when he learned that his father was at the church. This individual recalled how "Sherry Gensler came in and got us. We walked into a room and saw Paul and Tryone, along with Officer Robert Farmer. I was pretty young and didn't quite realize what was going on. We were in the same room for a little while, but then they asked me and Mrs. Taylor and Cody to go into a separate room. Cody had already been crying. Tears running down his face."

Paul Posey had either read about the funeral in the newspaper, or had heard about it through the grapevine, and he took some actions before he set one foot inside the church where the funeral was to take place. He phoned the Roswell Police Department (RPD) about getting his son back, and Officer Robert Farmer became involved.

Robert Farmer had been a police officer for sixteen years and on an antidrug and antigang task force. He regularly went to schools in the area for the D.A.R.E. program, which helped kids to stay out of gangs and off drugs. In the year 2000, Officer Farmer was summoned by a supervisor to talk with Paul Posey. Paul had requested police assistance in regaining custody of Cody. He said his son was possibly at a church in Roswell and was at the funeral of his mother. Paul related that Cody had been living with his mother, but she had been killed in a vehicle accident.

Paul had already spoken once to Cody after the accident. (It is unclear if this was in person or by phone.) Paul had been unable to see or talk to Cody since that time. "Mr. Posey felt he was being denied access to his son. He was afraid Cody would be removed from the state of New Mexico by his new stepfather," Farmer recalled.

Officer Farmer went to the local DA's office to discuss the case with ADA Alan Griffin. Part of this was because of a document in which Paul had relinquished custody of Cody to his mother. Farmer said later, "I wanted to be sure we were doing the proper thing."

The ADA looked at the document, and it was clear that Carla was no longer a factor in having custody of Cody. Cody's closest biological relative was his father, and because of that fact, Paul had more rights to custody of Cody than William Brust or Corliss Clees. (There was also some later contention that Paul never signed the agreement, but had merely handed it to Carla without a signature.)

Farmer and another officer went to the church in Roswell, and Paul and Tryone followed in another vehicle. Officer Farmer recalled that the church had some outer doors and then some inner doors. They all went through the outer doors and contacted a secretary at the front office. Farmer told the secretary that he needed to talk to Mr. Brust and Cody Posey. He said it was important, and needed to be handled in the right way. The secretary said that services for Carla Brust had just started and couldn't be interrupted. Farmer agreed and requested an office where he and Paul could wait. Then he asked her to inform the pastor that they were there.

Farmer said that Paul never did go into the sanctuary of the church, so it would have been impossible for Cody or Doyle Baker to have seen him. Farmer recalled that they waited fifteen or twenty minutes before one of the pastors came out of the services, and the pastor was pretty hot under the collar. The pastor told Farmer and Paul that they were trespassing and needed to leave. Officer Farmer explained why they were there, and was able to calm the pastor down.

Corliss Clees and another pastor came into the room after the services. Both Corliss and this pastor were also very upset. Corliss told both Paul and Farmer they had no right to be there, and Farmer stated that they were present because Mr. Posey was being denied access to his son, and it was to assure that Cody would not be removed from the state. Officer Farmer went from office to office to office trying to calm everyone down. At some point Carl Clees contacted Officer Farmer and said that he was Carla's brother and he was representing the family at the funeral.

After Farmer managed to calm Corliss and the pastor down, he spoke with William Brust. He asked Brust if Cody had been adopted, and Brust said he had been considering it, but hadn't done so, so far. Farmer informed him that to take Cody out of state would be against the law and Brust would be charged with a crime if he did. Brust said that he understood and assured Farmer that he wouldn't do that.

Finally Farmer contacted Cody and brought him into another office. "Two pastors were with me, Pastor Ramos and Pastor Reed. When Cody was brought in, he appeared to be a normal ten-year-old child. He wasn't crying at the time. He was quiet and respectful," Farmer observed.

Farmer explained to Cody that he was sorry he had to deal with this at the present time. Farmer also explained that there were a lot of people there who were concerned about his welfare. Cody seemed to be okay with that, according to Farmer. They made some small talk, and Farmer asked if he wanted to go live with his dad. Farmer said that Cody responded, "I don't know."

Cody did say that he wanted to spend more time with Carla's family, and Farmer said that something could be worked out in that regard. Then Farmer asked if Cody wanted to see his father now, and Cody said yes.

Paul was escorted into the room. As Farmer recalled, "Cody seemed pleased to see his father. They exchanged hugs and kisses. I stayed in the room with Paul and Cody the whole time. They talked for about twenty minutes. It was a lot of small talk. Paul stated that he loved Cody and wanted him to come back and live with them. Cody said that he would, but he wanted to live with his mom's family for a while longer. Paul said that things could be worked out with his uncle Carl Clees about this."

There were talks at the church between Paul and Carl Clees and both agreed that Cody could stay awhile with Corliss Clees. According to Farmer, this interchange seemed to be civil, and after the arrangements were made, all parties seemed to be satisfied.

"Paul seemed to be satisfied that he could trust Carl. At that point Carl and Paul and Tryone all left the church. There were no incidents. I watched Mr. and Mrs. Posey drive off in a truck. Cody remained in the church and there was no screaming or yelling or calls for help by him," Farmer recollected.

William Brust also had a take on what had just occurred. He said later, "Me and Cody were pulled into separate rooms after the church memorial service. The officer came in and told me what was going on. I was told that Cody had not wanted to go with his father, but after talking to Paul, he agreed to give his father a second chance and go back with him."

What is unclear are the events that happened after the funeral service that day. Doyle Baker would speak of Cody joining him and some friends at a swimming pool in Roswell later that day and saying that he did not want to go back and live with his father. Others would say that Cody and his dad went to a park for a while and talked some more.

As things eventually turned out, going back with Paul, Tryone, and Marilea would have consequences for all of them that would have been beyond their wildest nightmares.

Chapter 5

Heaven or Hell

The disparity of how different people viewed the Posey family only increased when they were at the Cross D Ranch near Weed, New Mexico. One of those people was a registered nurse named Emily Nutt. She taught Sunday school at a church in Mayhill, where the Posey family attended. Emily had both Cody and Marilea in her class of students who were in the fourth, fifth, and sixth grades. There were Bible studies on Sunday mornings just prior to church, a children's program on Thursday nights, and something called the "Clowning Ministry" for children, in which they would don face paint and appear as clowns. This program was on Sundays between 4:00 and 5:00 P.M. Cody attended Sunday school, came back at 4:00 P.M. for the clowning class, and stayed on between 5:00 and 6:00 P.M. for Bible drills.

"The first time I saw the Posey family, they looked like the perfect family. All four of them were standing there with grins on their faces. They were all perfectly dressed, starched and ironed, and looked so nice," Emily recalled. "I thought, 'Oh, how wonderful to see such a perfect family.' And yet something was wrong. About two or three weeks later, Marilea came up to me and asked why Cody was living with her and her parents. She said they didn't want him and had only taken him in because his mother had died."

Emily talked about the clowning classes: "The clowning was a program where they would dress as clowns in full costume and make up their faces. The kids entertained at church and twice a year there was a big production. They would also entertain at summer vacation Bible schools and at different churches. This was a way to witness to people through clowning.

"Bible drills was a Baptist program for children to learn the Bible. It was a competition on three levels. The first level was to find any book in the Bible within ten seconds. Then the participant would have to tell the name of the book prior to the one called and the one after. In the second level the participant had to memorize twenty-five Scriptures. The third level was to find ten key passages—things such as where the Ten Commandments were located. The kids started out with church competitions, where if they did well enough, they moved on to an associate competition. Finally, if they moved up far enough, they could compete at the state competition in Albuquerque."

Emily Nutt taught Cody and Marilea during the fall of 2000. The first regional competition was slated for April 2001, and the state competition for May. Cody and Marilea were almost always in Sunday school, and they didn't miss a clowning class or Bible competition that year. "Cody was an excellent student. He had a mind for the Bible. A great memory. He was just a delight to teach and he always had lots of questions. He was a fun student to teach because he always wanted to learn," Emily related.

"It depended on who was there as to how Cody was at Bible drills. Paul and Tryone became involved in the children's programs at church, and they helped with the clowning program. Tryone even became a clown and helped with skits and costumes. Paul didn't want to clown, but he helped with staging and lighting.

"Cody was a good child, and I never had to correct him for anything, but Paul was very, very strict with him. He didn't have to say anything to Cody, all he had to do was look at him. No matter if Cody was laughing or talking to a friend, he would instantly stop. If he was standing next to a friend and talking, he would walk away from that friend and go stand by himself. He'd stand with his head down. Sometimes Paul would go up and grab Cody by the back of the neck. He would say, 'Cody!' and Cody would stop whatever he was doing.

"As time passed, I really suspected things were not right at the Posey home. I never saw Paul or Tryone show any affection toward Cody. There was a very marked way that they treated Marilea as opposed to Cody. They were always loving on her. Smiling at her. Touching her. Telling her what a good student she was and how beautiful she was.

"I tried to encourage Cody. He did exceptionally well during Bible drill competition and only missed the answer to one question. But Paul got mad at Cody and pulled him out of competitions. I said, 'Oh, please, Paul, he's worked so hard at this. He's good at it. He's been punished enough.' Paul replied, 'Let me ask you this, Miss Emily. How does allowing a bad boy to compete in state competition glorify God?'

"I made attempts three times with Paul and Tryone to

have Cody participate in the association competition, and twice for state. Cody was exceptional. There was even a man at the state level who was willing to let Cody in, even though he'd missed associate competitions. But Paul said he couldn't go.

"After a while only Marilea was allowed to participate in the associate and state drills. Cody was made to sit away from the rest of the children and away from Bible practice. He was made to attend and watch, however. Cody's parents were there and kind of taunting him. They said, 'Cody, if you were a good boy, you could sit up here with us. But because you are a bad boy, you have to sit in the back.'"

Charlene "Charlie" Cooper had a very different take on the Posey family at the same Baptist church. Charlie taught the fifth-grade class at Cloudcroft, and was Marilea's teacher there. Charlie also knew the Posey family because they were considered to be "ranch neighbors." The families shared fences and boundaries, and the men would help each other with the cattle and welding.

"Tryone and Paul were in the adult Sunday-school class and I never heard them say anything derogatory about Cody. They never called him names or physically abused him. The clowning class was open to all the youth, and sometimes I attended the meetings. My granddaughter participated in that, and I even put on her makeup sometimes. My granddaughter was about the same age as Cody," Charlie said.

"The Poseys were a lovely family. We were happy to have them in the fellowship. I never saw Cody once sit by himself in the back of the room at the clowning classes."

There were several people at Cloudcroft Middle

School who also said they never saw Cody being abused by either Paul or Tryone. One of these was Cathy Miller, a teacher at the middle school. She knew the Posey family and lived about a mile from their house. "Cody was always with a group at school. Talking and smiling. He tended toward a popular crowd. He was a neat kid. I also saw the Poseys at the Baptist church. Marilea was kindhearted and always looking out for the underdog. She liked to get lots of hugs," Cathy stated.

"I saw Tryone at school and she helped out a lot there. I didn't see any differences in the way Paul and Tryone treated Cody or Marilea. For a long time I didn't know that Tryone was not Cody's biological mother.

"I had seen kids at school who had been physically abused and I knew the 'red lights' to look for. These included bruises, black eyes, and burns. They also included if a kid continually asked for more food or was a withdrawn loner. I didn't think Cody fell into this category. Usually, parents who are abusing children will not make contact with a school, but Paul and Tryone were interested in how Cody was doing at school. Cody always seemed to have lots of friends."

There was never a consensus about Cody or any of the rest of his family. Others would speak more and more of Cody's isolation on the Cross D Ranch. Especially disturbed were those who had known him in the past and wanted to keep in touch with him. William Brust recalled, "Once Cody moved back with Paul, I didn't get to visit him anymore. Cody was forced to stay at home when not at school, and he couldn't visit his cousins from his mom's side of the family."

Vicki Harrington said, "After Carla's funeral I tried phoning Cody during some weekends. I'd call and be told he wasn't available. Tryone would usually handle the calls. My son got through to him once. Brandon was very upset after the call. Tryone told him that Cody didn't want to be friends with him anymore. When I asked Tryone about this, she said that Cody had moved on and had new friends and that Brandon needed to do so as well. Then she hung up on me."

Lorrie Taylor tried getting Cody's phone number, and she e-mailed him. She never got a response. Jan Calloway ran into Tryone at a Wal-Mart after the funeral. She asked how Cody was doing. Tryone said he was fine, but never allowed Calloway to contact him in any way. Sherry Gensler also saw Tryone in a Wal-Mart. She tried talking to Cody, but Tryone was not welcoming, and Cody wouldn't speak.

In fact, there seemed to have been very few people who ever visited the ranch, and most of the comments about Marilea and Cody from this time period were later stated by teachers at school. Amy Lane was a schoolteacher at Cloudcroft Elementary, which taught kindergarten through fifth grade. She had Marilea in her class and every once in a while Tryone would come in as a volunteer, copying papers and assisting teachers on field trips.

"Marilea was very energetic and a bright student. She was always dressed like a little country girl. She wore jeans or denim skirts, long-sleeved shirts, and boots, and her hair was in long braids. She was a cute little girl," Lane stated.

Linda Munoz was a teacher at Cloudcroft Middle School and had Cody in her computer class. The kids in Cody's sixth-grade classes were taught the beginnings of word processing and spreadsheets. Of Cody, Munoz later said, "I vividly remember him sitting in my class. He was talkative, and always had a great respect for me.

He was always dressed very neatly and often had a smile on his face. I did sometimes have to get onto him to get his work done, because he loved talking so much. But I would tell him in a kind motherly way that he needed to settle down.

"Cody was not making good grades in my class. He had quite a few zeroes for not turning in his work. One additional thing I did for Cody, and I did not do this for many students, was to let him take a typing book home. This was in order to help him get a little faster with keyboarding. I believe he had a typewriter at home, so I would allow him to type lines. If he could have gotten his speed up, he could have been making wonderful grades that he should have been making."

Munoz discussed Cody's grades with his parents about eight weeks into the school year. She talked to Paul, and Paul surprised her with a comment he made. Munoz said, "Paul turned to me and said, 'Your class is not worth taking, because my son is going to own his own business someday. And he'll be able to hire a secretary to do the computer work.'

"I told him that a person has to know computer skills. Even if you have your own business, you've got to be able to run a computer. Otherwise, you could have a secretary who could steal you blind or misrepresent you."

Munoz wrote a letter to Paul and Tryone around Christmastime that year. She explained how she taught her class and her observations of Cody. The response from Tryone was that they did care about his grades, and that computer skills were important.

One other thing Munoz would mention later. She said she had taken a workshop in child abuse and knew the things to look for, like bruises. She said that abused kids were often bullies in school, acting out in the way they were abused. They were generally unkempt, often missed school, and didn't socialize well. In her estimation Cody didn't fit into any of those categories.

The middle-school principal at Cloudcroft was Fred Wright. He knew both Cody and Marilea, and said, "When I observed Cody, he was usually talking with or playing with other students. I didn't see him sitting off by himself at lunch. When you see that, you have some concerns. Cody was a very polite, well-mannered young man. He was about an average student. Good in some subjects, but low in language arts."

When Wright thought back on it later, he described Paul Posey as being very strict with Cody. Paul and Tryone wanted to hold Cody back from going into the seventh grade. In other words, Cody would repeat the sixth grade. Even Wright was concerned about Cody's performance. "The problem would have gotten worse when he went into seventh grade. He was getting work in late. There were meetings between a teacher, Paul, and myself about Cody. These went on from January to the end of the school year," the principal recounted.

Asked later if Paul might have abused Cody at home, Wright said, "I wasn't aware if he was or not."

Cody had his own recollections of the middle school at Cloudcroft, and not all of them were good. He said that at lunch break and PE time, he would play football or basketball in his cowboy boots because his dad wouldn't allow him to wear tennis shoes. He wasn't allowed to wear casual clothing, but rather Wrangler jeans and a button-down shirt. Because he played basketball on asphalt, he eventually wore a hole in the bottom of one boot.

"I showed Dad the boot, and he got angry and hit me across the face with the boot. 'That's what you get for playing basketball in your boots!' he said. He had put his fingers in the finger holes that you use to pull up the boot and slapped me across the face with it. It left an impression," Cody said later.

"Dad forced me to save up my money to buy new boots, and boots back then were anywhere from seventy-five to two hundred dollars. I only got paid ten-dollars spending money for working on the ranch, so it took me three or four months just to buy a really cheap pair of boots. Pretty soon I had the same problem as before. I had to put duct tape on the boots to hide the hole."

And yet middle-school principal Fred Wright would later say, "I never saw Cody wearing duct tape on his boots. If I had seen it, I would have asked Cody why it was there. If it was because he couldn't afford shoes, we had a procedure where we look for shoes that might fit the child."

Cody was getting over $600 a month in Social Security, because his mother had died, but he never got any of it. Every month he signed the check over to his dad, who placed it in his own savings account.

Cody related, "If I got in any kind of trouble at school, I'd get home and get it three times as bad. There were three swats at school for talking in class, and then the principal would call home and tell my parents. When I got home, Dad would give me swats with a belt. These turned into whippings all over the body. I was told to bend over and grab my ankles. He'd hit as hard as he could, and it hurt so bad, I tried to run away. As I tried running, he'd chase me around and hit me with the belt. Tryone belted me on occasion as well.

"As I got older, the beating and hitting and name-calling became progressively worse. Around the age of twelve, it wasn't taking off the belt to spank me, it was taking off the belt to hit me. I was getting hit with fists, rocks, and boards. When I first moved back with Dad, he said he'd stop hitting me, but it only got worse as time went on.

"Even at the age of ten and eleven, I was doing the work around the ranch that a twenty-one-year-old would do. I unloaded seven hundred twenty bales of hay in one day. I toted fifty-pound sacks of feed, and might ride horseback all day long. Sometimes I wouldn't even eat lunch until seven P.M. One time we were putting stays in a barbed-wire fence. Stays are pieces of wood you put into the fence to make it stronger. I used an ax and saw and tied over two hundred stays into a fence in two or three days. I was in the sixth grade."

School was at least a break from toiling on the ranch, but Cody dreaded weekends and summer vacations. At those times he felt that he was being treated as a slave and not a son. Overall, he did well in school, but he did not do well in typing class. He got a C in that. Cody said as a punishment he was sentenced to his room after school. "I had to stay in there all night and the heat didn't reach the room very well. I was cold a lot. In the evening I'd hay and water the horses and clean the stalls. Then it was straight back to the room. There was [a] bed, a nightstand, and [a] radio in the room, but at some point all three were taken away from me. All I had to lay on was a mattress with a sheet on it. I went through a whole school year that way."

Cody would later say that he had those things taken away because he was supposed to read *Robinson Crusoe* that year and pass a test, rather than something that had to do with typing class. He read a condensed version of the book instead of the actual novel, and didn't do well on the test. His poor performance made his dad very angry.

"I'd eat a lot of dinners in that room. Occasionally I was let out to eat in the dining room with everyone else, and occasionally I was allowed to sit and watch television with them. My clothes were kept in my parents' room and they would choose what they wanted me to wear the next day. I had no choice in the clothes I wore."

According to Cody, things only got steadily worse at the ranch in Weed. "One time I spilled a glass of iced tea in the kitchen," he recalled. "It was a small kitchen and I was putting the tea back into the refrigerator and my elbow hit a glass of tea on the counter. The glass fell to the floor and shattered. My dad knocked me down to the floor and pinned me down there and slapped me repeatedly across the face. He was yelling stuff like, 'Dumb-ass!' and 'Stupid fuck!' I heard those words a lot around the house.

"One time out on the ranch, we were making a tire trough out of a big tractor tire. My dad was cutting a steel bead out of the tire with a reciprocating saw and it was hard to cut through the rubber tire. It was my job to hold the tire still and the tire was triple my weight. My dad got mad at something and swung the tire around and laid me out on the concrete.

"Around that ranch I had to feed mineral blocks to the cattle. Each mineral block weighed about two hundred pounds. We'd roll them off an old railroad car that was used for storage and then up a loading ramp into a truck. One of these fell off the ramp while I was pushing it and rolled down the hill. Dad kicked me and rolled that block up over my foot. Three toes were really bruised when I looked at them that night, and I could barely walk on that foot. I learned to grow accustomed to pain.

"Dad always wanted me doing chores at top speed. After a long day of work one day, I was walking slowly and Dad ran up and kicked me in the shins with his spur. He bruised my leg and cut my pants. Later on in the day, I was reprimanded for having torn pants.

"We had a bunch of flatland on the ranch and saddles in between the mountains, where the trees and brush outgrew the grass. So we'd try popping the trees and brush out of there with a backhoe to allow the grass to grow. We'd been doing it all day long one time and I thought I saw Dad motion for me to come up and jump on the tractor with him. I went up there and Dad pushed me off and I fell into a hole, where a large tree had been pulled out. This hurt me emotionally. I had always liked riding on tractors. I thought he was going to let me ride home with him on the tractor. It was kind of an all-American farm boy's dream to ride on a tractor with his father or his family.

"When those kinds of things happened, I'd remove myself from my father and family. I'd go outside and go up into the mountains and sit and cry to myself. I'd talk to myself about what had happened. I had nobody to talk to."

Because of the incident on the 5 Mile Ranch, where a social worker had spoken with Cody, and nothing happened to make things get better, Cody was very leery at this point to talk with any adults outside the family. He said later, "I didn't talk to teachers or counselors or any adult about what was going on. I kind of held it all in."

Then in the fall of 2001, the family was suddenly on the move again. It was so secret, according to Cody, that his parents wouldn't let him or Marilea tell anyone that they were moving. Cody said by this time Marilea constantly spied on him at school, about his behavior and anything that he said to others there.

Not long before they moved, Emily Nutt was a substitute teacher at Cloudcroft Middle School and saw Cody standing at the upper level with his head down, alone. She went over to talk to him and told him how much she missed him. Cody told her that they were moving. All of a sudden Marilea ran up and said, "Don't tell Miss Emily what we're doing! It's a secret."

Emily related, "Marilea looked at me and said, 'He can't tell you and neither am I.' And then she said to Cody, 'I'm telling Mom and Dad.' Not wanting to cause trouble, I just walked away."

The big secret that Cody and Marilea were not supposed to tell was that their dad had just been hired on as Sam Donaldson's ranch manager, and they were all moving to Chavez Canyon Ranch in Lincoln County.

Chapter 6

Lincoln County

Lincoln County, which includes the small town of Hondo, is a historic area of New Mexico. Near Capitan, in 1950, firefighters found a small bear cub up a tree that had escaped a terrible forest fire. They nicknamed the bear Smokey, and the name stuck. Smokey Bear became a symbol of forest fire prevention all across the nation, and the real Smokey Bear lived out a long life at the National Zoo in Washington, D.C.

Even more famous was the "Lincoln County War" of the 1870s, with its most notorious participant, Billy the Kid. Billy was fourteen years old when he killed his first man—not unlike Cody—and he killed at least four others in Lincoln County. And not unlike Cody, Billy was seen by others as someone who either had been pushed into the killings as a form of self-defense, or as a cold-blooded killer. No one could ever quite decide who the "real" Billy was, and the same would hold true for Cody Posey.

Cody may not have been pleased about the new move to Lincoln County at first, but in time he said, "I liked the country around Hondo and the school and people there. It took me a little while to get used to the ranch. I wasn't used to riding that rough a country. I liked the land on the ranch, though. I never met Mr. Donaldson too often, but I was polite to him. I knew him by saying, 'Hello.'

"I really got along with my classmates at Hondo School. I started sixth grade there and it was one big campus. There were about two hundred kids total, and the classes went from preschool up to seniors in high school. My grades improved and I even got a couple of honorables in sixth, seventh, and eighth grades."

Cody progressed enough academically that he was even allowed into a few "Knowledge Bowls," which were an academic *Jeopardy*-type game between schools. Students in the "Knowledge Bowls" were on a panel and asked questions, to which they provided the answers. The questions ranged across a whole variety of subjects.

However, his isolation seemed to increase even more at Chavez Canyon Ranch than it had at the ranch near Weed. According to Cody, he wasn't allowed to be around his friends after school; he wasn't even supposed to be talking with them at school; he wasn't allowed to go over to their homes; they couldn't come visit him at the ranch; he wasn't allowed to go on field trips. Except for a very short period of time, he wasn't allowed to participate in sports or any kind of extracurricular activity.

Cody said there was an instance when he supplied items for a school party, but was not allowed to attend. He said that during the school party, he had to sit in the principal's office. As far as talking with friends after school, there wasn't any of that. Cody recalled, "After the last bell rang, I went to my locker, grabbed my books. and went straight home. Tryone drove me and Marilea to school and back."

Different friends that Cody had made at school would comment on this aspect of his life. Lawrence Gonzales recalled, "When Cody got out of the pickup that Tryone drove, he felt better. He went to the gym and played sports as much as he could. When school was over, he didn't seem like the same kid getting into that vehicle. I never saw Cody interact with his parents. I was gonna say hello to Paul once, but I didn't. He never gave me any respect."

Anthony Sanchez said, "I hung out with Cody as much as I could. During lunch we went out and played basketball together. I never saw him after school, or during the summers. He never got to come over my house, and I never got to go over his house. He never got to play in any games on the Hondo Eagles team, and he was good at sports. When Cody first arrived in the morning with Tryone, he was upset. During the middle of the day, he was okay. He had a sad face at the end of the day and wouldn't talk much. This happened every day."

Bryan Aragon remembered, "Cody was a normal kid. He was very polite. No confrontations with anybody. He was one of the best athletes in our school. During school he was happy and relaxed, but about thirty minutes before he had to go home, he seemed depressed. He'd go to the restroom and fix his shirt. He always had to wear long-sleeved shirts, no matter how hot it was. A lot of us would stay in the hallway and talk. But he'd immediately go to his locker, get his stuff, and go to his stepmom's truck."

If life on the ranch at the Cross D had been hard, it only got worse at Chavez Canyon, according to Cody.

He listed a litany of abuses that could happen anywhere and at any time. Cody said, "One time I was riding with a saddle that had a big post horn on it, and I was in a new part of the country, with rocks and ledges and cliffs. It was dangerous riding country and I grabbed the saddle horn. My Dad saw it and grabbed me by the back of the neck and slammed me down so my chest hit the saddle horn. I almost fell off my horse. It was a horse I didn't know well, a horse the ranch hands named 'Pendejo.' (Roughly translated, this means asshole.)

"There was another incident where somebody else missed some cows in the area, and Dad rode up behind me and grabbed his rope and started hitting me with the coils of the rope because he thought I had missed them. He hit me on the back and head with the looped rope and he was swinging it pretty hard.

"Another time we were dealing with new cattle, and Dad was pushing cattle up toward me. There was a cow running right toward me and I threw a rock at it to steer it away. I went to move a wire gate and my dad threw a rock at me and hit me right in the shoulder blade area. It left a cut and a bruise.

"Dad always seemed to be throwing rocks at me. We were working, cutting an alley, to push cows one way and calves another. I was in charge of working the calf gate, and Dad was on his horse doing the cutting. A cow and calf were coming my way, and I got scared because the cow was coming right at me. I was only twelve years old, and it was pretty big. I shut the gate, and the cow and calf went into the wrong pen. Dad got so upset, he grabbed the gate and shoved it right into me. I was squeezed between the barn and heavy gate."

Cutting cattle was a dangerous business for Cody. According to him, his dad could get mad at the least provocation. "We were cutting cattle once, and I put a cow into the wrong herd. Dad was on horseback, and he roped me, dallied up around the saddle horn, and rode off. My arms were pinned and I fell facedown onto the ground. I was dragged about thirty feet on my face and front side, until I could turn over. When I did turn over, I was hit on the back of the head as I bounced along. I had cuts on my face and bruises on my back. Dad was using a quarter horse, and it was a good runner. I was afraid the rope would come up around my neck and choke me while I was getting dragged. I'd heard from cowboys about people getting roped and dragged and dying of head wounds or a broken neck.

"When he stopped, and I got up and took the rope off, I was crying and didn't say anything to Dad. Whenever I cried, he called me 'gay,' 'fag,' 'pussy,' or 'queer.' I was forced to hide my emotions my whole life. I had to keep my emotions in. If I ever said anything back to him, I'd get slapped or punched. If he felt the need to punch or hit or kick me, he would do it at every opportunity. I couldn't count the times he'd do it. Two or three times a week. Two or three times a day on occasion. It might depend on how his day was going. It happened more on the weekends or during the summer. It was kind of a relief to be at school.

"Tryone, when she felt like it, she slapped me and hit me too. One time I was sitting in an office chair. She hit me so hard, it tipped both me and the office chair over. It was all because me and Marilea were calling each other names. I called Marilea a 'geek,' and Tryone didn't like that.

"Another time my Dad was hitting and punching me, and I guess he got tired of it, and gave up, but Tryone came over to the couch and pinned me down with her knees and started hitting me in the face with slaps and closed fists. She was wailing on me."

All outdoor work was a potential time for trouble on the ranch for Cody. According to him, any little mistake would not be tolerated by his dad, especially when it came to livestock. "We were gathering a pasture of cows, and when you gather a pasture of cows, you have two or three people riding on one side, and you ride zigzag and cover a lot of area. You sweep the whole pasture. I was riding in my area of the pasture where some cows were missed. Up in Hondo, there's a lot of places you can miss cows. There's draws, trees, rocks, and a lot of places they can hide behind. My dad came up to me on horseback, and pulled me by my ear and tried pulling me off my horse. I grabbed onto the horn. We were riding side by side, and I was pulled toward his horse. We were riding up toward some brushy country and I got dragged through a bunch of branches."

Anyplace on the ranch could be a location of abuse, according to Cody. Any job could bring on a tirade from his father. Cody said, "One time we were irrigating and it was my job to clean the irrigation ditch after the winter— to clean it of all dirt and leaves. My dad dropped me off down there and told me to grab a shovel. As I grabbed the shovel, he didn't approve of the type of shovel I grabbed and he took that shovel and threw it at me and hit me in the chest. It left a bruise on my chest. The next day he dropped me off to do the same thing, and the shovel he wanted me to use, he grabbed it and hit me in the leg with it. He told me that was the one to use, and I had a bruise and cut on my leg after that.

"One time I asked my father a question, and my voice was changing around that time. So when I asked the question, I guess he thought I had sassed him. He went to slap me, but he thought I was trying to hit him, when I was just trying to cover up. He pushed me down to the ground and hit me and started choking me. It got to where I couldn't breathe. He told me later in the truck he didn't know what he was doing until I started to turn blue.

"My dad always told me when I was younger, he should have tied me up in a sack with rocks and thrown me in a river, like with puppies you don't want. Since then, I didn't like my head stuck underwater for a period of time, and I don't want to be choked. I have a fear of that. I don't want to die that way."

The fear of water was only reinforced by other incidents. Cody recalled, "In the transition from fall to winter, it was getting colder outside. There was a water tank about four feet high, and inside was a lead (pronounced 'leed') pipe. Whenever the water gets low enough, the pump starts pumping water in there. Once it goes underwater, it will stop pumping. It's like a float. It was cold, and the lead pipe had dropped to the bottom and the water tank was overflowing. It was my job to go in there and get it out. My dad told me to strip down naked and get in there.

"I told him the water was cold, 'cause I felt it. It would be better if I went in there with my clothes on. When I said that, he grabbed me by my hair on the back of my head, and put my head underwater until I stopped blowing bubbles, and I couldn't breathe. As he pulled me back up, I took a deep breath, and as soon as I took the breath, he put me back underneath the water. He did that about three times. My chest hurt so bad, it felt like it was going to burst. After that, I ended up in the water with my clothes off, fixing the lead pipe."

Cattle, troughs, irrigation—anything was a potentially dangerous situation for Cody. There was a forty-acre alfalfa farm on one of Donaldson's ranches on the east side of Capitan. The ranch could put up around 1,200 bales of hay per year, and Paul, Cody, and some ranch hands would drive up there and get the bales of hay. There was a designated driver of the truck, who would move it at a slow speed, and three or four others "bucked" the hay. One or two workers would be on a trailer behind the truck, stacking the hay.

Cody remembered, "I was young then and learning to drive a stick shift. I would bring my foot up off the clutch too fast, and the truck would bunny hop and jerk people around. So my dad opened up the door and grabbed a hay hook and put it down at my crotch and told me, 'The next time you pop that clutch, this hay hook is going into your balls!' I learned real quick not to pop the clutch.

"Another time with a hay hook, well, there's a rail for strapping the hooks on. We were done stacking hay, and I hooked my hay hook in that area, but my hay hook fell down and the tire rolled over the hay hook. It popped a tire because of the sharpness of the hay hook. We had to strap down the hay, jack up the truck, and remove the tire. I told my dad that I didn't know a hay hook was sharp enough to pop a tire. He took the hay hook and put it on my hand and said, 'If this hay hook is sharp enough to cut your hand, it's sharp enough to pop a tire.' And then he jabbed the hay hook down into the top of my hand. I still have a scar there." Workers who were there included Steven Chaves, Slim Britton, and Pilo Vasquez, and they would later remember this incident.

At a young age Cody had to load, unload, and feed hay to the animals on the ranch. At Chavez Canyon Ranch the hay was hauled on a "gooseneck flatbed." Cody, along with the others, would stack the bales up three or four high and then haul it to the barn. From there it was thrown off the trailer and stacked in the barn.

Cody recalled, "We were tossing bales off the trailer. You'd throw it down on the ground, to what's called a block, and then it would roll to the stacker. The bales weighed about sixty-five pounds each. That's hard throwing that stuff. There were some bales on that ranch weighing ninety pounds. You don't want a ninety-pound bale of hay hitting you anywhere.

"I was on the trailer, throwing hay onto the block, and it rolled off and hit my dad in the leg. He got upset and told me to get off the trailer. As soon as I got down, he got up there and was dropping hay down right and left. There was one that came down and scraped my back. A couple of times he launched them at me. Some hit me in the chest. That was pretty hard after hauling hay all day long. When I thought about it later, I think he was letting out anger. He seemed to enjoy it. He was angry a lot of the time.

"I wondered why I wasn't the one who didn't have to have hay thrown at them. Why couldn't I be the person Dad liked? I always thought that I didn't fit in, and my dad didn't like me. I wanted so bad to please him. I was thinking, 'What can I do to please him? What haven't I done?' A lot of the time, because he pointed the blame at me, I looked for the blame in myself. But a lot of times, I wasn't to blame.

"It was the same with Tryone. I wanted to make her happy, because she was just as bad. She was mean and cruel and hit me. Called me names. She didn't like me at all for some reason. I couldn't say why. I wanted to have a real family. I had seen families on TV and I'd talked to kids about family. I wanted to please everybody that I could, to make a family. I wanted to be the

kid who my dad would say, 'Hey, look, that's my son!'
I wanted to be the kid who went out there and worked
hard all day, and got appreciated for it. I didn't want to
work hard all day, come back, and hear that I did something wrong. I wanted to be liked and loved."

Even being around sheep was not a safe place, according to Cody. "When I was working sheep, they were afraid
of humans, so they would go to the opposite side of an
area from the human. They would bunch up in a corner
and sometimes smother themselves. A couple of lambs
had been smothered one day because of that. Two of them
were dead, and one wasn't dead. I thought I might be able
to give it a kind of CPR. I'd seen that done before. But my
dad gave me a pocketknife and told me to kill the lamb. I
couldn't do it. I was just going to let the lamb go. Steven
Chaves was there at the time, and he said to me, 'You
know what, I'm not gonna let it go. 'Cause your dad will
see it later and probably beat you.' So Steven grabbed it,
took the pocketknife, and cut its throat."

Steven Chaves lived in Hondo and knew Cody at
school. He also spent one summer as a hired hand,
working with Paul and Cody on the Chavez Canyon
Ranch. Steven loaded hay trucks, built fences, and did
typical ranch work. "I heard a lot of verbal abuse from
Paul on Cody," Steven recalled. "It was bad. Very, very
bad. Paul was always cutting down Cody, and as far as
physical stuff, I saw Tryone slap him really hard when
we were picking up rocks from the horse corral. Cody
had suggested using the wheelbarrow. As soon as he
said that, Tryone just stood up and slapped him so hard
that his hat flew off. It left a huge mark on his face.
Cody just looked at her, didn't say a word, and picked
up his hat.

"I saw Paul, one time, grab Cody's fingers with a pair

of pliers and squeeze his finger very, very hard with the pliers. It left marks on his finger and Cody started crying. Cody had been in the toolbox on the truck and slammed the toolbox lid down. Paul walked over there, grabbed a pair of pliers and put Cody's finger in the pliers, and started squeezing really hard. Paul was saying stuff like, 'When you close that fucking door, you'd better watch where the fuck everyone is at, or you're gonna smash someone's finger! And if you do, I'll rip your fingers off!'" Cody's finger changed color.

"The very first day I started working there, I saw Paul drop a big rock on Cody's back. He told Cody to run down a canal at the hay field. When Cody did, Paul dropped that rock on his back. He tried to play it off as a joke. Cody faked a laugh, but he stood up and was rubbing his back. I can't remember anything else, but I know there was more.

"While loading hay, Paul would play games on Cody. While Paul was on the truck, he would drop hay bales on Cody as fast as he could. The hay bales weighed about forty pounds. They were being dropped from about ten feet up. They hit Cody all over—in the back, on his legs. Even on his head. We unloaded about four hundred bales of hay that day. Every other one, Paul would hit Cody.

"I didn't really talk to Cody at school, but I saw him there all the time. I saw him show up at school a few times with marks on his face. He had a scratch by his eye one time. He could play basketball at home, and he played basketball with Sam Donaldson's granddaughters a few times. But he hardly ever got to play. He mostly had to work. He was so happy when he got to play basketball.

"I didn't ever know of Cody being allowed to go to a

party. I played paintball, and I gave him a paintball magazine one time. I asked Paul if Cody could play paintball with me, and Paul kind of beat around the bush with his answer. He just said, 'You're a good kid, and I might let him play with you sometime.' But he never did.

"Cody was called names all the time. Paul would call him 'stupid' and 'motherfucker,' 'dumb-ass,' and 'idiot.' Tryone called him names all the time too. If Cody made any mistake, even a little one, they would call him names. Most of the time, if Cody asked a question they thought was dumb, or if Cody made a mistake, they made him feel pretty low. Marilea was never called names. She would occasionally be chewed out, but they never called her names.

"Cody worked harder than most men. He sometimes wouldn't even eat lunch, he'd just work all day. The only time I didn't see him working was when he was in school."

Cody couldn't even keep a pet for long. He said later, "Pilo Vasquez and I got along very well, and one time Pilo gave me a puppy. The puppy was big enough to jump over fences. It broke its leg, but it wasn't a bad break. He was still running around on three legs, having the time of his life. When I told my dad about it, I said, 'You know what, I think the dog's broken its leg. Can we set it and maybe get a stick to make kind of a little splint?' And he told me no. He said I was going to have to shoot it and kill it. I didn't want to. I'd grown real attached to that dog. I said, 'I have money saved up. I have about forty dollars. Maybe we can send it to the vet and maybe he can set the leg.' Dad wasn't having it. He told me to shoot the dog right in front of Marilea, Tryone, and him. Then he gave me a pistol, and I shot it."

Not only Steven Chaves told of abuse being handed out to Cody by Paul, other ranch hands would tell their own stories of abuse at the Chavez Canyon Ranch. Ysabel "Pilo" Vasquez was a friend of Cody's who helped work on the Donaldson ranch with Paul and Cody. Pilo said later, "There was this time at the ranch house, we were all eating, and Tryone, I don't know if she was watching Cody or what. Cody wanted to keep eating, because he was hungry, and there were some cookies, bread, small cakes, things like that in the kitchen. Tryone was coming toward him and he was going to get something, and she told him no, put it back, and he did. She came back to where we were, and turned around, and he was watching her. When she didn't look, he grabbed a cookie and stuffed it in his mouth, and he crossed his arms like nothing happened. He wanted seconds. We were working hard that day. Well, I'm poor, but I felt sorry they didn't allow him to eat. Tryone didn't say anything to anyone else about seconds, except Cody.

"On another occasion we were working on the other side of the ranch where I lived at. The time came to eat, so I told Paul, 'Let's eat,' because later we would have to move to another place. Paul said, 'No, I like to work a lot, and when I work, I don't like to eat.' So I said, 'How about Cody?' And Paul said, 'He doesn't need to eat.' So me and the other guy there had lunch. We put it on top of a pile of hay. We were there eating, and I asked Cody, 'Do you want a soda or a cookie?' He wanted to, you could tell he wanted to, but he would just look at Paul and wouldn't do anything. The other man said to Cody, 'Do you want a sandwich or a taco?' And Cody just looked at Paul. So he didn't get anything, because Paul didn't want him to.

"Another time Paul withheld water from Cody. That time we were working on another ranch with cows. It was late and it was a hot day. Paul told Slim Britton, the other worker, 'You and Cody and Marilea are going to have to move these cattle to another pasture, because Pilo and I are going to work on some other chores we have here at the corral.'

"Cody was already on his horse, and he told Paul, 'I'm going to drink some water.' But Paul said, 'No, first you're going to take the cattle.' The water was right there, but Paul didn't let him drink any. Slim was right by my side, and he didn't say anything, but he had a look on his face like he didn't like what Paul said. As a manager it seemed like Paul wanted us to do things the way he wanted, when he wanted. I could tell Paul was angry at me, because I said Cody should have some water. Paul's face was red."

Cody remembered this incident as well: "One day we were branding calves and it took about three hours. From that point on, we did pen work, and then had to drive a herd about two miles. Slim, Marilea, and me were sent on another drive of about two miles more. I had gotten up at three in the morning to start work, and didn't get home until about eight that evening. The only water me and Marilea had was when Slim Britton showed us how to drink out of a water trough. He did this because I was getting sick and Marilea was looking very pale. She looked like she was about to fall off her horse."

Pilo continued with tales of how Paul mistreated Cody. "One time Paul told Cody that he wished he'd been castrated, because he didn't want to have another kid like Cody. On another occasion Paul and Tryone invited me in for a glass of iced tea and cookies in the house. I was in the kitchen when Tryone came into the house. I understood the lady a little bit, but I mostly speak Spanish. She said, 'We're waiting for Cody to finish school. We're going to buy him an old truck when graduation is over. He's going to come into the house, pick up his things, his clothes will already be in the truck, and that's it for him around here. No more Cody in this house!'

"Paul came in from the bathroom. He heard what Tryone was saying. He said, 'Yes, it's true. Just an old truck, and when the graduation is here, we don't want him around anymore.'

"I never heard Cody answer back to Paul or Tryone. If Paul scolded Cody, and Tryone was there, she was next to scold him. I never saw Cody misbehaving. One time I was tending sheep, and I raised a stick toward a sheep. Cody thought I was raising the stick at him. He cowered down and said, 'Please don't hit me!' I put a hand on him and said, 'Cody, I won't hit you. I'm not your father.'"

Slim Britton was a ranch hand at the Chavez Canyon Ranch as well, and he later said of himself, "I've been a cowboy, ranch hand, and foreman on ranches all my life. Paul was the ranch manager on the Chavez Canyon Ranch, and my duties were to take over the Pajarito Ranch, owned by Sam Donaldson, near Picacho. I oversaw that one, but I worked on all three ranches. They were basically known as the Slaughter Ranch, Pajarito Ranch, and Chavez Canyon Ranch.

"Pajarito was about twenty-three miles from the Chavez Canyon Ranch, and the Slaughter Ranch was next to Pajarito. We all got together and worked—me, Paul, Pilo, and sometimes Cody and Marilea. Sam Donaldson had cattle and sheep at the time and a hay farm on the road to Capitan, just outside of Hondo. It was eighty acres of hay. There was a lot of cutting of hay per year, and we'd average two thousand bales of cutting. There were six to eight cuttings per year. Even then, there wasn't always enough hay from the hay farm for all three ranches. We ran about three hundred head of cattle and eight hundred to twelve hundred sheep on those ranches.

"I got to know Cody Posey pretty well. I spent a lot of time around him. I also spent a lot of time around Paul and Marilea, and some around Tryone. I saw how Paul and Cody interacted. Cody carried a lot of weight for a kid. He was called upon to do a man's work. Paul would work too, but Cody was called on pretty hard. He did all the chores and he was out there and worked like a man every day. He did very well.

"Cody was kind of the outside wheel in that family— he was the outcast of the bunch. The three of them would be over in one place, and Cody would be outside working. I'd go in to get something at the headquarters, and I'd drive up and Cody would be out cleaning stalls or moving hay or picking up rocks or filling water troughs, and they'd be in the house.

"They all talked down to him pretty bad. If he didn't get somethin' just right, Paul would call him, 'You wuss!' I heard Paul call Cody everything from 'stupid little son of a bitch' to 'nigger motherfucker.' Tryone wouldn't address him quite as bad, but she still said stuff like, 'ignorant,' 'stupid,' and 'worthless.' Marilea would tease him. He'd be in trouble and she would giggle at him.

"Most of these incidents occurred when we were working or when Paul didn't think anybody was watching. We were working cattle in what we call the 'brush pasture,' which is in Pajarito. The new man generally goes to the outside of the pasture, where they gather. You line up across the pasture, and the guy on the outside goes like a sweeping motion, and you're pushing the livestock around the pasture to a point where you're bunching them. You keep going to the inside man or to a point. I was on the outside, Cody was next to me at the canyon, then Marilea, Paul, and Pilo. The outside guy and the inside man really control the drive.

"That particular day Cody had picked up a crippled cow, and she was real slow. I'd seen it, and it was way up in the trees. He was comin' slow with her, which is what you do. I just kinda waited and I was sittin' there and Paul came down off the hill and rode up on Cody with his rope in his hand. He thrashed him across the back with the rope and yelled, 'You're out of the drive, you son of a bitch!' And hit him and tried to knock him off his horse. You take a lariat and hit somebody with one, and it really hurts. I've seen some people taken apart with a rope. They're hard, and it's like being hit with a piece of steel. I'm sure Cody cried, but he stayed in the drive."

There were others, however, that claimed that Paul did not mistreat Cody, despite what Cody and his friends had to say. One of these was Terry Winkler. He also was a man who lived the ranch life. He said later, "Slim Britton had an ax to grind against Paul. There was a drought goin' on, and Paul had to sell off more and more livestock, 'cause he'd run outta grass. It got to a point where he didn't have enough work for everybody. So he told Slim to start lookin' for another job. He didn't fire him, he just gave him the opportunity to be lookin' for another job. A lotta people will do that so a person won't get in a bind, but as soon as he said that, Slim said, 'Well, you can fire Pilo. We can run this better than he could.'

"Tryone was one of those special women who was so nice. When I was by there, I don't know if I was just lucky, but almost every time I was there, she had just made fresh cookies. And there was nothin' else but I had to come in and have some cookies. Cody had 'em too. If it was close to mealtime, she would insist that I stay and have a meal with them. Cody would eat at the same table as everybody else. I never heard a foul word come out of her mouth. She was as nice a lady as you could expect to ever meet.

"There was one time, Slim and Pilo were at a branding. We got there with the cattle, and Paul told me to start draggin', and I was gonna let Cody do it. It's a skilled trade. I said, 'If the young people don't learn how to do it, it will be a lost skill. We got plenty of time, and this is a good time for him to learn.' Cody started ropin', and like anything else, when you do somethin' for the first time, he missed a lot. He was gettin' flustered, and Paul walked up there while Cody was sittin' on his horse, and he put his hand on Cody's leg and was lookin' up at him, and said, 'Don't worry about it. All of us, we have all missed a lot more than what you have. You just have to learn how to do it.' And he was givin' him pointers on what to do. Through that whole day there was never a cross word outta Paul. We got through a little bit after dinner, and we had our dinner and went on our merry way."

Verlin Posey also said how proud Paul was about Cody's roping abilities. Paul phoned Verlin up and said how much Cody had improved in that area. "Paul was really proud of his roping skills, and told me so."

Winkler recalled, "There came a point where it was rainin', and Paul and me was in the barn goin' over some stuff. Cody was in the pickup. We heard a gunshot

go off. We went runnin' and got there and jerked the
door open and jerked Cody out to see if he was shot.
Our adrenaline was pumpin', and when that happens,
you do things harder than you normally would, but even
then, Paul didn't throw him to the ground.

"Paul asked Cody what happened. Well, there was an
automatic pistol in the pickup, and Cody had checked
to see if it was empty, and he had fired it. He had shot
the dashboard of the pickup. There was no cussin' on
Paul's part. No hittin' or anything like that. The only
thing Paul was stressin' was that there was never an
empty gun. You thought it was empty, and it still shot. It
was a teaching aspect. No threats, or name-calling."

Cody would remember this incident in a very different way. He said that the gun had gone off by accident.
When his father ran from the barn, he grabbed Cody out
of the pickup and threw him to the ground. According to
Cody, Paul was more upset about Cody having shot the
dashboard than he was about seeing if he was all right.

One of the most onerous tasks on the Chavez Canyon
Ranch, according to Cody, was something he called,
"Working on the Rock Pile." He related, "In Hondo
there was a joke that we grew rocks as a crop. There
were rocks everywhere. My duty was to go around picking up rocks, throw them off hills, cut trees, rake weeds.
I had to pick up rocks from the corral, dump them over
the fences, and it was a punishment job. If the family
didn't want me around, they sent me out to pick up
rocks. I had to pick them up by hand, put them in a
coffee can, and dump them over a fence.

"I would work all day long, picking up rocks, and
couldn't even have lunch until Dad came home. It got
hot in the corral and I wasn't sure if I could have water

out there. I wasn't told that I could, so I went out to the shop and grabbed the shop water, and hid it in the barn.

"Using the coffee cans on the rock pile occurred about three out of seven days a week. It happened during the school year, on weekends, and even during summer vacation. Every time I picked up a rock, there was another rock underneath it. There really wasn't any point to it."

Others would remember the rock pile project as well. One of these was Pilo Vasquez. He said, "There were a lot of rocks in the corral. I went over there to the ranch and there was a clean space. I asked Paul, 'How are you cleaning this?' He said that Cody and Marilea were there with a wheelbarrow. I told him, you have that piece of machinery (indicating a backhoe). You can put the rocks in there and drive it and take the rocks and place them the way you want them. But he said no, they needed the work, and they needed to learn how to work, so they were going to do it the hard way with the wheelbarrow."

Steven Chaves also spoke of the rock pile project. "The rock business was right in front of the Sam Donaldson house. I thought what we were doing was pointless. We had to load them in coffee cans. I guess it was just to make the place look nice, but there was always more rocks. A very pointless job."

School had always been a refuge for Cody, away from the ranch. Yet, even this was becoming less and less of a refuge as 2003 rolled along. Cody would find love at Hondo High School, but he would also find trouble and torment there as well.

Chapter 7

Girlfriend

John McCallum was the district superintendent of the Hondo Valley schools, and he knew both Cody and Marilea. The Hondo Valley School District was one of the smallest in the state, with 130 students, and forty staff members, if you included teachers, cooks, and bus drivers. All the classes—kindergarten through twelfth grade—were congregated on an eleven-acre campus in Hondo. There were only twelve other students in Cody's class during 2003 and 2004.

"Cody was a good student—a bright student. He wasn't a troublemaker. I knew Marliea as well, and sometimes I saw the students coming and going from school. Most of the students arrived there by bus, but not Cody and Marilea. They were driven there by Tryone, which was unusual," McCallum shared.

"It was demographically a poor community around Hondo, and lunches were free to the students, because many of them were below the poverty line. It was also a close-knit community, and Cody got along well with other students and teachers. Most kids who arrive from another district are not accepted right away, but that was not the case with Cody. He adapted very well. He was outgoing with other students, but when his parents were around, he was quiet and withdrawn. This was different than most children there."

Teacher Dale English also observed Cody and Marilea at the Hondo Valley School. He said, "I did a lot of bus duty and was there every morning when the bus came in and the parents brought their kids. One thing I really noticed when Tryone brought Cody and Marilea was that it seemed like the pickup had barely stopped, and Cody was running to school to see his friends. At the end of the day, before any students were allowed to go ride with their parents, they had to stay in the multipurpose room. The parents were on the other side of the street, waiting for their kids. All the buses with other students would leave before these kids were released. Then the students were allowed to go to their parents' car. I noticed that Marilea was always the first one to the vehicle, and thirty feet behind her was Cody, walking with his head down. I didn't see any other student acting that way.

"I never heard Tryone say anything good about Cody. One summer Tryone came and asked if Marliea could be in the summer tutor program, and we let her in. After this was over, we took a lot of kids to the lake on the other side of Roswell for a fun day. Tryone asked if she could come along. On the bus, maybe because she was a captive audience, I really started telling her about what a super kid Cody was. I saw so much potential in him, and we had no problems with him and he was an asset to Hondo. She kept telling me, 'He's not that way at home. He doesn't do his chores. He's always lazy. He's very disrespectful.' She was jumping on him so much, that one of our teachers broke in.

"Even elementary-school teachers knew about the way Tryone treated Cody. It was common knowledge. She once told me something I'll never forget. She said, 'I'm glad that Cody's mother died, because I don't know how he would have been raised.'"

Donna Crawford was a science teacher at Hondo Valley School and she had Cody and Marilea in her classes. Crawford noted that Cody was a B and C student in his seventh-grade year, but by the end of the year, he'd dropped to a grade of D in her class. He started out well in his eighth-grade year, and was getting A's, but as time went on, the grades kept slipping until once again he was getting D's.

Crawford recalled, "Sometimes kids would take things from other kids and hide them as a joke. On three occasions this happened to Cody. In one instance it was a watch, in another a cap, and in a third a backpack. When the bell rang, and he didn't have an item, he would panic. I would try to calm him down, but he would say, 'You don't understand. If I come home late to the truck and don't have my watch, she's gonna kill me! You don't know what kind of trouble I'm gonna be in!' His reaction was much greater than other kids when this happened.

"Junior-high classes are the most difficult to teach. Kids push to see how much they can get away with. Cody's class was pushing hard, and I threatened to call some parents in, which I eventually did. I called in five parents, and one of those sets of parents were the Poseys. There was a second time I threatened to call in Cody's parents, and he begged me not to. He said, 'Please don't call my parents, I'll do anything you want!' Eventually I gave in. Cody was normally a good kid. He thanked me over and over. I knew that his parents were overly strict with him.

"There was one instance where I overheard Cody say to another student, 'I hate my parents and my parents hate me.' I was very concerned about this, so I set up a meeting with Paul and Tryone to come in and talk about it. It was a parent-teacher conference. I brought them in and immediately regretted it. They started hollering and screaming at him, and Cody started crying. I was in shock. I hadn't expected that kind of reaction. I couldn't understand what Tryone was saying, because Paul was yelling so loud. Cody started denying it, and Paul shouted, 'Are you calling this lady a liar?' Cody said, 'No, sir,' and Paul said, 'You're gonna get it when you get home! You know what's gonna happen when we get home!' I tried calming things down by saying that Cody was a good kid, and that he was seldom in trouble. Tryone, however, pulled out a business card and handed it to me. She said, 'Take this, and if he does anything else, you call us immediately!'

"There was one occasion when I was doing bus duty, and Tryone yelled at me, 'How are Cody and Marilea doing?' I said they were doing fine. She said, 'He better be doing fine, or he'll know what's good for him!'

"By the end of the school day, Cody was a completely different person. In class he would be a happy person— laughing and joking. As soon as the bell rang, no more joking, laughing, or smiling. He transformed into a very solemn person."

Brandon Devine taught agriculture at Hondo Valley School, drove a bus, and was a football coach. He taught five classes of comprehensive agriculture courses, including woodshop and welding. Devine's classes included topics about animal science and plant science, and he was a Future Farmers of America (FFA) adviser. In that capacity Devine taught the kids leadership roles, public speaking, livestock judging, floraculture judging, and helped them in contests. There were many contests in the FFA, which included livestock showing at county fairs, and Cody was automatically enrolled as a member of the FFA when he took Devine's agriculture class and the dues were paid by the school district.

Devine said, "Cody was a fun kid. A good student. He was always willing to participate in discussions, and since he worked on a ranch, he knew a lot about agriculture. He shared an interest in horses, saddles, and spurs. Things of a cowboy-type nature. He didn't have an interest in livestock showing, but he did have an interest in livestock judging.

"I wanted Cody to participate as a judge at FFA contests. There was a meeting at the Hondo Valley School concerning this, and after the meeting Paul and Cody came up to me. I asked Paul if Cody could come out for FFA. And Paul said that he could if his grades improved, but Cody was never allowed to participate. Each time there was a contest, I would send a permission slip home with Cody, and it always came back with large letters written on it, 'NO!'"

Cody was good at sports, including basketball and football. Devine recalled, "Cody wanted to play football, and I wanted him to play football. Paul had come by the shop in the summer of 2003 and was looking for a kid to be a ranch hand during the summer months. I asked if Cody could come out for football in the fall, and Paul said that Cody was grounded from extracurricular activities for a full school year. I asked Paul to reconsider and I said that Cody would have little time for mischief and would be under my watchful eye. During the fall of 2003, while heading out to football practice one day, I saw Tryone waiting to pick up Cody and Marilea. I approached her and asked if Cody could come out for football. I said that his grades were very good at the time, and I would let him on the team, even though it was already late. Tryone acted upset and said in a loud voice, 'If another person from this school asks me that, he won't be able to play football next year either!' I told her Cody shouldn't be punished for our ignorance and left."

Cody did manage to play a few games of basketball for the school team while he was in the seventh grade at Hondo. Dale English recalled, "I knew it was the first time he ever played organized basketball, and I was amazed at how talented he was. Maybe not the best shot, but he was like a gazelle running up and down the court. Very good defensive abilities and leaping abilities. At such a young age, he was very talented."

Cody had an explanation for why he was suddenly pulled off the basketball team. "There were two kids in class talking, and I was accused by the teacher of being one of them. The teacher called my family, and after the game that night, my dad slapped me across my face and said, 'You're not going to play basketball!' I couldn't play any more sports after that."

Teacher John McCallum also recalled, "Cody played basketball briefly one year. I attempted to persuade his parents to allow him to be in more activities. I think that extracurricular activities are extremely important. They teach sportsmanship, teamwork, and leadership. We encourage the kids to do it. But that little bit of basketball was all Cody ever played."

Jack Nelson was a guidance counselor at Hondo schools. He tried to have a family mediation with Cody and his parents near the end of the school year in 2003. Cody had come to Nelson and said that he was having disagreements with his dad. His dad claimed that Cody was not taking care of his chores correctly on the ranch, and Cody disagreed with this. "The meeting lasted about thirty minutes," Nelson recalled. "Anytime a student came to see me, I would listen to him and look for nonverbal communication. In all fairness, Cody didn't say to me that he was being abused.

"During one lunch period, I came in and started talking to Tryone and Marilea. I explained that Cody and I had talked, and Cody had agreed to a mediation meeting with his parents. He was concerned that his dad was making him do too much work and he didn't have time to just be a seventh grader. Cody hardly had any free time at all. Tryone said she knew they had been working him hard on the ranch, and she could see where he might be concerned. She said she would talk to Paul and see if they could all come in as a family and they would discuss the situation.

"As it turned out, however, this was the last week of school. I was very busy with other duties at school that week. There wasn't enough time left in the school year to set up a meeting. I did tell Cody that if the relationship between himself and his dad got worse over the summer, he could call me and we would try to set something up over the summer months."

Sooner or later, according to Cody, anything he liked at school was taken away from him, even the "Knowledge Bowls." Dale English said, "Cody was academically astute. He was a good kid and a pleasure to have him on the 'Knowledge Bowl' team. After the first 'Knowledge Bowl,' Cody stopped coming, but Marilea would still bring in her permission slip with a signature that she could attend the next one. Cody would say, 'I can't go.'

"I did a lot of bus duty every morning, and when the buses came in and the parents brought their kids to school, I would talk to Tryone, saying that Cody was very good at the 'Knowledge Bowl.' 'He's an outstanding young man and I see a lot of potential in him.' I kept saying, 'Would you please let him go?' But it was all for naught."

Teachers weren't the only ones who said that Paul and Tryone made Cody's life miserable. Eli Salcido lived in San Patricio, had five kids, and one of them, Dorotea Salcido, was Cody's age. Eli helped with the 4-H Club in the area, and was also the yearly Santa Claus at Hondo. Eli was at a parents-teachers meeting at Hondo Valley School one time, and the superintendent had put the meeting together about how to help the eighth-grade kids. Cody, Tryone, and Paul were sitting near Eli.

Eli recalled, "I didn't know Paul or Tryone until then, and after the meeting I saw Cody and his father in the corner. Paul had Cody by the arm and was shaking him. I went over and said, 'Hey, this is your son. And what I been hearin' from you all night, well, I haven't heard you say anything good about him. I don't appreciate you shakin' him like you are now.' Paul told me to shut up and mind my own business. I took my hat off and said, 'I ain't gonna allow it here!'"

Eli didn't say whether he was ready to fight Paul then and there, but apparently the shaking of Cody stopped.

Because Paul was so irritated with Cody, he made him write an essay about his poor behavior and poor grades. Cody wrote something entitled: "My Former Years and Why They Happened." In this essay he wrote that in his early years he did all his work and was happy. Then as he got older, he started acting up in class, talking back to his teachers, and not paying attention. All of those things were problems, he wrote, *And when I wasn't doing wrong, you (Paul) had no reason to be mad at me, so life was great.*

Cody wrote that things got worse for him around the third grade, because he would not do his homework. He said that all he wanted to do was go outside and play and not finish his work. *In class I would talk and not pay attention to the teacher. I was always getting up and wandering around the room.*

Cody spoke of when his dad left Sandy and he was stuck with Tryone in a new place with a new family. He said that he goofed off even more at that point, not paying attention to lessons, and that he tried to emulate some bad kids at school as a way of getting back at his dad and Tryone. He wrote that he wanted to do things some of the bad kids did, and *When I couldn't, I got mad at you and was trying to get back at you.*

Cody said that he played games at lunchtime and day-dreamed in class about scoring points so *everyone would love me.* He also wrote that he would talk back to teachers because he thought he knew more than they did. By the fifth grade he had gotten interested in girls, and *I would start daydreaming about being with the hottest girl in class.*

Cody also wrote that he started seeing his mom more often on weekends, and she told him that he didn't have to follow Paul's orders. Cody said that when he came back to live with Paul, Tryone, and Marilea after his mother had died, he tried to be a better boy for a little while. But then he said he got worse because he hung around with kids who didn't get good grades and didn't care. These kids told him not to listen to his parents, but to do what he wanted instead. Cody wrote that he had to be in sixth grade twice because he was purposefully slacking off.

I have never changed before, because I didn't want to change. He said that he hadn't changed because he wanted to be like the "bad" kids in school. Then he added, *They have parents who really don't care what they do. I didn't want to do what you told me, because I hated you, and I didn't want you to win.*

All throughout the essay was a common theme of wanting to be like the popular kids in school who didn't care about their grades and didn't pay attention in class. Cody ended by writing that he would try to improve in school and be more obedient at home on the ranch.

Years later, however, Cody stated that he wrote what his father wanted to hear. He said if he hadn't written things that way, all he could expect was another beating. Cody related later that he felt like a prisoner in his own home.

One thing many teachers and students would see over time that might have been from abuse was Cody coming to school with a black eye. Brandon Devine recalled, "I saw Cody with a red puffy left eye. Me and my wife and son one time ran into Paul, Tryone, and Cody at a store in Roswell while Christmas shopping. We shook hands and said hello, and Paul asked me how Cody was doing in class. I told him very well, and Paul said that if Cody ever gave me any problems, to let him have it. 'That's what my ag teacher did to me,' Paul said. Tryone added that Cody was exactly the kind of kid who needed it. Personally, I never had one single problem with Cody."

Teacher Donna Crawford said, "There was one instance Cody came to school with a black eye. I asked him about it, and he gave me a plausible answer. He said he had been hit with a softball in the eye. Since this had happened to me once, I thought that was possible."

Students Patrick Gonzales, Anthony Sanchez, and Leo Salcido also spoke of Cody being verbally and physically abused. Leo Salcido told a story of what contempt Tryone held Cody in. Leo said, "There was a 'Knowledge Bowl' at Hondo, and other schools were there. These included Capitan, Ruidoso, and Cloudcroft. I was gonna talk to Tryone and joke around, because Cody was hangin' out with his old friends from Cloudcroft school. I was jokin' around, sayin', 'Hey, Cody's a traitor. He's over there with those guys. We should go beat him up.' And Tryone turned around and looked at us and she was serious. She said, 'If it was up to me, I'd have you guys do it right now!'"

Leo Salcido wasn't the only one who overheard Tryone say that. Cody's friend Joseph Brady did as well. He said later, "She seemed very serious."

If Cody was stymied in so many other things while at Hondo High School, the one thing he did find was romance. He met a girl there named Brenda Lucero, of San Patricio, and really fell for her. Brenda was cute and sweet and very personable. Others would remark later on her good qualities.

Brenda would recall, "I went to school with Cody from the sixth through the eighth grades. He was my boyfriend, but I only got to see him at school. I tried calling him at the ranch, but I could never get through to him. I wasn't allowed to talk to him. Tryone always answered the phone."

More than any other girl he met, Cody would adore Brenda Lucero. Yet according to Cody, there was one real impediment to Brenda Lucero as a girlfriend. He claimed that his father and Tryone were racist when it came to Hispanics. Cody said of an earlier incident, "I was down at the hay farm doing irrigation and it can take two or three hours. While I was waiting for the water to go down the row, I went across the field to talk with a farmhand's kids. Everyone called the guy 'Laro,' but his real name was Alvarado. The oldest kid was probably in third grade. I was over there talking to their family to see how they were doing. My dad showed up at the farm, grabbed me around the collar, and dragged me away from the kids. He threw me down on the ground, pinned my arms down, and straddled me, hitting me. He said, 'I don't want you hanging out with those Mexicans, 'cause you're probably smoking weed with them. My white boy isn't going to be hanging around Mexicans!' It upset me because we used to work on a ranch that Laro managed. He was a good man and worked hard.

"I wasn't supposed to talk to Brenda Lucero, Alicia Chaves, Gilbert Salcido, Leo Salcido, and Bryan Aragon. They were all Hispanic. I'd try talking to them, but Dad and Mom always seemed to find out and I'd get punched and slapped."

Just how Paul and Tryone knew so much about whom Cody was talking to at school would become a matter of debate later. To many in the area, there was a consensus that Marilea was spying on him at school and reporting back to Cody's dad and stepmom. Donna Crawford said, "In between classes Marilea would wander in and look around. She would walk around and look at things, and initially I thought she was interested in science. Then out of the blue, she would ask, 'How is Cody doing in your class?' This happened many times."

Bryan Aragon recalled, "If Marilea was around, Cody was very isolated from the group. At lunch we'd be talking, and if Marilea came around, he'd drift off. Other than at lunchtime, he didn't hang around Marilea. If

Marilea came around, he'd try to make it look like he wasn't with us.

"There were a couple of times that we had an awards ceremony at the end of the year. Tryone was having a conversation with my mom. Cody was right there beside her, and I said hi to him. He didn't say anything, he just looked at me. It was real strange, since he was a friendly kid."

Dale English said, "There was a reward system between Marilea and her parents. These parents were paying a young child to spy on Cody for things like talking in class. He'd come home and get a beating for it."

The greatest corroboration of this story was from Dorotea Salcido. She said, "I was friends with Marilea. I hung out during lunch breaks at school with her. We would follow Cody around because Marilea wanted to. She was spying on him. I did it because Marilea did it. She was looking at who he talked to and what he was talking about. And also to see if he was with Brenda Lucero."

Dorotea, more than anyone, seemed to corroborate what Cody was saying about Paul and Tryone disapproving of him having a Hispanic girlfriend, although others would also make reference to this. Then one day Cody recalled, "I was suddenly pulled out of Hondo School because I liked Brenda Lucero. The day I was pulled out, I didn't even know what was happening. I was told to turn in my books. I wasn't even able to tell my classmates why."

Once again Paul and Tryone were pulling Cody out of a school and transferring him elsewhere. This time it was to Capitan High School, about twenty miles down the road from Chavez Canyon Ranch.

* * *

Cody said that once he started going to Capitan High School, the rules were the same, except now he was riding on the bus to school and he wasn't supposed to talk to anyone on the bus ride there. Cody claimed that the consequences of talking were getting worse. "I would be punched harder by my dad or Tryone. One time I talked to my friend Teresa Goodman, and Tryone found out about it. She slapped me across the face."

Teresa Goodman recalled, "I was a freshman and Cody was in eighth grade when I met him at Capitan High School. I met him through my foster sister. The majority of kids at Capitan were from farms and ranches. I spoke with Cody sometimes during recess or lunches. I had met Marilea, but we weren't friends. I observed that when Marilea was present, Cody wouldn't say anything to anybody. He would stop talking if Marilea walked up. If he was on the bus talking to someone, and he saw Marilea looking at him, he wouldn't say anything for the rest of the ride. Marilea would sit across from him on the bus."

Cody claimed that eventually he did learn that Marilea was tattling on him to his parents, and there did seem to be a reward in place for her if she told on him. Cody recalled, "It upset me, because quite a few times there were things told about me that weren't true. I would come home and be asked several questions about something. If I didn't know about it, they would assume I was lying. I would get slapped and beaten. But even if I knew about something, and was truthful about it, I'd still get slapped and hit with things."

In time Cody made a new girlfriend at Capitan High named Erin McCallahan—though he would later claim he never stopped loving Brenda Lucero. At least as far as Paul and Tryone were concerned, Erin was more acceptable to them; she was Anglo. Even with that in mind, they still didn't allow Cody time off the ranch for any kind of dating.

Cody would write a remarkable letter to Erin's parents at one point, and it called into question many of the claims he made later against Paul and Tryone. The letter began: *To the Family of Erin—Pardon my expression, but all I am is a screw up.* He wrote that his stepmom and dad had done everything they could to keep him from being a screwup. He said that he had stolen, cheated, taken illegal drugs, failed subjects, disobeyed them, and many other things. *Now that you know this, I can understand if you don't want your daughter to see me, but I assure [you] that my mother and father will have to worry no more. I will do right and straighten out. Sincerely, Cody A. Posey.*

Later he would claim to have written this letter because Tryone had told Erin's family what a bad boy he was, and he wanted to set the record straight.

Even as he thought of Erin Lynn McCallahan as a girlfriend, he still said that Brenda Lucero was his "real girlfriend." And Brenda, for her part, recalled, "Even when Cody went to Capitan, I tried contacting him by phone. I tried contacting him by letter. I wrote three letters to him and got one response."

Brenda's mother, Rita Lucero, worked at a Wal-Mart, and one time Tryone approached her in the store and said, "Cody isn't going to see Brenda anymore. He has a white girlfriend in Capitan, and he doesn't need any Mexican girlfriends." Rita was stunned and outraged by the remark. She definitely thought that Tryone was a racist.

Cody recalled, "There was one time, I said, 'Why do

I have to call Tryone 'Mom'? She's not my mom.' Dad stood up, came around the table, hit me in the eye, and knocked me and the chair to the floor. I often went to school with black eyes, busted lips, and bruises on my arms.

"The beatings got a lot worse when I started going to Capitan. I was scared even to be around my dad. I was wondering why things were getting worse. I thought maybe it was me doing something wrong. I couldn't please him. I always tried to get away from him as quick as I could. I'd eat breakfast as quick as I could. Walk as quick as I could. I tried to remove myself from them, so situations wouldn't come up to be hit."

As the school year for 2003 to 2004 came to an end, Cody braced himself for another summer on the ranch. That summer of 2004, there was another young man there who witnessed what life was like for Cody on the Chavez Canyon Ranch. His name was Clint Skeen, he was seventeen years old, and he'd grown up on a ranch that bordered Sam Donaldson's ranch. Clint rode the school bus to Capitan with Cody and liked him. Clint said that Cody was a good student and hard worker.

Clint said of that summer, "I hadn't worked for Paul before, and I was mainly irrigating and windrowing the hay. They'd come down to the field, and we'd all work together to pick up bales of hay. Cody would come and irrigate with me sometimes. He was down there every day for a while.

"I saw Cody and Paul interact many times. I could tell there was a lot of tension between them. Cody around me was happy, but when Paul entered the picture, he was like a whipped dog. He'd put his head down. He was real nervous around Paul. Paul would verbally abuse him, and call him names like 'shithead,' 'dumb fuck,' 'fuckup.'

"I saw how Tryone treated him too. I was eating lunch one day at their house, and I was sitting at the dinner table. Cody got something without asking Tryone first, and she blew up at him. She cussed him, and he wasn't doing anything improper. She screamed at him and called him a shithead.

"I saw the relationship between Cody and Marilea in the fields when they were together. They would get into little arguments, but nothing unusual. Cody was expected to do a lot more than was expected of the usual ranch kid."

For the most part there were many who agreed with Cody that he was being mistreated by his stepmom and dad. But not all. Charlie Cooper recalled, "I saw the Posey family at the Joneses' fiftieth wedding anniversary in 2004 in Ruidoso. Cody danced with my granddaughter at the party, and my other granddaughter visited with Marilea. We all interacted around the dinner table. I didn't see any signs of abuse of Cody, and I had been trained to look for those kinds of things with my school work."

Cooper's recollection may have been a little bit too rosy. Even Verlin said later that there was a lot of tension between Cody and his dad in the summer of 2004. Verlin remembered, "Paul was very upset. He talked to me for two hours on the phone and he was at his wit's end. It seemed that Cody had lost interest in wanting to do anything. Cody said that he didn't want to be a cowboy, and that was fine with Paul. So Paul had asked Cody what he wanted to do and said, 'You have to be interested in something.' Cody told him he just wanted to hang out with his friends and get high. Paul said he couldn't allow that."

Even Cody would admit later that he did smoke marijuana a few times with some of his high-school buddies. According to Verlin, this was the real reason Cody had been pulled out of Hondo High School, and not because Paul was prejudiced against Brenda Lucero. Yet, Cody insisted that it was because of Brenda and his relationship, and not for another reason. The separation from Brenda seemed like just one more impediment to his happiness heaped upon him by abusive parents.

Cody was incredibly unhappy in 2004. Just before the school year had ended at Capitan High School, fellow student Raymond Zamora saw Cody sitting alone on a bench, crying. Cody had bruises on his head, and he covered his face with his hands as he was crying. Zamora asked Cody what was wrong. Cody responded, "I want to kill my parents!"

Chapter 8

Meltdown

Verlin Posey recalled that in the year 2004, Paul started locking up his guns. Verlin said later, "A gun that is not loaded is just a piece of steel. We had all been raised around guns, and knew how to take care of them. Paul started locking up his guns in a gun cabinet. I was surprised when I learned about this, and asked him why. He said that he was afraid that Cody might use a gun on him."

In June 2004, Verlin picked up a horse at the Chavez Canyon Ranch that was for sale. He took the horse to his own ranch to see how well it would work out there. The horse was not to his liking; so on July 4, 2004, Verlin and his wife, sons, and a couple of friends took the horse back to the Chavez Canyon Ranch. Later in the day they were all going to a rodeo in Capitan. It was the "Smokey Bear Rodeo," one of the most popular in the state.

Verlin remembered, "Paul and Cody came outside and we visited awhile. I got the horse from the trailer and turned it loose in the corral. We were there about an hour, visiting, and I didn't see any problems with Cody and his dad. They were standing shoulder to shoulder, and Cody was joking and visiting with the rest of us."

Cody would also recall the events of that Fourth of July weekend. The next few days were a watershed in his life. Cody said, "I woke up on July fourth, and it was a normal day for me. I went out and fed the horses, then came back in the house and ate breakfast and went out to clean the corrals. After the corrals were cleaned, my dad stepped out, and we started breaking a horse. This was a way to get a horse to behave around saddles, noises, and people. We were breaking a young filly that morning. As we were messing with her, she had a problem with kicking, and I didn't like the way my dad was handling her. He wanted to tie her tail to her leg, so when she kicked, she'd pull on her tail. I had a better idea that would get her used to people making noises behind her and people walking behind her. It would stop that habit. But Dad didn't agree with my idea and we got into an argument about it—a very heated argument. We ended up doing it his way. After we were done, we went into the house and Verlin, Shanda (Verlin's wife), and some other people came by the ranch, bringing back a horse that Verlin had thought of buying, but brought back.

"We stood there and visited a good ten or fifteen minutes. From there, I was outside playing basketball until Tryone and Marilea showed up later on that night. When they showed up, I was unloading boxes off a trailer, down into the basement. During that time I heard my dad and Tryone get into a pretty heated argument. Yelling back and forth, back and forth. After the trailer was done, I went back outside to play basketball.

"That evening I went into my room and was lying

down, waiting to fall asleep. I heard my name called, and I stepped out of my room. I was being called into my parents' room. I knocked on the door, and as I entered their room, my dad was standing there to the left of the bed. Tryone was lying on the bed and she was covered up at the time. I stood at the foot of the bed and my dad had a little butane tank with a regulator at the end. You can strike it with a striker and a little flame will come out. It's like a little torch. He also had a little dowel rod used for welding.

"As I stood in front of the bed, Tryone pulled down the covers and she was lying there completely naked. My dad struck up the torch and told me I was gonna have sex with Tryone. I refused to do it. As I was telling him, he was heating up the rod. He walked up to me and burned me. They were fairly good-sized burns at the time. As he burned me, he told me to do it. I said no. Tryone scooted down the bed to the foot of the bed, grabbed my head, and put it into her breasts. At that time, to make her let go of me, I bit her. As I bit her, I got burned another time with the rod. Then I just ran out of the room.

"I had a little corner of my room between the nightstand and my bed. I lay there in the corner, asking myself why this was happening to me. I knew this was wrong. I felt really disgusted. Dirty. I felt like I was lying and rolling in dirt.

"Thinking, that night, was a whole mixture of emotions—fear, disgust, and why my life had been like this. Tryone had said something like, 'We're not really family. It's an okay thing to do.' I sat there in between the nightstand and wall. It was kind of a safe spot. I was wondering if they were gonna chase me down. What were they gonna do? What's gonna happen next?

"I woke up the next day, lying on my bed on top of the covers. The alarm clock rang. I woke up, put on my clothes, and hurried out the door as fast as I could to avoid being around my father and stepmother. I went out and did my chores and fed the horses. I came back in, and my father and stepmother were not in the kitchen. I fixed myself a bowl of cereal and ate that cereal as fast as I could. As soon as they came in, they came in as if nothing had happened. They didn't say anything to me.

"I went back outside to clean the corrals. This time, instead of using a shovel, I used a rake. My father didn't approve of that. He said it took too long to use the rake, but that's how I did it that morning. My father came out of the house, stepped up to me, and asked me why I was using the rake. I told him using the rake gets it clean. He said, 'It's not clean enough.' I told him, 'It gets cleaner than you've ever done it.'

"I got backhanded and was told to go into the house. Then he said something like, 'I need my cup of coffee.'

"As he backhanded me this time, I had the same emotions going through my head as the night before. I lost control of my emotions. I felt overwhelmed. I walked into the barn, put up my tool, and was just asking myself questions, 'Why was I the one who had to be hit? Why was I the one who had to have the situation the night before?' I lost control. I didn't know what I was doing. I more or less lost my mind."

Cody happened to notice Marilea's saddlebag in the barn. Inside the saddlebag was a pistol with snake shot in it.

What happened next would have to be pieced together by evidence and Cody's recollections. There were no other witnesses to the carnage on Sam Donaldson's ranch that day. They were all dead.

Chapter 9

Deconstructing Cody

After Cody's interview, and what seemed like a confession to the murders, he was arrested and taken to a juvenile facility. And two key people would become part of his life in the court system for years to come. The first was Gary Mitchell, a lawyer who became Cody's defense attorney. Mitchell had a law office in Ruidoso, and had been practicing law in New Mexico since 1976. He took on cases that spanned from DUIs to death penalty cases, and he'd handled over two hundred murder cases by 2004. Of the seventy death penalty cases he had taken on, Mitchell had only lost one. He was president of the ACLU in New Mexico, and not afraid of tough or complicated cases, which Cody's case was sure to be.

On the other side of the aisle was ADA Sandra Grisham. A former judge in the region, she was now the main deputy DA who would handle Cody's case as a prosecutor. Ironically, Grisham would often stress her record with children's rights in the years to come. She chaired the New Mexico Council on Crime and Delinquency, and cochaired the subcommittee on Child Abuse and Neglect. She brought court-appointed special advocates (CASA) for children to the Twelfth District courts and served on a Court Rules Committee regarding children. In the upcoming Cody Posey case, however, it soon became apparent that Grisham would not be seeking leniency for Cody.

From very early on, the defense and prosecutor could look at a given set of events and see very different things. There was never any doubt on anyone's part who had shot and killed Paul Posey, Tryone Posey, and Marilea Schmid. The overriding factor in the upcoming case was not who—it was *why*.

Even the tape of Cody's seeming confession would bring forth different responses from the district attorney's office and that of Cody's defense counsel.

ADA Sandra Grisham wrote in the initial stage of the proceedings, "The court can see that the child is competent to stand trial. The court can see the child manipulate in the videotape."

Yet, always in the background, the question was: How badly had Cody been abused by his parents? Even Sergeant Shepherd would later admit, when he testified in court, "Cody spoke of abuse when I spoke with him. He also indicated he had not been taking his medication."

The issue of Zoloft was just one piece of small evidence that would be tallied, categorized, and analyzed—like all the other hundreds of pieces of evidence, both physical and verbal—until they almost took on a life of their own. No part of Cody's fourteen years would be excluded in the search for the truth as to what factors had driven him to kill his family on July 5, 2004.

One of Gary Mitchell's first strategies was to contend that Cody had not been adequately told of his rights before making a confession. The chief contention was whether Cody had proper adult guidance with him at the time that he was interviewed. Even the place chosen for the interview would come under question. The CYFD safe-house room was supposedly just that, a place where a child could tell what happened about an event without repercussions. Mitchell contended that if officers wanted to seek a confession from Cody, they should have taken him to a police station interview room.

On the other hand, Sandra Grisham said that Cody understood full well his rights when he had been Mirandized, and that he had an adult with him at the time, Mr. Salcido. Not only that, Cody had even told the officers that he was an A and B student. In Grisham's estimation, an A and B student certainly understood the implications of a Miranda warning.

In many ways the four psychiatrists who eventually interviewed, tested, and evaluated Cody would make the difference in whether he would gain his freedom once again, or be incarcerated for life. And not unlike Sandra Grisham and Gary Mitchell, each would take into account certain events in Cody's life, and see them in very different lights. Cody was always like a prism to those around him. Depending on where a person stood would define the image he perceived in who Cody Posey was and continued to be.

Dr. Christine Johnson was a clinical and forensic psychiatrist, and she had gone to Virginia Commonwealth University, then to the University of Vermont, and finally did postdoctoral work at the University of Southern

California. Johnson finished her postgraduate work in 1986 and became board certified in juvenile forensic psychology.

In 1993, she began working for the University of New Mexico (UNM), teaching and doing court-ordered evaluations of adults and juveniles. She had close contact with juvenile facilities in the state and over the years had conducted more than two thousand forensic evaluations by the time she saw Cody. Dr. Johnson had done these evaluations for both the prosecution and defense. She later said, "Usually one side or another wants to know, how did this kid get to the point where he did what he did." She also realized that many times the agency wanted a risk assessment of the defendant, to make sure that the community would be safe if the person was let back into society.

In 2004, Johnson was working at the UNM forensic evaluation service when she got a request from Gary Mitchell to do an evaluation of Cody Posey. In the state of New Mexico, anyone under the age of eighteen was to be legally considered as a child. Johnson said, "We look at children and consider that their behavior may not be that of an adult. Their judgment is still distorted by their age development."

Johnson noted that adolescents came into their own in rational thought, more like that of an adult, at the age of sixteen. At the time of the killings, Cody was only fourteen. He was still in years a part of what could be termed "junior-high mentality." Johnson said, "I think of junior high as a black hole that kids fall into. Expectations are changing for them, and junior high is very stressful."

As far as abuse went—and Cody and many others certainly thought of him as being an abused child—

Johnson stated, "An abused child is one who has had any kinds of harmful things happen to them. The most common ones are physical or emotional abuse. The abuse is usually intentional by the abuser. Verbal abuse can be extreme or as mild as calling a child 'stupid.' Sexual abuse, which is forced on a child, is an over-arching category, and may involve all the other forms of abuse, and demeans the child. It makes the child think they are not worth anything. It puts responsibilities upon a child beyond their years, and the children feel low about themselves and unsafe in the world.

"Children look to adults to learn who they are and what they're worth. Once you instill those ideas in a child, it's hard for the child to get rid of those feelings of inadequacy. Children are so self-conscious and so insecure. In some ways, around this period of life, fourteen and fifteen, denigrating stuff is extremely harmful. Vulgarity around a child can be frightening to them. When that combines with physical abuse, it just compounds the trauma for the child.

"Isolation can affect a child in two main ways. Kids need to be exposed to other children and other adults for things that will help them grow and become socially adept. They need to be involved in team efforts. Isolation cuts them off from normal development, and it doesn't allow a child to get help elsewhere. The child starts to shut down and take care of things in their own way. In abused children we often see children being isolated. The abuser needs to keep control of the family and also because of the abuser's insecurities.

"Some of the classic symptoms of child abuse are clusters of symptoms. With severe abuse, anxieties, overactivity, or overalertness is prevalent. There can be sleep problems and the inability to get certain thoughts

out of one's head. You can see a kid filled with shame—
an erosion of self-worth. They tend to feel powerless
and there is nothing they can do to change their situation. Some kids will just try to stay safe and not make
waves. There is a quality of untrustingness. They can
learn that talking to others about their abuse won't help.

"Some kids erupt into anger. Some escape psycholog-
ically—they just detach. They learn ways not to feel.
In most people the response to a threat is to fight or run,
but kids can't do that against an adult, especially their
parents. So they turn inward. Older kids might fight
back or run.

"Children, twelve, thirteen, or fourteen, might search
out relatives, friends, or teachers to help them. But often-
times parents of abused children will constantly be with
them, so they can't make strong bonds with other
people."

In the days to come, Mitchell would ask Dr. Johnson
certain questions, and both the questions and answers
were enlightening as they related to Cody.

Mitchell: How important is it for a person of
junior-high age to participate in activities outside of school?

Johnson: I think it's hugely important. Peers
become exceedingly important at that
age. It's an intense need that kids have,
and given the right peers, it's good for
them.

Mitchell: Would it be good to participate in
FFA, 4-H and basketball?

Johnson: Those are ideal things.

Mitchell: What about church activities and Sunday school?

Johnson: Those are the kinds of activities a lot of parents would love to have their children participate in.

Mitchell: Will abusive parents restrict those kinds of activities?

Johnson: Yes. And I've also seen it with misguided punishment where parents will use things that the children want, to punish them. To deprive them of things that are good for them is really self-defeating.

Mitchell: In abusive families, do we see one child held up in front of the other as the bright one, the smart one, et cetera?

Johnson: That is a form of emotional abuse. It's bad enough not to be able to live up to a parent's expectations, but having another child held up as perfect, it's like living proof of your own inadequacy. Early on, they view it as a problem in themselves. At some point they begin to feel it's unfair. It's easy to see that kids in that situation would feel like an outcast. The black sheep.

Mitchell wanted to know if abused children often thought of themselves as worthless, liars, and cheats. By this, he was getting at Cody's letter to Erin Lynn McCallahan's parents.

Dr. Johnson answered, "That is a common characteristic of a chronically abused child."

Asked if abused children tried to find safe havens, Johnson said, "Yes, but sometimes only in their minds. Sometimes, if the ability to find a safe place is not there, kids learn to retreat and keep away from painful feelings."

Mitchell wondered what effect there was when one child in a family was treated differently than the other. Johnson replied, "It's another piece that feeds into their powerlessness. It's unfair, and they know it's unfair, but there is nothing to be done about it."

Mitchell asked if in abused families there could be one child who monitored and then reported back to the parents about the other child. Johnson said, "It's a tragic, unwelcome dynamic of an abusive family that harms all the children. It sets up one against another. It puts one kid in an adultlike position. It's harmful to both."

Mitchell wanted to know what a "unit of abuse" was. Johnson replied, "A unit of abuse refers to whichever persons are involved in abusing. There can be more than one person in a family who are abusers, and it just compounds the problem, especially if the abused kid doesn't have a sibling as an ally. It makes them more isolated."

In her evaluation of Cody, Dr. Johnson took into account different sources of information. First among those were interviews with Cody. Her first interview with him occurred in September 2004. The interviews were about his history and detailing of his reactions during the interviews—how he thought, how he felt, how he related to people. Dr. Johnson also spoke with third-party sources and looked at records concerning Cody. These included school records, legal records, and postarrest records. She interviewed friends and family related to Cody, as well as reading over one thousand pages of discovery on the case.

Dr. Johnson did four interviews with extended members of Cody's family, and interviewed ten of Cody's friends. She also interviewed fourteen people who worked with Cody at the detention center, where he was housed in Bernalillo County, and psychiatrists who saw him there. Some of the people Dr. Johnson talked to were Corliss Clees, Don Ward, Verlin Posey, Sandy Schmid, Bryan Aragon, Brenda and Rita Lucero, Sherry Hobbs, Gilbert Salcido, Slim Britton, Pilo Vasquez, and Jack Nelson.

Dr. Johnson also performed psychiatric tests on Cody to try and find out certain traits and behavior patterns he might possess. There was a common test for adolescents that took into account how they were the same or different from other adolescents. It factored in patterns of feelings and social skills. The testing had a large population of those tested to give it a good measure of statistical accuracy. These tests were an accepted tool within the psychiatric community, though Dr. Johnson acknowledged, "What you get from a test is a possibility—it is never absolutely clear-cut."

Once Dr. Johnson did all of the interviews and testing, she formulated what she had learned into "a story in context about Cody. It was a big picture of the kid—a formulation of who this kid was and how he got to where he was." With this in hand she put it into the context of the legal question of whether Cody was legally competent to stand trial, and had he been able to form an intent to kill on July 5, 2004.

Dr. Johnson said, "There are recognized mental disorders found in the DMS. Things you look for are depression, fatigue, and post-traumatic stress disorder (PTSD). Kids who are abused chronically often have PTSD. PTSD first came to attention because of what veterans suffered after combat. This had been termed in earlier wars as 'shell shock' or 'combat fatigue.'

"Another thing to look for was attention-deficit/ hyperactivity disorder (ADHD). This disorder starts to show in kids before the age of seven. There are different clusters of behaviors that are a problem for them and other people around them. There can be inattention, trouble concentrating and memory, a disorganized lack of focus and hyperactivity. It's not the child's fault, and it's not the parent's fault. If not dealt with, it can be frustrating for everyone around them.

"In my evaluation of Cody, I reached a diagnosis. I thought Cody showed a combination of disorders that would reflect that he had extreme stressors in his life, but he didn't have them to the degree of a veteran's disorder. Cody suffered chronically from an adjustment disorder. An adjustment disorder was a reaction to stressful things in his life, and he showed a combination of disorders that came from responding to stressful things since childhood. He had a few stepmothers and the loss of his own mother. The death of his mother happened right in front of him. He also probably suffered from excessive discipline. In addition, resulting from the stresses, was depression. It was probably severe at different times in his life. When he was first arrested, he was diagnosed with severe depression.

"Family dynamics were active in his case. There were issues that should have been addressed earlier. The amount of emotional abuse seemed severe to me, as was the physical abuse. There was chronic conflict with his father and possible sexual abuse, as stated by Cody. Isolation from his extended family members, isolation from his friends and girlfriend, the death of his mother, all of these things had ongoing influences in his life. As I see it, he had a temporary loss of control, on July 5, 2004. A loss of control is caused by circumstances that arise out of a situation, but is not permanent. An example would be losing one's temper under extreme stress. You act out of situational stuff instead of how you usually are.

"Terror and fear are emotions, and you can have tendencies to experience these emotions over and over again. They can be chronic, like depression, so that sadness is always with you. There are mental disorders that are associated with a present distress or disability and increased risk of suffering death, pain, disability, or an important loss of freedom." Dr. Johnson believed that in Cody's case he was reaching the point in July 2004 where he feared that his father might beat him to death.

Dr. Johnson surmised that the sexual abuse that Cody had talked about that occurred on the evening of July 4 had ratcheted up his anxiety, depression, and sense of losing control. When he reacted to his father chewing him out about not cleaning the horse stalls properly, it was one bit of emotional abuse too many, as far as Cody was concerned. With the events of sexual abuse from the previous evening still in his mind, Cody reached for the pistol in Marilea's saddlebag with an intent to stop the abuse once and for all.

Another significant player in the analyzation of Cody Posey was clinical and forensic psychologist Susan Cave, from Santa Fe. She had earned a bachelor's degree in psychology from the University of California Los Angeles, and later a doctoral degree, with an emphasis of forensic evaluations at trials. She was involved with CYFD for twenty-five years, made referrals to child protective services in cases of abuse, was involved with the New Mexico juvenile justice system, and worked at the detention center in Santa Fe. She also held a teaching post in psychology at the University of New Mexico, worked for the Department of Corrections, and was a director of services at Las Vegas, New Mexico, where criminals with mental-health issues were sent for evaluation.

Dr. Cave was contracted to do an evaluation of Cody, and conducted a similar procedure to that of Dr. Johnson. In fact, she used parts of Johnson's report and said that it was very detailed on Cody. Dr. Cave viewed Cody's interview with officers Shepherd and Armstrong, and also reviewed police reports. Dr. Cave interviewed Cody as well, and performed a trauma symptom test on him.

Dr. Cave said, "A child's developmental level needs to be taken into account. Around the age of sixteen, they start thinking like adults, but before that, they think as children. There is a stage from seven years of age to ten, from ten through twelve, and thirteen through fifteen is its own stage. One of the most difficult stages for a child is the thirteen-to-fifteen period. They focus on peers and changes that are happening in their bodies. It is a time of transition, and if a child is abused, their emotional development is stunted. They become stuck. The emotional part gets stuck in childhood, even though their bodies are growing.

"Symptoms of an abused child include sleep disturbance, emotional withdrawal, lack of trust, and hypervigilance. Hypervigilance is when a child doesn't feel safe, so they are always on guard for the next bad thing. The child may be emotionally flat, so they learn to over-control themselves. It's not safe to laugh or cry, or show any emotion. Abandonment by a biological mother can lead to stunted emotions. Depression can become profound for the child with a sense of loss."

In her diagnosis of Cody, Dr. Cave basically agreed

with the assessments of Dr. Johnson. She said, "Cody had a major depression, probably going back to early childhood when his mom abandoned him. This was exacerbated when he lost Sandy as a stepmom. That was like a double whammy. Then there was post-traumatic stress disorder after he saw his mother die in front of him. There would be bad dreams and recurring thoughts about that.

"Cody also had an adjustment disorder in reaction to stressors in his life. This led to conduct problems. The PTSD can be seen in rape victims, combat veterans, abused children, children exposed to war, and hostages. They all show the same kinds of symptoms. For Cody, PTSD was chronic. Because of witnessing the death of his mother in a car wreck, it led to a sense of helplessness and extreme loss. Abuse only intensified the symptoms for Cody.

"At an early age he suffered from ADHD. Children who have ADHD have a hard time focusing, especially at something they are not interested in. They are kind of bouncing off the wall. It can be treated with medication, but the family needs to be involved to help minimize distractions. They need to vary tasks and give the child frequent breaks. The child can't be made to sit there and do the same thing for hour after hour. Kids aren't behaving the way they are with ADHD just to be bad. They can't help it.

"'V' codes are not a diagnosis, but there were three 'V' codes for Cody. Parent-child relational problems, physical abuse, and sexual abuse. There was physical abuse and Cody said there was sexual abuse. With a fourteen-year-old, that is more serious than to other older children. It's never easy. It's always catastrophic. It has serious emotional consequences.

"Cody had endured years of physical and emotional abuse. The name-callings and the put-downs by his father and stepmom Tryone were a constant. He had decided that he would just try toughing it out and would just put up with it. Enduring it and trying to do the best job that he could. But that began deteriorating, especially in the summer of 2004.

"I believe a contributing stressor was what made Cody act out at the time of the killings. I think it was the attempted sexual assault that created intense emotions and an upwelling of fear and anger—feelings like he couldn't tolerate it anymore. I think that was one of the precipitating circumstances. Strong emotions were generated from that incident and overwhelmed his self-control.

"As to the loading of the gun—I'm not saying he was out of touch with reality. He wasn't hallucinating or operating under delusions. He was experiencing a flooding of emotions that were overwhelming."

Mitchell wanted to know why Cody crawled into a corner of his bedroom, after the alleged sexual molestation. Dr. Cave told Mitchell, "That was a child looking for some kind of safety. He was very emotionally wounded and frightened by that experience. There was probably some anger about it, and all the other countless incidents. I think it was probably a very intense period of time when he didn't know what would happen next."

Mitchell questioned, for a child who was in a situation like Cody was in, did the danger ever disappear? Dr. Cave answered, "I think given the history and the information that we have, Cody was basically walking on eggshells. Sometimes his father would go off on him in unpredictable ways. Cody might not have done anything to bring it down on him. The stepmother was the same way. She would also kick him, slap him, and belittle him. It could happen at any moment in time, as long as he was there in that environment with no allies, cut off from the rest of the world. And that was what every summer was like for Cody."

Mitchell wanted to know how things were affected if Marilea was an ally of the parents and gave them information about Cody. Dr. Cave replied, "Anyone who has had two children probably knows that kids experience what psychologists call 'sibling rivalry.' That is pretty normal in most households. But when you have a dichotomy where one child is all good, and the other child is all bad, that is totally unrealistic, because nobody is all good or all bad. We all have strengths and weaknesses. The ostracized child is out there, isolated and alone. The child who is the ally of the parents becomes a tattletale. So they are not seen as even being friendly by the victim of abuse."

Mitchell asked if Cody had any safe havens. Dr. Cave said, "It appeared the only safe haven was at school, but the report is that Tryone took them to school and back. During the summer Cody's parents had total control of him on the ranch. If someone else was working on the ranch, then he did have an ally for a while. He could talk to them and seek protection."

Mitchell told Dr. Cave about the rock pile incidents, where Tryone had Cody picking up rocks by hand. Dr. Cave said, "What comes to mind are meaningless tasks, like polishing the doorknob for the hundredth time during a day. It is abusive."

Asked about Cody and his isolation on the ranch, and whether that was abuse, Dr. Cave replied, "I think it is especially so when it involves adolescents. That is a very social time of life—where the peers start to become important, where extracurricular activities become important. Those are socialization experiences that all young people in our society need to become fully functional adults. The isolated kids become adults who don't know how to act in a social situation."

Mitchell: When abused kids who don't have intervention by outside people, do those children feel danger is always present?

Cave: They have hypervigilance. Police officers have this—they are always on alert for something bad that might be happening that needs their attention. They're always on guard. They're always waiting for the next bad thing to happen. They always have the fear.

Mitchell: Do abused children readily relate the actions of abuse to others?

Cave: Not necessarily, because they've lived with it for so long, they don't really know what normal family life is like. When they're young, they think this is the way it is in everybody's household. When they get older, they do gain friends, and begin to realize that what happens in their household doesn't go on everywhere. They begin to sense that's not the norm. And I have seen it in the past, when children are taken out of a violent, abusive environment, they've had to go into treatment and it took some time before they felt safe enough to recall the abuse and talk about it and give detailed information.

I think it took Cody some time to feel safe, to be away from the abuse, and start readily bringing it to mind and talk about it. Most of this stuff is not fun stuff to talk about to others. Most of us take our most painful memories, put them away, shove them down, and keep them down. You can't function if you go walking around, recalling the most painful thing that happened to you. So that's what Cody did.

Mitchell asked about what might happen if Cody was put into a safe, supportive environment: "At some point, might he talk about what had occurred on the ranch?" Dr. Cave said, "Yes, because you want them to be able to talk about it. It needs to stop being a deep, dark, hidden secret. It needs to be exposed to the light, so they can heal. They need to talk about it as they're ready to deal with it."

In this regard Mitchell wondered: Was there a conflict with doctors between healing and getting information from an abused child? Dr. Cave replied, "Yes, if I'm interviewing a child, I don't want to cause further harm. It's very hard to have a rape victim go back and give you a blow-by-blow description. Basically, I don't do that. I may ask them about circumstances and how they are feeling about it now. With abuse victims it's basically the same thing. We don't want to harm them. We want to do it in a thoughtful and careful way, so as not to cause further harm."

Asked by Mitchell if she thought Cody had suffered

from a mental disease or disorder on July 5, 2004, Dr. Cave answered, "Yes."

Mitchell then asked, "Do you have an opinion as to whether Cody Posey formed a decision to take away the life of another on July 5, 2004?" Dr. Cave replied, "Yes, but we can't forget he was fourteen years old at the time. Fourteen-year-olds do not think like adults. So there is a developmental component. With his history, and the very recent attempted sexual assault, the burning by his father, he was overwhelmed by his emotions at the time and felt in imminent danger. He felt that these things could happen at any time."

There were two other psychiatrists, as well, who dealt with the psychology of Cody Posey, and they essentially looked at the same material as Doctors Johnson and Cave, and came up with very different conclusions. In a commonly used analogy about viewing a glass of water as either half full or half empty, the essence of Cody Posey depended a lot upon the eye and mind of the beholder.

Dr. Wade Myers was a psychiatrist from the University of South Florida. He had gone to Temple Medical School, did an internship in general surgery, and residency training at the University of Florida. He also had been in two fellowship programs—one in child psychology and the other in forensic psychiatry. He served as head of the Florida Psychiatry Society and headed an ethics committee in the American Psychiatry Association.

Dr. Myers had worked on the investigation of several murders, was on a committee for juvenile justice reform, and conducted seminars dealing with adolescents. He'd been published in many papers and journals, some dealing with treatment for youths who had killed.

Sandra Grisham wanted to know about various aspects of conduct disorder versus a personality trait. Dr. Myers told her, "A conduct disorder is a pattern of antisocial behavior by children that is persevering and has symptoms like lying, stealing, running away, acting aggressively, bullying, and truancy. Under Axis 1 of the DSM, personality traits are more enduring than a conduct disorder. Conduct disorders are basically for children under eighteen years of age. Only after that age can a person be diagnosed with a personality disorder. That is because they haven't fully developed yet."

Grisham asked Dr. Myers what he'd specifically done in the realm of children who had killed someone. Myers told her, "I've been interested in that subject since the 1980s, and have written two books on the subject. One was *Sexual Homicide by Juveniles,* the other, *Serial Murder by Children.*" He'd also done more than fifty presentations about adolescents and murder.

Dr. Myers was asked by Sandra Grisham to conduct a psychiatric evaluation of Cody Posey. Dr. Myers eventually conducted interviews with Cody on three different occasions. He gave him various tests, including a mini mental exam to get a general idea of his mental functioning, a digit test, attention span test, verbal fluency test, and personal assessment test. Myers also administered an incomplete sentence test, where Cody filled in the missing words, and a psychopathy test that was geared toward adolescents. Besides these tests Dr. Myers read over one thousand pages of discovery material and Dr. Johnson's notes. He also reviewed letters written by Cody.

In one interview, Dr. Myers asked Cody about his thoughts prior to July 5, 2004, and thoughts about killing his parents. Cody admitted to Dr. Myers that he'd had thoughts of killing them prior to the events of July 5.

Grisham: Did Cody have any psychological symptoms, prior to July 5, 2004?

Myers: Essentially, he had a negative history of mental illness before the events of that day. He was always having a feeling of sadness since the death of his mother, and that's understandable, but that's not a mental illness. I didn't see any relationship between the death of his mother and the violence of July 5, 2004.

Grisham: Did depression cause violence in this case?

Myers: No. In fact, he had a very good response from the use of Zoloft. He was essentially back to normal by April 2004.

Dr. Myers said, "There were some notations that at an early age Cody might have had ADHD, but he did not meet the criteria for that by the time I saw him. He was generally a good student, who got along with teachers and classmates. He said he liked hiking in the mountains, riding his bike, shooting hoops, watching movies, and playing video games. He had friends and a girlfriend. He felt his father was too strict with him and didn't let him have enough social outlets. He was concerned because his father would not let him have friends over at the ranch."

Grisham wanted to know about how many times Cody

said that he'd been abused. Dr. Myers had asked him about this and made a tally of the times Cody said that he had been abused and what the circumstances were. The tally came to about 150 instances of abuse from his father over his lifetime, according to Cody. Twenty times being backhanded, fifty to sixty times shoved, fifteen times hit with a board, five times hit with a pipe, three times hit with a shovel, whipped with a rope two or three times, thrown down and choked ten times, kicked fifteen times, punched ten times, pushed out of a truck once, pushed off a fence twice, and pushed in front of a cow once. As far as verbal abuse went, Cody said that he'd been called names at least once a week.

As far as Tryone went, Cody said that she'd slapped him five or six times, and punched him in the face about five times. Cody related that he and Marilea once had a physical fight, but that was all. He did not tell Dr. Myers of Paul, Tryone, and Marilea ganging up on him.

Cody described his relationship with Marilea as being good. He said he liked her, and when they were young, they played well together. They would play with Legos and have good conversations, according to Cody.

Cody spoke to Dr. Myers about being a good worker on the various ranches, but that he thought he'd been asked to do too much hard work. Cody said that during the summer months he would work ten-hour days. Then on school days he'd work thirty minutes in the morning and thirty minutes at night. He said that on a few occasions he purposefully screwed up his work to get back at his father in an indirect way.

Cody told Dr. Myers about a couple of dangerous things he had done in the past, such as riding a mountain bike off some very steep declines, where if he had not made the drops, he would have been seriously injured. He also spoke about his temper and controlling it. Cody said that he'd had a short temper all his life and he thought that maybe he had inherited that trait, since both of his natural parents had short tempers as well. He spoke about the depth of his emotions and said that he didn't have strong feelings about most things. When he started to have strong feelings about something, he would push it out of his awareness.

Cody told Dr. Myers that he had two teachers and three or four friends whom he had told about physical abuse at home. Some of those teachers had seen bruises on him, according to Cody. Cody also talked about getting into at least three fistfights with his dad. On those occasions he ended up quitting the fights, and had bruises and cuts on his body. He explained that his father was five-seven tall and weighed 240 pounds, whereas Cody was shorter and much lighter. He said that his father would mock him in regard to these fistfights, because Cody would say, "I'll fight you or die trying," and his father would respond, "You'd better pack your lunch because you're never gonna beat me."

Cody didn't speak about having nightmares because of the abuse, which are symptoms of PTSD. He did say, however, that he'd had bad dreams about his mother's death. He told Myers he'd climbed out of the vehicle in which they were riding and saw her on the ground in convulsions. During the three weeks he'd spent with Corliss Clees, after his mother's funeral, he cried a lot. He told Myers, "I loved my mother to death." He said that his father had not been very supportive of his feelings after Carla's death, and his father seemed to have an attitude of "just get over it. Don't wallow in your misery. Just move on."

Cody spoke of having dreams where his mother was

still alive. Dr. Myers agreed that this showed some signs of PTSD, as did the fact that Cody became afraid when he was in a vehicle that took a sharp corner.

Cody described personality conflicts with his father and said, "My dad was an ex-army, macho, tough guy. He was a perfectionist and had very high expectations of my behavior." Cody said that his father was emotionally abusive toward him on a weekly basis since Cody had been a small boy. He also said that his father had been physically abusive toward him since Cody was small as well. Cody related that his father was not an emotional man, and it was hard to talk to him about personal or emotional issues. Cody felt that his father didn't like him.

Dr. Myers asked Cody about his sexual preferences and if he'd had any sexual experiences. Cody said that he liked girls, and that Brenda Lucero and Erin Lynn Mc-Callahan had been his girlfriends. He hadn't had sex with either one of them, because he thought they were "good girls," and he respected them, but he said he'd had oral sex on three different occasions with other girls. These had occurred on school campuses, according to Cody. In one instance it had happened with a girl in an art class. They were casual affairs, according to Cody.

Cody spoke of the alleged sexual abuse against him on the night of July 4, 2004, and said that before the shootings his parents had called him into their bedroom. His father had a small welding torch, had come over to Cody, and essentially had told him that Cody was going to have to have sex with his stepmother. Cody said no, so his father heated up the welding torch and touched it on Cody's arm. Then, according to Cody, his dad told him once again to have sex with Tryone. Cody refused, and his father heated up the rod and touched him a second time on the arm. Cody said that Tryone grabbed his head and pulled it down to her breasts. Cody said he had bitten her and ran from the room.

Dr. Myers related, "Cody told me the next day he woke up, had breakfast, and was nervous about what happened the night before. At the breakfast table his parents didn't bring it up, and everything seemed fairly normal. Cody then went out and was doing his chores. Cody said he was in the process of cleaning out a pen, and his father told him he should be using a shovel, not a rake. Cody responded that he was doing a better job than his father could do. In response to that, he said, his father slapped him in the face and left a red mark there. After that, his father made a remark about wanting to go into the house and get some coffee.

"I asked Cody how he was feeling at that time, and he said, 'I was mad.' Cody said he did not go into the house, where his father had gone, but instead went into the barn. He said he saw his sister Marilea's saddlebag and saw a bulge in there. It was the bulge of a pistol. At that time, he said, various alternatives came into his mind— Should he run away? Should he call CYFD and report being hit? Should he tell his teachers? Or 'Should I just live with it?' But nothing had worked in the past. So he told himself, 'I might as well just kill them.' And he did.

"Later, he said, he buried the family using a backhoe. The ground was fairly hard, so he buried them in a manure pile. He went back to the house, thought he changed his clothes there because there was blood on the clothing, and took the truck and went to the store in Hondo and got a Sprite. He went to see his friends, Gilbert and Leo Salcido, and they went and played basketball for two or three hours. They explored along the river, they fished, and they swam. They shot off some fireworks, they grilled some hot dogs on the grill, and he helped the Salcidos work on a house on the property. He also saw his girlfriend Brenda Lucero for a brief time at a neighbor's pool.

"He told me he had planned to run away to Mexico and either get a job or go into computer science as a technology coordinator, setting up computers for businesses and schools. I asked him how he felt during that time, and he said he didn't feel joyful because of what happened—'But it was partly fun. I was having fun, but in the back of my mind, I knew things were screwed up.'

"Later when he spoke with the officers, Cody said, 'I was busted, so I started telling the truth. I knew if I didn't tell the truth about what happened, I risked going to jail for the rest of my life. So I figured at that point, honesty was the best policy.'"

Dr. Myers asked Cody about the legal system, and he said that he understood about how it worked. The topic came up about computers, and Cody said that he had once spoken with his uncle Bryan Basham about some site on the Internet that dealt with murder. One site in particular was about the Menendez brothers, who had killed their parents and then claimed they had done so because of abuse. Dr. Myers said, "Cody thought the Menendez brothers had not done a very good job, because they had waited too long in killing their parents."

Dr. Juan Sosa was mainly in agreement with Dr. Myers in his findings. Sosa had received his B.A. degree from the University of Puerto Rico, and a master's at the University of Florida. He'd done a research paper on aggressive/passive behavior in prisoners. He replicated this study for his Ph.D.

From Florida, Sosa moved to El Paso, Texas, for a while, and then into private practice in Las Cruces, New

Mexico, in 1980. In this practice Sosa saw all age groups and had seen thousands of adolescents over the years. Many of them had been abused, so he'd treated hundreds of abused kids.

Sandra Grisham asked Dr. Sosa to evaluate Cody. Sosa had read Dr. Johnson's report and asked Cody about his history, the death of his mother, his extended family, and the day of the crime. Sosa said later, "Cody was very verbal. Very bright. His use of language was very good. This was a clinical interview to try and see how much major trauma he had suffered. I only tested Cody on one scale, because he had already been tested to death by the other psychiatrists. My test looked into the possibility of psychopathy in Cody. I wanted to find out what was happening with him at the present time. It was a test for juveniles. You score the test on a computer and it will give symptoms from mild to moderate to severe. The only severe score on Cody concerned his sleep patterns. He had moderate stress levels and no mental disorder or disease according to the DSM-IV.

"I viewed Cody's videotaped confession, and I noted internal inconsistency. His stories kept changing, and they shouldn't have. Hypothetically, if someone said they first got burns from a welding accident, and then said later that they were intentionally burned by someone else, that would be an internal inconsistency."

Grisham asked him, "If someone had spoken of ten instances of abuse, and then changed the number to one hundred instances, is that an internal inconsistency?" Sosa said that it was. For all intents and purposes, "internal inconsistency" was a fancy word for lying.

Grisham wondered what Sosa thought had contributed to Cody and the events of July 5, 2004. Sosa answered, "There was a history that led to it, and Cody seemed very angry and frustrated. He had made a decision prior to the murders to proceed to the murders. As far as mental illness, or any kind of psychological deficit, or dysfunction to make him do what he did, he didn't have those."

Grisham asked, "Did he have characteristics that led up to the events of July 5, 2004?"

Sosa replied, "In looking at the evidence, and looking at Dr. Johnson and Dr. Myers (their reports), it is quite clear that they showed an antisocial disorder and budding psychopathic tendencies on Cody's part."

Grisham asked, "What are the traits of a psychopathic person?"

Sosa answered, "One of the most prominent ones is the fact that this individual is flat. They are cold and unemotional. They tend to dehumanize people. They can do terrible things without emotion. There is a lack of remorse. A lot of times they have grandiose feelings about themselves."

Grisham wanted to know what a grandiose sense of self-worth entailed, and Sosa said, "An individual feels that they are better at something than another. You see it at a workplace a lot. Some employees think they know better about things than their supervisor does. Cody said that his father called him a smart-ass for talking back to him."

Grisham: What other psychopathic traits did Cody have?

Sosa: Lies and making up stories to create a sense of endangerment to himself. These characteristics create a sense of worries and woe. The person will say things to elicit sympathy.

Grisham: What traits did you see in Cody that he was lacking in feelings and emotions?

Sosa: I watched the videotape. The one thing that was consistent throughout the tape was his calmness. He was able to present whatever happened, by being very cool. The only time he showed emotion was when he talked about the death of his mother. That impressed me that a fourteen-year-old expressed himself so calmly and so cooly. The fact that he was calm and cool and collected while talking about a highly emotional situation was something I noted. There was no sense of feeling of guilt, excitement, or high emotions. He was very calm and very directed. That was disturbing.

If a sliding scale was made of these psychiatrists and how they viewed Cody and his responsibility in the murders of Paul, Tryone, and Marilea—Dr. Sosa would have been the farthest at one end, believing that Cody knew what he was doing at the time of the crimes, and already showed signs of psychopathy. Next in line on the scale would have been Dr. Myers, followed by Dr. Johnson. On the scale farthest from Dr. Sosa was Dr. Cave, who believed that Cody had almost no control over his emotions at the time of the murders and was in a state of overwhelming emotional loss of control.

In the end these four psychiatrists would be very important as the legal matter of *State of New Mexico* v. *Cody A. Posey* moved forward. And in the end it was crucial as to whose viewpoint a jury and Judge Waylon Counts believed the most, as far as the guilt and sentencing of Cody Posey.

Chapter 10

Opening Shots

From August 2004 on, both prosecution and defense were compiling very long potential witness lists—everyone from Verlin Posey to Slim Britton to Gilbert Salcido. Various letters and documents were also being subpoenaed, such as Tryone's personal journal entries, letters from Cody to Erin McCallahan, and Cody's essay to his father.

In early October 2004, it was decided that Cody's case would stay in children's court, and that same month there was a preliminary hearing concerning exhibits that detailed Sam Donaldson's ranch, a diagram and photos of the Posey residence, and a videotape of the crime scene. The court also was taking in media request forms from many New Mexico television stations, as well as *Dateline NBC,* Court TV, and CNN. By now, this was a big case on nationwide television and the Internet. It was even getting noticed overseas.

In July 2005, Sandra Grisham put in a request for a

change of venue from the Eleventh District Court in Carrizozo, New Mexico. This was unusual in the respect that it is generally the defense that puts in change-of-venue requests because the local population is unfairly prejudiced against a defendant. In Cody's case, however, the public opinion in Lincoln County and the surrounding area was overwhelmingly pro–Cody Posey.

Grisham filed a Change of Venue Motion with Judge Counts stating several points.

1. *The case had received a huge amount of media coverage that included television, radio, newspapers, and on the Internet.*
2. *"Because of public excitement or local prejudice" that pertained to Cody's confession and activities, it was not expected that an impartial jury could be seated in Lincoln County.*
3. *The media exposure had become a problem in itself, in that several reporters and news agencies had become a part of the witness list.*
4. *The prosecution ran an independent poll of potential jurors in Lincoln County and discovered that from 42 percent to 55 percent of the people had already formed opinions as to whether Cody had killed Paul, Tryone, and Marilea. Thirty-six percent to 48 percent had already formed an opinion as to whether he had been abused as a child.*

On October 12, 2005, there was a hearing on the issue of a change of venue, and Sandra Grisham argued, "It's easier to seat a jury in Otero County than in Lincoln County. There will be a problem with no-shows in Lincoln County. One-third of the people who live in Lincoln

County are transients. Mr. Mitchell is well-known in Lincoln County, and some jury respondents have not been truthful about whether they knew Mr. Mitchell."

On the other hand, Gary Mitchell said that Cody Posey was entitled to a trial in the county where he had resided. There were now over one hundred witnesses from Lincoln County, and that would cause a problem if they had to go to the court in Otero County. "We can get a fair trial in Lincoln County," Mitchell emphatically stated.

In the end Judge Waylon Counts ordered a change of venue to Otero County. He cited the fact that because of extensive press coverage, 94 percent of the jury pool in Lincoln County knew about the case. Thirty-four percent of the jury pool had already formed an opinion, and there was not a large population from which to draw a jury pool. By comparison, Otero County had a much larger population from which to make up a jury.

During November 2005, Grisham was trying to have Dr. Myers and Dr. Sosa evaluate Cody once again, but Mitchell was fighting that. On December 5, Grisham wanted the court to hold Mitchell in contempt for refusing the evaluations. She said to Judge Counts, "The respondent (Cody Posey) informed the state's expert (Dr. Myers) that his attorney (Mitchell) told him he was not allowed to discuss anything that happened regarding the shootings or what he did shortly before and afterward, up to and including the time of his confession.

"Dr. Myers asked the respondent (Cody) to confirm that instruction with his attorney, as it would be impossible to complete the evaluation without the information. The respondent phoned Mr. Mitchell or his office and confirmed the instruction. The respondent also informed Dr. Myers that the reason for not cooperating with him was that he was not on his team. Mr. Mitchell's instructions were contrary to the court's order and resulted in an incomplete evaluation of the respondent."

Once again, on December 8, Grisham asked Judge Counts to hold Gary Mitchell in contempt and that Mitchell should pay Dr. Myers for the time he'd spent with Cody. Mitchell, for his part, said that there had been some confusion about what he had actually told Cody concerning this, and Judge Counts replied, "You were incorrect in your instructions to Cody Posey." Dr. Myers was instructed to evaluate Cody once more and ask any questions that he wanted to ask.

Anticipation of the upcoming trial sparked a lot of media interest. Both NBC and Court TV had camera crews in Alamogordo, and Court TV planned to televise the entire proceedings live. Judge Counts was going to allow two photojournalists to be present during the trial, and they could take whatever photos they thought would be relevant to the case. In a trial with such explosive issues, and the murders of three people by someone who had only been fourteen years old at the time, there were sure to be moments of high drama in the Otero County Courthouse.

The actual trial for Cody Posey began on January 17, 2006, when Sandra Grisham faced the jurors in a packed courtroom and began her opening statement. She told them that on Monday, July 5, 2004, it was a sunny morning on the Donaldson Ranch, but that the morning would soon be eclipsed by a horrible deed perpetrated by fourteen-year-old Cody Posey. She said that Cody decided that his world would be better off without his father, Paul, who was a hardworking man, devoted husband, and family man. Grisham called Paul a "cowboy extraordinaire."

Cody also decided that his world would be better without his mom, Tryone, who was also a hardworking individual, dedicated mother, and beloved daughter to her parents. Grisham said that Tryone could brighten up a room by her mere presence.

Lastly, Cody decided that his world would be better without his thirteen-year-old sister, Marilea: a bright, cute, bubbly girl. A girl who loved living on a ranch, school, her family and life.

On that morning, Cody made a cold-hearted and selfish decision to snuff out each and everyone of these individuals. Grisham said that Cody turned his back on the most important of the Ten Commandments—"Thou Shalt Not Kill." Before the morning was over, Cody took a pistol from Marilea's saddlebag and executed his father, Paul, his stepmom, Tryone, and his stepsister, Marilea. He ushered them out of his world and into a pile of manure, leaving them there to rot.

Grisham said to the jurors, the first thing they needed to know, was why Cody had done these terrible things. And she warned them that they might never have the perfect answer as to why, but in the legal system a perfect answer why someone would murder was not necessary in order to convict them. In part, she said, Cody Posey answered the questions of why. He had opportunity to murder when he received a phone call from Sam Donaldson that he and his wife and family members would not be on the ranch over the Fourth of July holiday.

According to Grisham, Cody went to the barn and got the only gun on the ranch that was not locked up in a gun safe. He took the snake shot out of Marilea's pistol and reloaded it with .38 caliber ammunition. He tucked the pistol in the back of his pants, where it couldn't be seen, and walked past his dad and Marilea who were working on a truck. He passed them by because he knew if he shot them first, Tryone, who was in the house, might be able to get to the phone and call 911.

So he passed them by, walked into the house, found Tryone in the living room and exchanged a few words with her to put her mind at ease. Then he pulled the gun out of the back of his pants and shot her in the head. Not content with a single shot to her head, he pulled the trigger again and shot her a second time. In fact, he said about this later, "It was just to make sure that I got her."

Cody covered his stepmom with a blanket so that Paul and Marilea couldn't see her when they first came into the house, and he ran and hid behind a refrigerator. As his dad ran into the house, Cody pulled back the trigger and shot his dad in the head. Right behind Paul, Marilea came running in, and Cody stepped out from his hiding spot and shot her in the face. Since she was still moving, he pulled back the trigger and shot her a second time to make sure that she was dead. Then he dragged the bodies outside, wrapped them up in a blanket, got a backhoe, and put his mom and Marilea in the bucket of the backhoe. He drove a short ways, dumped their bodies on the ground, and returned, placing his dad in the backhoe bucket as well. He dumped his dad's body near the others and tried to dig a hole, but the ground was too hard there. So he put his dad back in the backhoe's bucket, and drove down a road to a manure pile on the ranch.

Cody dumped his dad's body into the manure pile, and returned to pick up the bodies of Tryone and Marilea. Bringing them back to the manure pile, he started to bury them in it, and in the process nearly flipped the backhoe over into a little ravine. According to Grisham, it was the only time that morning that Cody was afraid. Abandoning the backhoe, he got a shovel and entombed the bodies in the manure pile, making sure that they were buried deep enough to make the pile look natural as possible.

Cody put the backhoe back where it usually was, changed his clothes, because they were bloody, and broke a window in the kitchen door. He did this to make it look as if someone had broken into the house and killed Paul, Tryone, and Marilea. Then he wrote a short letter, supposedly from this unknown person, to be left for the police.

Cody drove toward the hay farm, threw the gun and cartridges in the river, but didn't throw the ammo box there because he knew it might float and somebody would notice it. He turned off an irrigation pump on the hay farm so that it wouldn't flood a field and draw attention that something was wrong. He did all of these things, Grisham said, because as he'd stated, "I didn't want to go to jail for the rest of my life."

Cody washed up, went down to the Hondo store, and even talked to teacher Todd Proctor there, calmly telling Proctor that his dad and family were fine and they'd gone to Roswell for the day. After getting a Sprite at the Hondo store, Cody went to the Salcidos' place and lied to them about why he was able to come over to their house. During the next couple of days, Cody played basketball with the Salcido boys, went swimming, set off fireworks, shot rifles, and had a good time. All while Paul, Tryone, and Marilea's bodies were rotting in the manure pile.

By Wednesday, however, his cover-up began to unravel—the bodies had been found and Sergeant Shepherd and Investigator Armstrong came out to the

Salcido place to talk to him. He was shaking with fright until he thought they were buying his lies, and then he began to calm down. Shepherd and Armstrong left the Salcidos, but returned an hour or two later, and took Cody to the Children, Youth and Family Department office in Ruidoso for a taped interview. Cody continued his lies there, according to Grisham, until he realized that Shepherd and Armstrong were no longer buying his stories. At that point, he began to tell the truth.

Grisham concluded her opening statements by saying, "At the very end of a very, very tragic case, ladies and gentlemen, the state will have proven beyond a reasonable doubt, and all the necessary elements, how these killings occurred, when they occurred, who committed them, and who tried to cover them up. All the elements which will convince you of tampering with evidence and three counts of first degree murder."

Chapter 11

Foundations

Gary Mitchell did not present his opening argument right after the prosecution's, instead he was waiting until the beginning of the defense phase. During the trial there weren't real surprises about what the prosecution would ask their witnesses, or questions that the defense would ask their witnesses. And the statements by the witnesses would basically corroborate themes that either the prosecution or defense wanted to get across to the jurors. The real battle—contentious questioning and surprises—would come on cross-examination, where the opposing sides attempted to tear down what the witness on the stand had just said. There were hints of what was to come during the cross-examination of Sam Donaldson, the first witness for the prosecution. During direct Donaldson told of the events of July 4 through 6, in chronological order. It was on cross by Gary Mitchell that the first of many objections was put forth.

Mitchell:	When you learned that Cody Posey had shot his family, did that come as a surprise to you?
Grisham:	Objection. Whether it was a surprise or not is irrelevant.
Counts:	Overruled.
Donaldson:	Yes, it did surprise me.
Mitchell:	Did you want a proper investigation?
Donaldson:	I certainly did.
Mitchell:	Did you give names, to the state, of people who they ought to go investigate?
Donaldson:	Names of people?
Grisham:	Objection.
Counts:	Counsel approach.
	(There was a short whispered conversation between Mitchell, Grisham, and Judge Counts. At the end of it, Judge Counts pronounced, "Sustained.")

Donaldson gave a recitation of events as they had concerned him and his family on July 4 through July 6, 2004. And more contentious proceedings began right after Sam Donaldson's testimony. Grisham had her witness Sergeant Robert Shepherd take the jurors through the first days of the investigation and the interview of Cody at CYFD, where Cody first admitted to killing his parents and Marilea. On cross Mitchell brought up the use of the CYFD safe room. "That room is normally used for children who have been abused, isn't that correct?" he asked. Shepherd said, "Yes, sir."

Mitchell contended, "It can be difficult to have kids

relate about issues they don't want to recall?" Shepherd answered that was correct.

Even Shepherd admitted that he heard from some people in the Hondo area that Cody was being abused. Shepherd said, "The community of people out there, they know one another." Asked if he had questioned any of the ranch hands, who had worked with Paul Posey on the Chavez Canyon Ranch, about abuse, Shepherd said that he hadn't. And Sergeant Shepherd admitted that at the Salcido residence, Cody had spoken about going to school with a black eye. Cody had said at that time that his dad had warned him he'd better tell everyone that he'd been hit in the eye with a softball, if he knew what was good for him.

At this juncture someone's cell phone in the gallery went off. Judge Counts was incensed and proclaimed, "Get that cell phone out of here! If it rings again, you go to jail!" There wasn't going to be any nonsense in his courtroom—from the gallery, media people, or anyone else.

Mitchell asked Shepherd what lawyers were present at Cody's interview. Shepherd said that DA Scot Key was there, as well as Sandra Grisham and Cody did not have an attorney present. Cody had, however, voluntarily come down to the office to be interviewed, and Faustimo Salcido was there with him.

Mitchell wondered what computers had been seized from the Posey residence. Shepherd said that three had been seized, one from Cody's room, one from Marilea's room, and one from the ranch office. Computers, and what was on them, would eventually be a fiery point of contention later in the trial.

Verlin Posey, Paul's brother, testified what he knew of the family dynamics among Cody, Paul, and Tryone, and said that he'd never seen either Paul or Tryone abuse Cody. On cross, Mitchell wanted to get into some family history with Verlin, which brought an objection by Grisham. Mitchell, however, told Judge Counts that he would not go into the family's genealogy, just Paul's marriages and divorces. Judge Counts overruled Grisham, stating that it was okay to lay a history of the family background, but Mitchell couldn't stray into the area of how Paul and Verlin's parents had treated them as boys. Mitchell did ask a little bit about who was married to whom, and when those marriages had occurred. The main questioning of Verlin Posey was being saved for later in the trial, however.

An important part of the case was about the gun that Cody had used to shoot Paul, Tryone, and Marilea. Grisham took Katarina Babcock, step by step, into every aspect of the gun. Babcock testified that in the testing one anomaly occurred—when the hammer was pulled back, it was supposed to stay and the gun would not fire until someone pulled the trigger. But in this gun, because of possible damage or defect, someone could now touch the hammer with their thumb and it would fire the gun, without having to pull the trigger.

The bullets recovered from Paul, Tryone, and Marilea's bodies were of the same class that could be fired from the pistol in question. There was no exact match to the bullets having been fired from that particular gun, but the probability was that they had been.

After Babcock, and after the jury had been dismissed for the day, came the first of many arguments by Grisham and Mitchell to have key evidence admitted or excluded from trial. Without the permission from Judge Counts, the jury was never going to hear certain evidence. Like all good lawyers, both Grisham and Mitchell were persuasive and tenacious. They knew a lot of what they argued might determine the outcome of Cody Posey's fate later in the proceedings.

One issue right off the bat was the admission of certain photos of the crime scene and manure pile, where the bodies were discovered. Mitchell didn't contest that Cody had killed Paul, Tryone, and Marilea, but he said, "The issue is what is the degree of homicide in this case. Those photos [of the bodies] don't need to be shown. They are inflammatory. The state is deliberately being provocative to inflame the passions of the jury."

Judge Counts wanted to see exactly which photos Mitchell was talking about, and Grisham showed him the photos in question. The photos dealt with three stages of the bodies being uncovered from the manure pile. Judge Counts admitted one, which displayed just a partial showing of a body beneath the manure. Counts did object to the most graphic photos, which showed the face of one victim after it had been pulled from the manure pile. There was a great deal of decomposition present. Judge Counts left the third photo up for discussion later.

As for autopsy photos being shown to the jurors, Mitchell said, "For me, it's impossible to judge these types of photographs anymore. I see these kinds of photos all the time. I don't like it, but you get to be like a doctor. You tragically get used to it. The four you have in front of you, those are extremely inflammatory, because of the decomposition that has taken place, and because the nature of the injuries is not in dispute. I don't know if I'd do this if I was the prosecution. I mean, it's good lawyering, but the Supreme Court has tried to warn us time and again, the way the body is disposed of after the offense is not an issue in these types of cases. These photographs make it an issue. In America it's as if the way we treat bodies is a crime, even though it's never charged—"

Judge Counts interrupted, "But it is charged."

Mitchell responded, "I kind of blew off those four counts (witness tampering). There won't be any denying from me in opening that Cody did the shooting or disposing of the bodies."

Grisham responded, "I think the state is entitled to using a limited number of photographs that are relevant to the crimes, the crime scene and the testimony before the court. The ME will be testifying about things that are relevant to the case. Case law shows that autopsy photographs are valid and admissible, such as in *State* versus *Valenzuela.*

"We have to corroborate the defendant's confession. The defense is trying to sanitize what he did by saying the photographs are inflammatory, and that does not do justice to the victims in this case and to the people who had to work on this case. We have to go to intent. By burying them in a pile of manure, his intent was to defile and demean these people. It shows his state of mind when he buried them in a manure pile. He knows the manure pile in the summer will help decomposition."

Grisham said that the medical doctor would have to testify that decomposition made it difficult to track the paths of the bullets, and cited *State* v. *Zamora,* which helped to clarify and illustrate testimony. As far as Marilea went, Grisham argued, "Her eyes were wide when she saw the gun. And where does he shoot her? In the eye. A photograph will corroborate that. He disposed of the bodies in a particularly heinous and ruthless way. That is not something that should be kept from the jury. The photos display what happened. This is the result of his actions. The photos are nasty, but there is nothing in there that is overreaching."

Judge Counts did some research on the subject and said that he thought an argument that was most relevant to the issue at hand fell under section 403 of the New Mexico penal code. This concerned prejudice versus probative value, and he was going to study the issue overnight.

Other key issues were at stake as well, including the years of alleged abuse upon Cody by Paul and Tryone. Grisham said, "There was the incident where Paul supposedly gave him a black eye, but Cody told his friends he got it from playing softball. It should be disallowed. There's another incident where Cody said that his father broke a board on his back when they were living in Roswell. Somebody left bruises on his buttocks, but these were not made by breaking a board over his back! There was no record at the time of this board abuse and no admission that Paul did it. Not even Cody's mom said this, and the alleged incident happened seven years before the killings.

"There is no direct evidence of a choking incident. To have Mr. Mitchell say that Cody was abused all his life is extremely inflammatory. This doesn't even begin to address the sexual abuse fairy tale." Grisham cited case law from *New Mexico* v. *Lefevre.*

Mitchell responded, "No one should be presumptuous as to what I will say in opening statements. Let me say as emphatically as I can, when I present evidence of battery and assaults, whether they are abuse in some people's eyes, or not abuse in some people's eyes, I assure the court, I'm going to have direct evidence of those incidents. There were witnesses who heard or saw those incidents. The child has as much right to testify as anyone else. I label this child abuse.

"I may dance to the rules, but anyone who has been around me knows I won't disregard a court's order. I have a pretty good idea what I need to be doing. It strikes me as a great irony that I will have a tape of this trial the next time the state does a child abuse case. I've done a lot of child abuse cases in this state. And I've never heard of *Lefevre* being cited the way it is here. I mean, that ol' dog doesn't hunt.

"I don't think I have to go through every incident here today with the court, and have the court rule on it. If the state has information that I'm not going to act in good faith, they can bring it to the court. But I don't think they have that. They've been trying cases with me for years.

"It goes to self-defense and the degrees of homicide in this case, whether or not Cody acted on a rash impulse on that day. Whether or not his capacity was diminished. In battered women's cases in New Mexico, we have been allowed to go back to the aggressor and all the incidents that have occurred that led up to the tumultuous event. We can talk about the aggressor and his battered childhood, because we know the connection between kids who are abused and become parents and abuse their children.

"All of the attorneys in this courtroom are aware of it. We live with it every day. In the state of New Mexico, I don't think you can abuse a child, can attempt to rape him, can have him work twelve to fourteen hours a day in the hot sun without any water. I wouldn't treat the livestock on my ranch the way this kid was treated! That's how bad these incidents are. If you restrict us in this case, I don't think that is fair. We must let the jury decide."

Grisham was right back with, "There is no evidence of beating. This is not an issue about a battered woman. A battered woman doesn't kill their husband, and then turn around and kill her sister and their kids. You can't analogize a battered women's syndrome in this case. And that he (Mitchell) be allowed to go into the childhood of a victim! Mr. Mitchell has said, 'If I was the prosecutor, I'd be trying to get those pictures in. Well, if I were the defense attorney, I might be trying to put the victim on trial. But there has to be a limit, Your Honor! They try to tie in incidents that supposedly happened seven years before the killings. That's ridiculous!

"He's trying to smear the victim by talking about his childhood? The victim's not here to talk about his childhood. The victim's not here to defend himself. Cody Posey made very, very sure that there would be no witnesses to come before this jury to tell what really went on in that house.

"To go back to the father's childhood has to be far more prejudicial than probative. You have to draw the line somewhere. There is nothing specific in any report that Cody was bruised on the buttocks by Paul using that paddle [she may have meant board]. I can understand a defense saying, 'We want to try the victim, we don't want to try the kid.' But there are three victims in this case."

This issue would not die down, and Mitchell replied, "There are photographs of Cody's bruises in Chaves County. He was taken to the hospital and there are eyewitnesses. Chaves County did an investigation when the child was seven or eight years old. With this child there was an escalating factor, and things got progressively worse. They never got better."

Judge Counts told Grisham and Mitchell, "Opening arguments are an opportunity to give counsel a chance to tell the jury what they expect the evidence to be. It is what counsel believes they have good faith to present.

Mr. Mitchell has a good-faith belief that he has direct evidence to discuss in opening arguments. The court will not restrict him from mentioning these incidents. The state opened the door by presenting evidence about the incident when the child was seven years old, by way of presenting the confession tape.

"New Mexico does embrace the concept of imperfect self-defense. There may not be a perfect self-defense argument. There is going to be some testimony of what may be considered in the lay mind as cruelty to Cody by Paul and Tryone. Those go at least to imperfect self-defense.

"All of this is subject to laying a proper foundation. I will not find it inadmissible at this point. I will give the defense the opportunity to prove those matters. And there may be the wild card of the child testifying to the various incidents."

This was a huge boon for the defense. In essence, imperfect self-defense *was* their case. Neither Mitchell nor Cody was denying that Cody had shot Paul, Tryone, and Marilea. The crux of their case was *why* he had done it. Without the alleged incidents of abuse being heard by the jurors, it would be an almost impossible task.

There were still other issues to tend with before the jury came back in. Grisham noted that there were fourteen new defense witnesses that she had to voir dire. Among these were Anthony Sanchez, Courtney Taylor, William Brust Jr., Lawrence Gonzales, and Mary Harrington. Grisham said she did not want any of these people testifying before she heard what they had to say, and that the defense had only handed those names over to her just before trial. Mitchell countered, "The DA should have had most of those names on their list since December."

As Mitchell was saying this, Judge Counts was looking

at the list, and Mitchell joked, "Well, Your Honor, maybe I'll just keep my mouth shut while you work."

Judge Counts shot back, "If all lawyers did that, my life would be a lot easier!"

Almost any aspect of Cody's and Paul's lives could become a point of contention as the introduction of evidence continued. One of these was how much importance the document in which Paul supposedly disowned Cody came into play. Mitchell argued, "It shows relevance that Paul disowned his own biological son. It shows how much dislike Paul had for his son." Grisham argued just as strongly that it was irrelevant and prejudicial. She also said that it was only a memo about Cody between Carla and Paul and never had any legal validity, because it had never been signed by both parties. Grisham claimed, "It is not something we can erase from the jury's mind if it comes into Mr. Mitchell's opening."

Judge Counts replied, "The question is whether or not it can be brought up during an opening argument. Even though, if a foundation is laid, it could come in—but not during an opening argument."

Mitchell said that he believed he could establish a foundation and would eventually do so. "These are theories we can prove."

A lot of effort was put in by the defense and prosecution about the computer that had been seized at the Posey residence. There were some key areas that could be vital to their cases, and some real pitfalls as well. Agent Jack Henderson, of the DA's office, had looked through Cody's, Marilea's, and the ranch office's hard drives on the computers, and Mitchell said, "This is a critical portion of the defense. Days upon days the office computer had pornographic sites regarding father/daughter incest and mother/son incest. There had been searches on Google about these types of sites. And that is only the stuff that was saved. We can show through Henderson and Joe Burchett when that computer was accessed for those sites. School records will show that Cody couldn't have looked at them, he was at school.

"Sometimes these sites were accessed at two or three A.M. And sometimes the porn sites would be looked at after checking out ranch property on the computer. Cody would not be looking at that. Circumstantially, I can show that this was an isolated ranch, and they didn't have a lot of visitors. (Mitchell's implication was that a visitor would not be accessing the pornographic Web sites on the ranch computer.)

"The children were at school at certain times. And it is highly unlikely that two schoolkids were up at two or three A.M. All of this goes to what Cody claims happened on the night before the murders, that Paul wanted him to have sex with Tryone.

"I also want Paul's second wife, Sandy, to testify that he had a fascination with porn. There was porn on the Internet and pay-for-view porn on television. There was no porn on either Cody's or Marilea's computers. In fact, Cody's computer was not even hooked up to the Internet."

Then as a pro forma motion, Mitchell said to Judge Counts that all the charges should be dropped because there had not been sufficient evidence given for the trial to proceed. Judge Counts dismissed this fairly readily, saying that there had been more than enough sufficient evidence for the trial to continue.

Chapter 12

Window into Cody's World

Mitchell told the jurors that it was his pleasure to be representing Cody, and that the prosecution had asked them why certain things had happened that led up to the murders of Paul, Tryone, and Marilea Posey. Mitchell said that various witnesses and Cody would tell them why.

Mitchell introduced his law partner in the case, Tim Rose, and Mr. Akenfeld who was their investigator. He also introduced two Lincoln County deputies, Bob Cranson and Gordon Johnson who escorted Cody into court everyday. Then Mitchell started with a chronology of events in Cody's life, starting at around the time he was two years old when a man named Jim Forrester claimed he saw Paul pick up Cody and toss him across the room for no reason.

Mitchell said the first abuse Cody could remember occurred when his father spanked him with a board so hard that the board eventually broke. Cody was taken to a hospital in Roswell and photos were taken of the marks on Cody's back and buttocks. Later a report would be filed with CYFD in Chaves County that Cody was not getting lunch in grade school because his father would not allow him to have money for lunch there.

Mitchell told of Cody's recollection of an event in East Grand Plains, when his father made him fill up a watering trough, one Dixie cup full of water at a time. It was so hot on that day, that Cody nearly passed out from the heat. His stepmom Sandy finally intervened and told Cody to fill up the trough from a hose, because Paul wouldn't know the difference.

The list of abuses went on and on, from Paul knocking out Cody's teeth if they were loose, to hitting him with a flyswatter on his face, which left marks. One day Cody tried helping his dad, who was on a four wheeler, plowing a garden. Cody tripped in front of the plow and his dad nearly ran him over. Cody had to run all the way down the row to get out of the way, because his dad would not stop the four wheeler.

In 1998, Paul left Sandy for Tryone, and Cody was forced to live with them. According to Mitchell, Cody did not get along with Tryone right from the start. He said that she constantly belittled him, and Paul would join in the verbal abuse. When they moved to the 5 Mile Ranch it was very difficult for Cody, because he had never been on a real working cattle ranch before. He was too young and too short at the time to get the stirrups adjusted correctly, but when he left his feet outside the stirrups, his dad would reach over and either jerk him into the saddle horn or knock him to the ground.

Even just getting out of bed in the morning for Cody could be a succession of abuse. At times his dad would either throw cold water on him or shock him with a cattle prod. There was also an incident at a cattle trough with ice on its top, and Mitchell recounted Cody's own words about the incident. Cody said to his dad, "Can I borrow your gloves? Mine are too small and I'll get my hands all wet and cold." Instead of giving him the gloves, his dad reached down, stuck a loop of rope into the water until it was cold and hard, and whipped Cody with it.

Mitchell recounted Cody being knocked off a fence into a cattle crowding chute on the Corn Ranch, where Cody was pushed up against the fence by a cow and kicked in the ribs. Later at the calf table, Paul didn't like the way Cody was working, so he stuck Cody's arm underneath a bar and pinned him there for over a minute. When Cody looked later at his arm, there was a crease left by the weight of the bar.

Mitchell spoke of the agreement between Paul and Cody's mother, Carla, in which Paul would disinherit Cody and give him back to her custody. Part of the agreement stated, "No contact shall be made by either party for any reason at any time. All past due child support is canceled." Carla remarried a man named William Brust Jr., and Cody liked his new stepdad. The whole family planned a new life together in Washington state, but tragedy intervened on a Wyoming Interstate highway. Near Ranchester, Wyoming, while William was driving, he drifted across the road and the pickup flipped over. William and Cody, who were wearing their seat belts, survived. Carla, who was not wearing a seat belt was killed, dying right in front of Cody as he witnessed her death throes. The psychological damage it caused would haunt Cody for years to come.

Even the funeral for Carla back in New Mexico was a nightmare. Cody's father, Paul, came to the memorial service unannounced, and sent Cody into shock. According to many who were there, he began crying and said that he never wanted to go back and live with his father, Tryone, and Marilea. But in the end, that is exactly what happened.

According to Mitchell, things only got worse for Cody from that point on, with physical abuse incidents such as being hit with a three hundred pound tire by his dad, knocked off a tractor into a hole, kicked with spurs, hit with ropes, rocks, fists, and pieces of wood. Even Cody's blankets were removed from his room at the ranch house when Paul and Tryone became angry at his school grades, and Cody spent an entire year with only a sheet on his bed.

Mitchell said that Cody was constantly cursed and hit by Paul, and when he was done, Tryone would do the same. There wasn't even any relief from being around Marilea. In fact, according to Mitchell, she was part of the problem, spying on Cody at school, tattling her stories to Paul and Tryone, knowing that Cody would be punished when he got home.

Things only got worse for Cody when the family moved to Sam Donaldson's ranch. Mitchell spoke of Cody being roped and dragged across a corral, of being constantly hit with rocks, punched, kicked, and beaten. Even as something as innocuous as Cody joking with Marilea and calling her a "geek" drew a slap from Tryone that was so hard that it tipped Cody and his chair over.

Cody was not alone in speaking of these incidents of abuse. Steven Chaves recalled Cody being sent to clean rocks out of a corral as punishment, and he called the task pointless. Chaves also spoke of Paul dropping forty pound bales of hay on Cody and laughing about it. One of the worst incidents occurred when Cody was just learning how to drive a stick shift and he continuously popped the clutch on the truck, making the passengers who were stacking hay move around. In response, Paul took a hay hook, jabbed it at Cody's genitals, and yelled, "I'll jerk your balls off if you pop that clutch again!"

Pilo Vasquez recalled Cody being forced to shoot his own dog, when it broke a leg, and being told to slit the throat of a lamb. Slim Britton remembered Cody being forced to drive cattle in the hot sun without water, until he nearly passed out, and constantly forced to work all day without any food. Even at the dinner table, Cody was often denied seconds, while everyone else there got extra helpings of food. Slim said that Cody was "cussed at pretty hard" by both Paul and Tryone.

School was the only relief for Cody, according to Mitchell, but even there his torment didn't stop. He was denied a chance to play basketball, something he was very good at, for a minor infraction, and denied a chance to participate in Future Farmers of America events, as well as Knowledge Bowls. Marilea stilled spied on him at Hondo High School, and tattled if Cody spoke to kids of whom Paul and Tryone did not approve. He was made to ride to school with Tryone in the morning, picked up by her in the afternoon, and forced to work on the ranch as nearly a slave, according to Mitchell.

Because Cody chose a Hispanic girlfriend at Hondo, his parents suddenly without warning pulled him out of school and made him go to Capitan High School miles away. He was instructed not to talk to other kids on the bus, and Marilea was there to keep an eye on him. The punishment by the time he reached Capitan was worse than before, a spanking with a belt replaced by Paul hitting him with closed fists. Paul even threatened that if Cody told outsiders about this, especially social workers, he would eventually get out of jail and "I'll come and get you."

Mitchell said that by the summer of 2004, Cody feared for his life. He knew that no help would be coming from Marilea, and he was a virtual prisoner on the ranch. And then on the night of July 4, everything spun out of control when Paul called Cody to his bedroom, and Cody opened the door to find Paul standing in his underwear and Tryone lying naked under a sheet on the bed. Paul told Cody he was going to have to have sex with his stepmom, but Cody replied, "No, I can't do that! It's wrong!" He started to leave but Paul detained him and burned him with a small butane torch. Then Tryone grabbed Cody's head and pulled him down toward her breasts. He couldn't stand it, bit her, and ran away to his room, where he hid in a corner all night.

Mitchell said that the next morning, Cody got up early, ate a hasty bowl of cereal so as not to be around Paul and Tryone, and went outside to clean the corral with a rake. Even this brought his dad's ire, and Paul told him to use a shovel instead of a rake, and then he hit him. At that point, according to Mitchell, Cody snapped. All the years of abuse, and the unexpected insistence that he have sex with his stepmom, became too much for a fourteen-year-old to handle.

Mitchell concluded by saying, "He no longer wanted to be beaten, abused and raped. Extreme emotions overwhelmed him. Ladies and gentlemen, Cody's been called stupid most of his life. In fact, he's above normal when you let him be. We're not denying he did it. I guess the real question is, how much are we going to demand of a child? When do we allow them to finally fight back?"

Chapter 13

In His Own Words

Cody related on direct many of the instances of abuse by Paul and Tryone that Mitchell had talked about in his opening statements, and Cody added a few more that hadn't been heard before outside of court. But for Cody, as it would be for most witnesses, where the sparks flew was on cross-examination and redirect.

Right after Mitchell finished with Cody, Sandra Grisham told Judge Counts, "Ninety-eight percent of what we heard from Cody on direct is new to me. I need to get various documents to be able to cross-examine this witness." Grisham wanted a recess until 1:00 P.M. to accomplish that. Judge Counts gave her until 11:00 A.M. instead.

When trial resumed at eleven, Grisham and Cody squared off from the witness stand and prosecutor's table.

Grisham: Good morning, Cody. I'm the children's court attorney. You say your first memories are of living with your mother and aunt in Roswell?

Cody: Yes, I believe so.

Grisham: When did you live with your stepmom Sandy?

Cody: Anywhere from the ages of four to nine.

Grisham: How old were you when your dad married Tryone?

Cody: I believe I was nine years old.

Grisham: After your dad divorced Sandy, how often did you see her?

Cody: I believe three times after the divorce.

Grisham: While you were still living with Sandy, where were you going to school?

Cody: I attended a private school at Roswell named Abundant Life Christian. I was moved to East Grand Plains.

Grisham: Was there a time you got into trouble in school by bringing a knife to school in your backpack?

Cody: I believe so. I remember having a knife on me at that time.

Grisham: Did you have some kind of counseling after that?

Cody: I remember going to a counselor. I went for two sessions. I was pulled out after that.

Grisham's questioning might have seemed innocuous at times, but she was attempting to get Cody on record saying certain things that she planned to disprove later by the statements of other witnesses and possibly by contradictions in Cody's own statements.

Grisham wanted to know while Cody was living with Sandy, if he had been tested for a gifted program in the school. Cody said he thought he had been, and Grisham replied, "Do you recall saying, the school tried putting you in a gifted program but your father refused?"

Cody answered, "I remember taking the test, but I don't know why I didn't get in."

This was just one example of trying to catch Cody in lies with his own words. Grisham would later show documents that would state Cody had not scored well enough to make it into a gifted program.

Grisham said, "There was a picture of some bruises on your buttocks, and a mark farther up your back. Now, according to your mom, that mark on your back wasn't from your dad. It was from playing. Do you remember that?"

"No, ma'am, I don't," Cody replied.

"You do remember the name of the officer who talked to you about that incident, right?"

"I believe her name was Sharon Barry."

"Do you remember talking to someone at the hospital?"

"I remember talking to a photographer who had a camera with him at that time."

"Do you remember talking to a doctor?"

"No, not to my recollection."

Grisham asked Cody, "Do you remember talking to a doctor about how you liked living with your dad? How he'd take you rapeling, and you weren't afraid of him?"

Cody answered, "No, ma'am. I don't think I'd been rapeling at that time in my life."

Grisham asked if Cody recalled the incident when living in East Grand Plains of having a loose tooth, and his father hit him in the jaw and knocked it out. She asked how many times that had happened. Cody answered, "I remember it happened three times."

Grisham said, "Sandy was living there at the time, and you remember being slapped across the face if you didn't eat your food?"

"Yes, ma'am."

"Sitting up all night, if you didn't eat your food?"

"Yes, ma'am."

Grisham queried if Cody recalled being on the 5 Mile Ranch, also known as the Corn Ranch, and wanted to know what year the incident happened where Cody had described being in the chute with the calves. Cody thought the year had been 1999.

"Who was there during those fall works?"

"It was the Corn brothers."

"B.A. Corn saved you from a cow?"

"B.A. Corn helped me jump over the fence to get the cows off me. When he did that, he ended up getting a finger broke by a gate slamming back on it."

"Who did you say threw you into the pen of calves?"

"My father."

"Who else was there besides B.A. Corn?"

"I believe it was just me and B.A."

(Later, Grisham intended to have the Corn brothers on the stand to refute this testimony.)

Grisham asked Cody to recall the incident where he had supposedly been vaccinating a calf, and his father slammed a bar down on his arm. Cody replied, "On a calf table there's what we call a 'squeeze.' There's bars you can use to open up a certain area that you want to work. As I did that, my dad slammed the bar down across my arm. If there's pressure on the bar, you can't get loose. My arm was closed between one bar, and the other two bars were pressing on that bar."

"Who was there during that?"

"I believe the Corn brothers were there during that."

Grisham asked Cody about being hit and his head slamming back into a wall on the 5 Mile Ranch, creating a hole in the wall. She asked him where it was in the house and how he had fixed it. She got fairly specific about this incident.

"What part of the house was this in?"

"It was in the hallway, near a side door."

"How did you fix it?"

"I had to go and find some putty to put in the hole."

"How big an area was that?"

"About six inches."

"Did you use anything but putty to fix it?"

"No, ma'am."

"What tools did you use?"

"I used what's known as a 'putty knife' and just stuck as much putty in there as I could to make it look even with the wall."

"How much putty did you use?"

"I believe I used the whole tub."

"Did you paint over it?"

"No, the putty was white and so was the wall."

Grisham asked if Cody remembered telling Sandy that Paul and Tryone had been calling him names, so CYFD workers came out to the 5 Mile Ranch. Cody said that he did. Asked if the CYFD worker had spoken with him, Cody replied, "The CYFD man did not talk to me. I remember them driving up to the house and they talked to Paul and Tryone at the gate."

Grisham said, "You're absolutely sure they didn't talk to you?"

Cody answered, "Yes, ma'am, I am."

Grisham wondered why Cody had to write an essay. He replied, "My father told me to write an essay. It was a two-thousand-word essay."

Grisham asked, "At the funeral, what was your first contact with your father?"

"I believe my first contact, well, I saw him at the front of the church. I vaguely remember an argument about custody."

"You told an officer that your father was mean, abusive, and cruel?"

"Yes, ma'am. That was after the argument. The preacher at the church told us to enter his office and we could talk to an officer there. And Officer Farmer asked me if I wanted to live with my father, and I told him no, because of the fact he was abusive. He beat me and was mean."

"Did you tell the officer any details?"

"I'm not sure."

"What was the meeting like with your father, after the funeral?"

"He picked me up in the truck. We went to a park. I sat on a swing. I don't remember if words were exchanged. I just remember the time at the park."

"In the meeting at the office of the preacher, what was said and done at that meeting with your father?"

"After I told the officer that my dad used to beat me, the officer said by law I had to live with my father. I believe once again I told him I didn't want to. He gave me a phone number to call him in case something happened."

"You didn't go with your father for another three weeks, correct? That's because he agreed you could stay with your uncle?"

"I didn't stay with my uncle. I stayed with my aunt Corliss. I'm not sure what kind of agreement was made."

"When you were staying at your aunt's house, did your dad call every day?"

"I'm not sure."

"Did he call a lot?"

"I don't know."

Grisham asked Cody what grade he was in when he had been sentenced to his room for a year. Cody said he thought it was during the sixth grade at Cloudcroft. Asked if he meant a school year, in other words from August until June of the following year, Cody answered that it had begun three or four days after the school year had started. The reason it had started was because he got a C in his computer class, and everything was taken away from him after that.

"When you say everything," Grisham said, "you mean everything but the mattress and sheet, and they never gave anything else back to you?"

"During the summer, after the school year was over, I started earning things back. Things like my bed frame, a pair of clothes, and my books back. Stuff like that," Cody replied.

"Weed's pretty cold in the winter?" Grisham asked.

"Yes, ma'am."

"The incident about being slapped across the face with the cowboy boots—what year of school were you in?"

"I believe I was in my sixth-grade year."

"Did you have PE then?"

"During PE, I had my PE shoes to wear."

"So when you said you had to play basketball in your boots, that wasn't during PE?"

"That was during the lunch break."

Grisham asked if he remembered what months of the

school year he had to wear duct tape on his boots. Cody replied that he didn't remember which specific months, but this had gone on for three or four months. Grisham wanted to know if it bothered Cody that his parents were receiving Social Security money from Carla's death, but that he didn't get any of it. Cody said that it did bother him. She wanted to know if he thought it was fair they had done that, and he answered no. Asked if he had any discussions with Paul or Tryone about it, Cody replied, "I asked them what the Social Security money was for, and they said it was to help raise me."

"You say you didn't know you were going to Hondo until they pulled you out of school in Weed, but you-all had discussed about moving to Hondo prior to when you left?"

"There had been a discussion that we were going to move, but I hadn't been told for sure we were going to move."

"You knew it was in the works, though?"

"No, ma'am. I didn't know they were actually going to do it."

"Didn't you talk to a few friends about the move to Hondo?"

"I believe I talked to a few friends that they had talked about it."

Grisham brought up the subject of Cody using a saddle with a big saddle horn on it. She wanted to know who used that saddle as well. Cody said that he and Marilea both used it at Hondo. Then Grisham said, "You talked about an incident in Hondo when you were working cows, and your dad roped you and dragged you facedown all the way across the corral before you were able to turn over on your back?"

"No, ma'am," Cody replied. "That's not what happened. I was roped and I was dragged a good ten feet before I could turn around so that I wouldn't be dragged on my face. I was then dragged about the length of this courtroom that way."

"Who else was working cattle that day?"

"I believe it was Pilo Vasquez and another ranch hand, who we later fired. I can't remember his name."

"Do you remember what time of year that was?"

"I believe it was early spring."

"Do you remember what grade?"

"I believe it was the middle of my second 6th-grade year."

"Could it have been in the seventh grade?"

"I don't think so."

Grisham told Cody that he had laughed a little bit while testifying about the incident when he had popped the clutch and thrown people around on the truck. She asked him who had been there that day, and he answered Pilo Vasquez, Slim Britton, his father, and Marilea. Asked who was on the truck, Cody said that it had been Pilo Vasquez. Grisham asked if Pilo was the only one thrown off, and Cody replied, "He wasn't thrown off. He was just shaken up. It's not that I threw everybody everywhere—it's just that the truck jumps and makes people get moved around from the original place they were standing."

"Your dad and Marilea were throwing hay to Pilo and you were driving?"

"Yes, ma'am."

Grisham reminded Cody that he had talked about a scar on his hand, and wanted to know who was there when that happened. Cody said that Pilo was there. Grisham added, "Oh, and I believe you said that Slim and Steven Chaves were there also." Cody said that they were, and Marilea might have been there as well.

Grisham asked Cody how old the puppy was when it had been dropped over a fence and hurt its leg. Cody said he didn't know for sure, but it was the size of being in between a puppy and grown dog.

Grisham asked if Cody was the only one picking up rocks out of the corral, and Cody said that he hadn't been. Grisham added, "Tryone picked up lots and lots and lots of rocks, didn't she?

Cody replied, "After I picked up the rocks, she went over and raked the area."

"You never saw Tryone picking them up and putting them in buckets?"

"No, ma'am, I didn't."

"Steven Chaves was picking up rocks and putting them in buckets, right?"

"Yes, ma'am. When the job started, it was Steven and I."

"What was Steven being punished for?"

"I'm not sure, ma'am."

Grisham wondered if Cody remembered going to a Christmas party and an end-of-the-school-year party. He answered that those were the only two parties he recalled attending. She asked if he had been on any field trips, and he said that he had been on a few. Asked where the field trips had been, Cody answered that one had been to a park in Alamogordo.

"Why were you pulled out of the clown deal at church?" Grisham asked.

"After I had been told I was going to repeat sixth grade, I was told I wasn't going to be able to participate in the clowning or the Bible competition," Cody replied.

Asked about the time he shot the hole in the dashboard of the truck, Cody said, "I was looking at a .45 my dad had, and as I cocked the hammer back to see if a round was in the chamber, I dropped it and it fired." Grisham wanted to know if it was an automatic, and Cody said it was a semiautomatic. Asked where he was sitting at the time, Cody answered inside his father's pickup parked outside of a barn on the forty acres of alfalfa farm.

"What did your dad do when this happened?" Grisham said.

"He was inside the barn talking, and when he heard the gunshot, he ran around to the other side of the pickup, grabbed me by the collar, and threw me to the ground. Then he was looking at me to see if I'd shot myself," Cody replied.

"Where did you land?"

"I ended up on the side of the road, which is pretty rocky."

"Did you get any bruises from that?"

"I landed on my back. I'm not sure if I did or not. I remember my back being sore."

Grisham said that when Cody was at Hondo, one of the discipline measures was that he couldn't take driver's ed, and that he couldn't talk to certain people around Hondo. She asked, "Isn't it true that your dad didn't want you talking to Gilbert Salcido because you two had smoked marijuana?"

"Yes, ma'am. One time."

"Just the one time?"

"Yes, ma'am. That I can remember."

"Do you remember you said you smoked marijuana on several occasions, mostly at school?"

"Yes, I recall saying that."

"So where else did you smoke marijuana besides school?"

"That was it. May I say something real quick?"

"Sure."

"That was it. It was at school, and it was the only occasion."

"Who'd you smoke it with?"

"The one time with Gilbert Salcido. The other times I was given it by a certain other individual. I can't remember his name. Robert something. He was from Albuquerque. He had just moved down there at the time."

"You don't remember his last name?"

"No, ma'am."

"Marijuana was pretty common around Hondo?"

"I believe so, and around the valley."

"Is that one of the reasons why your dad wanted you going up to Capitan High School?"

"I'm not sure. I wasn't given any reason."

Grisham asked if Cody was afraid of his dad, and he answered yes. Then she wanted to know why on several occasions Cody had told his dad that he ought to turn his father in to CYFD, if he was so afraid of him. Cody answered, "I thought maybe he would stop doing what he was doing if he thought I was gonna turn him in."

Grisham wanted to know about the incident of being thrown into a wall by his dad on the Chavez Canyon Ranch. Cody told her that his dad had thrown a punch at him and missed, and then tackled him and they both went into the wall. He added, "I remember breaking the wall. I had scratches on my back, where I went through. It was in the kitchen. I believe it was the wall between the laundry room and basement. My dad and I fixed it. He had some drywall sheets, and we just put those up there."

Asked if he remembered what they'd used to fix the

wall, Cody replied, "My dad cut some pieces down off the barn, but I don't remember what all he used. I helped him cut the pieces, but actually putting them up on the wall, I don't remember." Asked if they'd used a big piece of drywall, or a little piece, Cody said that he couldn't recall.

"But you helped him cut it, right? Do you remember how many cuts you had to make?"

"We cut out a fairly good size, but I don't know the exact size." Cody held up his hands and described an area about two feet by two feet square.

"Do you remember what shape it was?"

"All I remember is helping him pull it down."

"Do you remember when that happened?"

"It must have been about 2001."

Grisham wanted to know why Cody had gone to talk with Jack Nelson, and Cody said it was because he didn't want to call Tryone "Mom," and Paul had hit him in the eye and given him a black eye.

Grisham said, "Do you remember telling Dr. Johnson that—"

This brought an immediate objection from Gary Mitchell. Judge Counts asked Mitchell and Grisham to approach, and Mitchell told Counts, "Jury instructions cite a specific rule that no information of an evaluation may be used."

Grisham replied, "I'm able to use statements in a psychological evaluation that go to his mental state. All that led up to the killings and what caused them. I'm not talking about events of the day in question. I am talking about mental state and how he got to it."

Judge Counts excused the jury for a lunch break, and the discussion continued after lunch outside the presence of the jury. Grisham argued that Dr. Johnson spoke with Cody about things that happened before the killings, and her questions were going toward the aspect of diminished capacity, which was the basis of the defense case. Judge Counts agreed and said that Grisham's line of questioning was within rule 605 of the penal code.

When the jury was seated once more, Grisham asked Cody, "Didn't you tell a psychiatrist, 'Why should I do what Tryone says I should do, since she's not my real mom?' You had been calling Tryone 'Mom' since your own mother died, right?"

Cody replied, "No, I hadn't."

"Around when did you start calling her 'Mom'?"

"I'm not sure."

"You can't even give me an estimate?"

"I can't."

"But you'd been calling her 'Mom' for some time before this incident, right?"

"I had. And I didn't like to. But I was told to."

"You had a black eye at other times too?"

"I'm not sure."

"What grade were you in when you talked to Jack Nelson?"

"I believe I was finishing up my second 6th grade."

"Did you talk about other incidents of abuse that we heard about in the courtroom, yesterday and today?"

"I don't think so."

Grisham asked him about the letter he had written to the parents of Erin Lynn McCallahan. It was the letter where he had called himself a "screwup" and said that he had "lied, stolen, and cheated."

Cody said that he had been trying to explain things to the family, because Tryone had spread lies about him.

Grisham had Cody read the essay he had written. Cody had even drawn up an outline for the essay, which included: *my former years and why they happened, my*

good years gone bad, the years before—things I did and
the reasons, the good years slowly slipping away, why
I started doing and not doing things, and why it all
happened and why it changed.

"You say you never got a telephone call from anyone on
those ranches? Not in your entire life?" Grisham asked.

"I wouldn't say my entire life. I talked to Carl Clees
once or twice," Cody responded.

"You talked about the Sunday before the killings,
breaking a young filly, and you told your dad you had
a better idea?"

"Yes, ma'am."

"Did you have a lot of ideas that were better than your
dad's?"

(There was a long pause.) "I believe so."

"Did you tell a psychologist that all the problems with
abuse had started a couple of years ago?"

"I don't remember saying anything like that."

"When you were at Hondo, how did your family
spend its evenings?"

"Usually Paul, Tryone, and Marilea were inside watching TV or a movie. Usually I was in my room or outside
playing basketball."

"You never played board games?"

"During dinner it was kind of a ritual where everyone
would sit down and we'd play a board game."

Grisham said that there was a poem by Marilea that
hung up on a wall, speaking of a good family life.
Grisham claimed that in Marilea's mind, family life was
not torture. Then Grisham stated that Cody had planned
to escape to Mexico for a few years after the killings
until things cooled down.

Getting to the alleged sexual abuse on the night of
July 4, 2004, Grisham asked, "Do you remember what

your dad was wearing that night?" Cody answered he was wearing black briefs.

Grisham questioned, "When he first burned you, did you scream or cry out?"

Cody said, "I just stepped away."

"You turned around one time and hit him when he pulled your hair, but you didn't hit him when he burned you?"

"No, ma'am."

"He heated it up a second time? How long did that take?"

"I don't know. It was probably hot from the first time."

"And all the time you were just standing there?"

"The second time he burned me was when Tryone had scooted down the bed and pulled my head to her chest."

"Was the burn before or after you bit her?"

"Slightly before I bit her. And then I ran from the room."

Grisham then said, "Your Honor, I'm expecting an objection." Judge Counts had Grisham and Mitchell approach, and Grisham said, "I want to get into the motive of what Cody was thinking when he went to kill Tryone."

Mitchell responded, "Do you intend to use statements Cody told a psychologist? Then there will be an objection."

Grisham replied, "Not necessarily, but it's already been established on direct what he's said. I just want to go to what he's said."

Judge Counts, however, sustained the objection, and Grisham could not approach things in that way. Instead, she asked Cody, "Did you tell them (and here it's not clear if she meant investigators or psychologists) about all the guns in your household, except the murder weapon?"

Mitchell immediately objected, and it was sustained.

Grisham, however, countered to Judge Counts, "I want to ask him why all the guns were locked up in the safe. I want to show that Cody intended before the murders to accidentally shoot his parents one night when they came into the house. After that, they locked up all the guns."

Mitchell said, "There is no foundation as to time and place."

Judge Counts asked, "What door swinging open would let you walk through there?" (In other words, what door had opened so that she could ask such a question?)

Grisham responded, "Cody's general talk about what went on in that household."

Obviously, this was not a big enough door swinging open, in Judge Counts's estimation, and he sustained the objection.

Grisham asked Cody, "In all the times you talked to Doctors Johnson, Cave, Sosa, and Myers, did you relate to any of them the number of abusive acts you've related to this jury?"

Cody answered, "I believe I did to Dr. Johnson."

"You believe you talked to Dr. Johnson about being beaten two or three times a week, being banned to your room for a year, having your head held underwater in a trough until the bubbles left?"

"I'm not sure if I told her specific incidents."

"When did you remember all these incidents?"

This was greeted by silence from Cody.

Grisham finally said, "Never mind—pass the witness."

Mitchell on redirect asked why Cody had written that letter to Erin McCallahan's parents. Cody said, "I wrote the letter to Erin's family because Tryone had talked to

Erin's stepmom and I knew Tryone had bad-mouthed me. I wrote the letter so they would think I was a good person. I didn't know for sure what had been told. I wasn't sure what Tryone had told them, but she often told people I was a bad boy."

Mitchell got into a discussion about Cody's mother, Carla.

Mitchell:	When you lived with your biological mother, how was it?
Cody:	It was the best time of my life.
Mitchell:	Did you get hit?
Cody:	No, sir, I didn't.
Mitchell:	Did you get cursed at?
Cody:	No, sir, I didn't.
Mitchell:	Did you get punched or slapped?
Cody:	No, sir.
Mitchell:	Did you get somebody to tell you they loved you?
Cody:	Yes, sir.

Mitchell asked about the two-thousand-word essay his father had made him write, and wondered if Cody knew the reasoning behind it. Cody said that he didn't know the reason, but that he was told to write it by his father. Asked if everything he wrote was true, Cody replied, "No, sir, it's not. There were times when I messed up, but in the whole paper it told how I messed up all the time, and that's not true. My friends weren't bad people."

Mitchell wanted to know what two or three years Cody was referring to in the essay, in which he didn't have problems. Cody said those years were when Sandy was his stepmom. He was allowed to see more friends then. Cody continued, "Sandy had pretty much been my mother through my younger years. My mother at the time was in the navy. I was placed with a person I didn't like, Tryone, and she didn't like me. Tryone hit me and cursed me."

Mitchell asked Cody about his friends in third grade, and if they got to do things he didn't get to do. Cody said that they did, that they were happy, that they laughed a lot, and were loved. Cody added, "I wanted to go outside to play with my friends. I wasn't allowed to. They were allowed to wear T-shirts and looser pants. I was always forced to wear long-sleeved shirts and cowboy-cut Wranglers, cowboy boots, and a belt with the shirt tucked in. I was expected to sit down and eat lunch, and just sit and watch the other kids."

Mitchell: You said that things had not changed. You wrote, "I was as bad, if not worse back then."

Cody: I was writing what my father wanted to hear.

Mitchell: You said you've never changed, because "I haven't wanted to change."

Cody: I was acting that way, because I didn't think anything I was doing was wrong. And I didn't want to change to fit my father. I wasn't a bad boy.

Mitchell: Up until the time you wrote this letter, tell me the amount of times your father congratulated you on doing something well?

Cody: A couple of times. I might rope something and he'd say, "That's a nice loop."

Or playing basketball, I'd make a shot, and he'd say, "That was a good shot."

Mitchell: You wrote, "I hated you and didn't want you to win." Who was that written for?

Cody: Again, it was written for my father.

Mitchell: The whole tone of the letter. Who was it for?

Cody: My father.

Cody said that he did argue with his father on occasions, but he did so because he'd been told to stand up for what he thought was right. He had learned that concept from his father. Even by doing what his father said he was supposed to do in such a situation, it would lead to a fight, anyway.

Mitchell wanted to know if Cody had ever told Dr. Johnson that he wanted to be a cop or an assassin. Cody responded, "I said I wanted to be a cop or in the CIA. I don't remember if I used the word 'assassin.'" Asked about his father, mother, and uncle Carl—all having been in the military—what did that mean to him? Cody said, "It meant that they were standing up for what they believed was right. And they were standing up for their country." Along those lines, Cody said, police officers stood up for what they believed in and were doing their civil duty. It was another form of helping one another and helping their country.

Mitchell asked what a typical evening was like at home. Cody answered, "Typical was, we would get home and do chores, homework, and most of the time homework was done in our rooms. After that, we ate supper. During supper it was mandatory to play a card

Paul Posey, Cody, Tryone (Cody's stepmother) and Marilea (Cody's stepsister) appeared to be a happy family. *(Photo courtesy of Pat Basham)*

Cody, however, claimed that it was three against one in the Posey household, with Paul, Tryone, and Marilea against him.
(Photo courtesy of Pat Basham)

Cody said that although in public, it looked like he and his dad got along,
on their ranch his dad cursed him, beat him, and a lot worse.
(Photo courtesy of Pat Basham)

Cody claimed Tryone hated him and made his life miserable on the ranch.
(Photo courtesy of Pat Basham)

Some family members, including Pat Basham, said that Cody was treated kindly by Paul and Tryone, just the same as Marilea.
(Photo courtesy of Pat Basham)

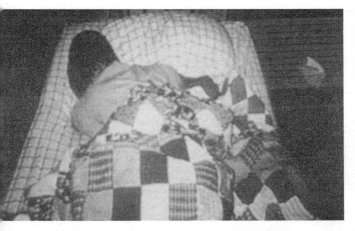

Cody claimed that at one point, all of his bedding was taken away as punishment for not doing well in school. Leona Basham, however, said that Cody had this quilted blanket that her mother had made on his bed, and said this photo proved it. *(Photo courtesy of Pat Basham)*

On July 6, 2004, Sheriff's deputies were called to the Chavez Canyon Ranch owned by television journalist Sam Donaldson. Paul Posey was the ranch manager and lived on the ranch with his family.
(Ellis Neel/Alamogordo Daily News)

Donaldson called the Lincoln County Sheriff's Office when he spotted a large amount of blood at the Posey residence and could not find any family members on the ranch. *(Ellis Neel/Alamogordo Daily News)*

Officers found a large puddle of blood and blood streaks in the kitchen area of the Posey residence. *(Lincoln County Sheriff's Office)*

Cody Posey shot Paul, Tryone and Marilea to death and loaded their bodies in a backhoe bucket before burying them in a manure pile. *(Lincoln County Sheriff's Office)*

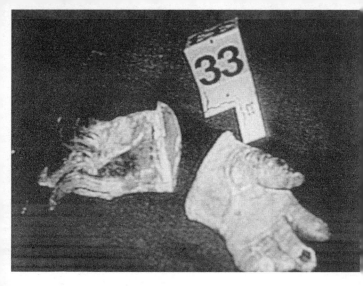

Investigators found bloody work gloves that Cody had used to bury his family members in the manure pile. *(Lincoln County Sheriff's Office)*

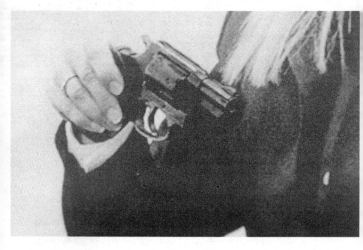

Investigators recovered a .38 caliber revolver that Cody had used to kill Paul, Tryone, and Marilea. *(Lincoln County Sheriff's Office)*

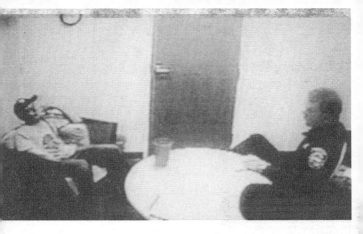

During questioning in an interview room, Cody initially made up a story about what he'd been doing since July 5, 2004. Eventually, however, he admitted to killing his dad, stepmom, and stepsister.
(Lincoln County Sheriff's Office)

Fourteen-year-old Cody was arrested on July 7, 2004 for the murders.
(Ellis Neel/Alamogordo Daily News)

At Cody's trial, Sam Donaldson testified as to the things he saw on July 6, 2004, when he discovered blood at the Posey residence on his ranch. *(Ellis Neel/Alamogordo Daily News)*

Verlin Posey, Paul's brother, and his family wore ribbons in court to honor Paul, Tryone, and Marilea. Verlin and his family said that Cody was making up lies about Paul, Tryone, and Marilea to shift the blame from himself as to why the murders had occurred. *(Author photo)*

Sandra Grisham headed the prosecution in the murder trial of Cody Posey. *(Ellis Neel/Alamogordo Daily News)*

Cody was represented by Gary Mitchell in his trial, which received a change of venue from Lincoln County to Otero County because of so much publicity. The prosecution asked for the change because so many citizens in Lincoln County were pro-Cody. *(Ellis Neel/Alamogordo Daily News)*

Cody lowered his head as an overhead screen in the courtroom showed photos of Paul, Tryone, and Marilea's bodies being recovered from the manure pile. *(Ellis Neel/*Alamogordo Daily News*)*

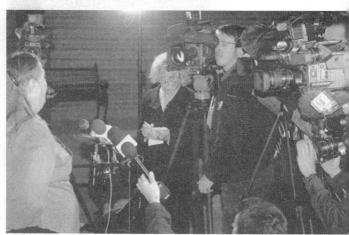

The trial of Cody Posey drew worldwide attention and media descended on the small city of Alamogordo, New Mexico.
*(Ellis Neel/*Alamogordo Daily News*)*

Sheriff Tom Sullivan of Lincoln County testified about what investigators had found at the Posey residence and on Sam Donaldson's ranch.
(Ellis Neel/Alamogordo Daily News)

During the trial, Judge Waylon Counts rendered decisions on numerous objections made by the defense and prosecution.
(Ellis Neel/Alamogordo Daily News)

Cowboy Slim Britton, seen here facing reporters, testified to many incidents of Paul and Tryone abusing Cody. *(Author photo)*

Cody always liked his first step-mom, Sandy, and Marilea's father, Jake Schmid (shown here facing reporters). Even Jake spoke up for Cody, despite the fact that Cody had killed Marilea. Both Sandy and Jake testified to incidents where Cody was physically and mentally abused. *(Author photo)*

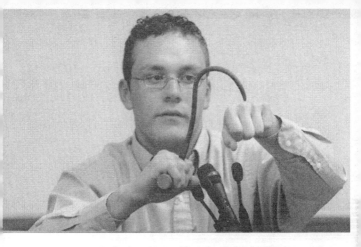

During testimony, Cody demonstrated how his father had hit him on the hand with a hayfork, leaving a permanent scar there. He also said his father had threatened to cut his genitals with it.
(Ellis Neel/Alamogordo Daily News)

Various psychiatrists and psychologists, such as Dr. Henry Gardner, testified for and against Cody, as to whether he had lost control of his emotions at the time he pulled the trigger and whether his claims of abuse were valid or not. *(Ellis Neel/Alamogordo Daily News)*

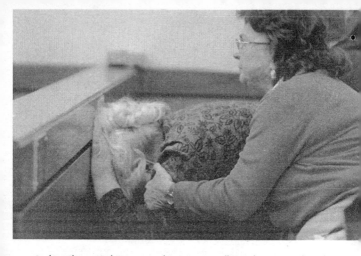

Corliss Clees, Cody's aunt and supporter, collapsed in court when three verdicts of guilty on murder charges were announced.
(Ellis Neel/Alamogordo Daily News)

As the sentencing phase for Cody got underway, area residents stood in front of the courthouse with "leniency for Cody" signs. They also asked people driving by to honk their horns in support of Cody.
(Ellis Neel/Alamogordo Daily News)

When Judge Counts pronounced that Cody would not be imprisoned, but instead would be incarcerated in a juvenile facility that helped kids, Corliss smiled and raised her hands heavenward.
(Ellis Neel/Alamogordo Daily News)

Verlin Posey and his wife had a much different reaction when the sentence was pronounced by Judge Counts. *(Ellis Neel/Alamogordo Daily News)*

Even former juror Norman Patterson, who had been among those who had found Cody guilty of the murders, was glad when Judge Counts sentenced Cody as a juvenile. *(Author photo)*

Mitchell was congratulated by Britton and other citizens outside the courthouse. Mitchell said, "This is a great day for the children of New Mexico." *(Author photo)*

game or board game at the table while eating. After dinner was done, it was free time. I spent most of my time outside playing basketball, riding my bike, listening to music in my room. Most of the time the rest of the family was in the living room watching a movie or TV."

Mitchell wanted to know why Cody wasn't with the rest of them. He said, "I didn't want to be around my dad or stepmom in case any kind of trouble would come up. I'd remove myself from them as much as possible."

Grisham took another shot at Cody during recross.

Grisham: Did you have video games?

Cody: Yes, ma'am, I did.

Grisham: What video games did you have?

Cody: I had some Tom Clancy games, war games, racing games, a fighting game, car games.

Grisham: Did you have any games that involved being an assassin?

Cody: I'm not sure if it was being an assassin. The Tom Clancy game was called Shadow Ops.

Grisham: How about Grand Theft Auto? You had that, and it involved shooting cops, didn't it?

Cody: In certain parts of the game, yes, ma'am.

Grisham: You get extra points for head shots, isn't that right?

Mitchell: Objection!

Grisham: Withdrawn, Your Honor.

* * *

Grisham said that Cody had stated that he never got in trouble in third grade, but that was the year he had brought a knife to school and got into major trouble. Cody replied that it was an accident. He didn't even know the knife was in his backpack at the time.

Grisham asked about the letter to the McCallahan family, and stated, "You said that you lied and you had a lot of problems with lying." Cody admitted that he had lied in the past, and Grisham asked him if he'd stolen anything. Cody said that he had stolen something once. Asked if he had cheated, he replied that he'd cheated in a card game.

"You did illegal drugs?" Grisham asked.

Cody's response was "I experimented with marijuana."

"What about acid?"

"I found some acid. I didn't know what it was at the time."

"Where'd you find it?"

"At a drawer in my mom's house."

"And you actually took it. Do you remember how old you were?"

"I must have been ten years old."

Grisham asked him about failing subjects, and Cody said that he had received some F's on a few papers. Asked if he was allowed to wear clothes like other kids, he did admit that near the end of his eighth-grade year, he was able to wear T-shirts to school once in a while.

As far as never saying anything good about Cody, Grisham said, "Your dad told a cop once that you were a top hand on the ranch, didn't he?" Cody admitted that had happened.

"He was pretty damned proud of your grades except for that one D, and that you managed to bring your grades back up at Capitan, wasn't he?"

"Yes, ma'am."

Grisham:	Your dad bragged about what a good shot you were, didn't he?
Mitchell:	Objection.
Judge:	Overruled.
Cody:	Yes, ma'am. I've been known to shoot well.

After two grueling days the statement about being able to shoot well was Cody's last remark on the stand.

Chapter 14

Cowboys and Teachers

The next day before the jury came into the court-room, Sandra Grisham asked Judge Counts to instruct Cody's family members and supporters in the gallery to control themselves. According to her, they were being demonstrative during certain parts of Cody's testimony. Before Judge Counts made a ruling on this, Gary Mitchell said that he would personally tell those people to control their emotions.

There were other issues to address as well before the jury came in, and Grisham wanted Mitchell's upcoming witnesses to not speak of any alleged cruelty to animals on Paul's part. She said, "A general character assas-sination is not appropriate. The prejudicial effect far out-weighs any probative value." Mitchell, however, re-sponded that many of the heated arguments between Cody and his dad had been about the way Paul handled livestock. "The witnesses know about Cody's treatment of animals as opposed to Paul's treatment of animals."

Grisham replied, "I know they (the defense) some-times attack the victim, but this is going too far!"

Mitchell retorted, "When abusers are abusive to ani-mals when they're young, it carries over to when they are older."

Judge Counts said, "Without an establishment of pro-bative value, I'd be inclined to grant the motion," so Mitchell continued his argument by saying that Paul had forced Cody to kill his own dog, even though the dog could have been saved by a simple veterinarian proce-dure. Mitchell added that the ranch hands, such as Pilo Vasquez and Slim Britton, had taught Cody how to handle horses properly. Mitchell said, "There was one in-stance where Paul did not like the way a cow was head-ing, he lost his temper, pulled out a gun, and shot the cow. This will show the abusive nature that he had, and show his character traits."

Grisham argued back, "You say that Mr. Vasquez will testify to that, but when the officers talked to him, he never told them that. This is just an outrageous charac-ter assassination for someone who is not here to defend himself!"

Judge Counts pondered all of this for a long time, and then replied, "There has been some specific testimony previously about the incident with the horse, and that will not be excluded. The objection about the other parts will be sustained."

That being said, Ysabel "Pilo" Vasquez took the stand, and a translator was needed to translate for him, since he mostly spoke Spanish and very little English. By the time of the trial, Vasquez had worked on Sam Donaldson's ranch for thirteen years. He had a wife named Diana, and a fifteen-year-old daughter named Leticia. The ranch Vasquez lived on with his family was owned by Donaldson, but was twenty miles from the main Chavez Canyon Ranch, where the Poseys lived. Nonetheless Vasquez had a lot of contact with Paul, Cody, Tryone, and Marilea.

Vasquez, like the others, repeated many of the stories of abuse that Cody had told. He said to Mitchell, "From what I saw, Paul and Cody didn't get along very well. The first time I saw something was when we were horse riding. We were going to gather cattle. Before we separated, because Paul was giving an order, Cody had his hand holding the saddle horn, so Paul hit him with his bridle. I heard him hit Cody on the hand. Paul told Cody, 'That's not what a cowboy does.' Cody wasn't doing anything wrong. A lot of cowboys do what Cody was doing. I was even doing that. I thought this wasn't right."

Regarding another incident, Vasquez said, "One other time Cody dropped the reins and Paul took a rock and threw it at Cody and hit him. We were just sitting there. Any cowboy could have dropped those reins. The rock was pretty big.

"I saw Cody cry twice. That was because Paul had hit him. On one occasion we were branding calves, and Cody did something that Paul didn't like. Paul told Cody to get off his horse, and told him, 'When I tell you something, you say, 'Yes, sir.' And Cody said, 'Okay.' Paul grabbed him and threw him on some new wire. He pushed Cody through a little hole in the wire. Cody started crying.

"The second time Cody cried, I don't know what started the conversation, but Paul was talking about cops. Paul said when a bad man has a knife, the police will use a baton on him. If the man won't drop the knife, the cop will hit him with the baton. Paul told Cody to come, and said, 'Look, this is the way the police do it.' Paul had a pipe or something and hit Cody on the chest.

Then Paul said if the bad man doesn't let go of the knife, the police hit him like this, and hit Cody on the shoulder. And then that's when I saw Cody crying. Paul wanted to show us how it was done, but he didn't have to do that to Cody."

Mitchell asked Vasquez about the hay hook incident, and Vasquez said of that scenario, "Once we were picking up hay, and Cody was the driver. The vehicle had a reverse and first-gear shift that were close together. It was hard to drive. The truck got stuck and died, and when he tried it again, it did the same thing. Paul didn't like that, so he went and opened the door on the driver's side and hit him with a hay hook. He said, 'The next time you do that, I'm going to pull your balls off!' I saw this."

Vasquez also spoke of a second hay hook incident. He said, "We were stacking hay in the hay barn, and there were four of us. You try to stack the hay very high— almost to the roof. Cody was all the way to the top, and he was on his knees up there. It was hard for him, since Cody was a child. Cody tried to handle those bales while he was on his knees, but it couldn't be done fast. It was very hot and the roof was of metal. It was hard for Cody to breathe with all the dust, but Paul told Cody to work faster. We could all see that Cody couldn't do it faster. But Paul said, 'I'm telling you to do it faster!' I told Paul, 'I'm going up there and Cody can come down here.' But Paul got mad at me, and talked pretty hard to me. He said that Cody needed to learn to work hard so he could become a man. So we passed some more hay up there, and Paul told him to work faster again. When Cody bent over to grab the hay, I saw Paul hit Cody with the hay hook. He hit him on the hand."

Once again, the real battleground was on cross and redirect. Grisham took Vasquez back, point by point,

about the hay hook incident, the weight of the hay bales
being thrown on Cody, and other incidences of abuse.

> Grisham: Was Paul your supervisor?
> Vasquez: Yes, he was my boss.
> Grisham: You didn't have a very good relation-
> ship with him near the end of his life,
> did you?
> Vasquez: I had a good relationship, until he
> started treating me like Cody.
> Grisham: In fact, there was a letter of reprimand
> against you, wasn't there?
> Vasquez: To me?
> Grisham: Withdrawn.

Slim Britton was also a ranch worker on a Donaldson
ranch, known as the Slaughter Ranch, and he had extensive contact with Paul, Cody, Tryone, and Marilea. Britton told Mitchell, "One time Cody missed some sheep,
and Paul was raggin' on him, and Paul was right up in
his face. I don't care how many years you been cow-
boyin', you're gonna miss some sheep. Paul was raggin'
at him, and all of a sudden, he had his leather gloves in
his hand, and just reared back and slapped Cody across
the face with those gloves."

Mitchell asked Britton how isolated Cody had been
on the Chavez Canyon Ranch, and Slim said, "The
ranches were fenced in, and the Pajarito and Slaughter
ranches, you could drive right in there. County roads
went in there. But the Chavez Canyon Ranch, the gate
was locked all the time. It was a big double metal gate
that went across a cattle guard."

Then Slim spoke of the rock pile incidents. He recalled, "The ranches are all different, and the Chavez Canyon Ranch is a very steep, rocky, rugged ranch. The pens have a lot of rocks in 'em. On numerous occasions I'd find Cody out picking up rocks in the pen. No tools—all he had was a wheelbarrow. Cody told me he was in trouble and that was his punishment. Cody was out there by himself, pickin' up rocks by hand. He was supposed to pick up all the rocks out of a wheelbarrow and stack 'em by hand by the fence. There was plenty of equipment around there to do that. A blade and a backhoe, and I never saw that equipment used, but I saw Cody out there bunches of time pickin' up the rocks by hand. Lots of times I'd be out there midday, and I'd see Cody pickin' up rocks till dark. There was no water jugs or food out there with him."

Asked about propane torches, Slim said, "There were plenty of torches around the ranch. Mainly, they were used on plastic water lines and you had to heat them up when repairing them. I saw one of those torches in the house. It was a little specialty propane torch. It was kinda like a butane torch. It sat up on top of the gun case in the dining room. There was one in Paul's truck as well."

Asked about an incident with Cody on the Pajarito Ranch, Slim recalled, "There was a lot of cholla cactus there on that ranch. It was hard to pen sheep there. You would have spills where some of 'em would break out of the bunch. You had to just go around them and then drive 'em back into the bunch. We had a lot of trouble that day. They just would not pen, would not pen, would not pen. We finally got 'em penned and Paul was mad. I was sittin' on my horse and Paul was sittin' on the ground and Cody was on the ground. I was gonna start around the sheep and Paul said to Cody, 'Go around.' So Cody started around the sheep, goin' one way, and Paul yelled at him, 'Not that way!' And Paul picked up a rock and threw it at Cody. He reared back and threw it right at him. And Cody was running away not to get hit. I just rode my horse in front of Paul and it stopped."

Slim said, "Cody was very good with stock. Over the years he learned how to take real good care of stock. You can handle 'em rough, or you can handle 'em gentle. And if you handle 'em rough, there's just problems. I tried to teach Cody an easier way.

"Cody was real good with dogs. I had a border collie dog I took around with me and Cody was good with it. I was present when there was a lamb incident. We found a lamb that a coyote had got. The coyote stripped it down and ripped the hide off the lamb. There was nothing you could do for it—it was really suffering. Paul told Cody to get down and kill the lamb, and you do that with a knife. You cut its throat. Cody couldn't do it. Cody had his knife out, but he couldn't do it. He was shaking real bad, so I finally told him, 'Cody, go.' And I did it."

When asked about Tryone, Slim said, "She belittled him. Called him stupid and dumb. We were there one day and right in front of him she was telling me about how bad he was. She said she'd be glad when he was eighteen years old so she could throw his stuff out."

Then Slim started to say, "One time Tryone with me—"

Grisham immediately objected, and wanted to know where this was going. Mitchell said it was going to concern "swinging sexual activity"; in other words, Tryone was coming on to Slim. Grisham was beside herself. She said, "This is brand-new information, and I object. This is ridiculous!"

Mitchell, however, responded, "Slim Britton will

show this happened on several occasions. He will substantiate what Cody said."

Grisham replied, "The state doesn't believe this has a scintilla of relevance and it is outweighed by its prejudicial effect."

Judge Counts agreed and sustained the objection.

The hay hook incident was important, because Cody had demonstrated it, and now Slim Britton spoke of it as well. Slim said, "It was very hot, and the bales were heavy. Cody, he was a kid, and he couldn't pick the bales of hay up right to put them on the trailer. His dad reached over and hit him across the hands with a hay hook. Not once, but several times. We'd switch up and try to change the situation. Me and Pilo kind of short-cutted a bale so Cody wouldn't have to put it up toward his dad."

The only trouble with this hay hook incident described by Slim was that it did not match the one Cody had spoken about. Cody had said that the time his dad struck his hand with a hay hook was when a hay hook had fallen off the truck and punctured a tire.

Still, Slim was very persistent about the incident and he recalled, "Cody was just learning to bump hay up. You use a hay hook to catch the bale, and when you go puttin' hay up on the trailer, you generally catch one wire with your hand and use the hay hook in your other hand to put it up. Then you bump it with your knee to put it up there. Well, Cody was just a kid and he wasn't physically strong enough to do it that way. A kid will try and put it up there with both hands while the trailer is moving.

"Paul would hit Cody on the hand with a hay hook and call him dumb-ass. Cody was fussed at and it was hot. He was expected to do a man's job. On that particular day we had hauled hay at both the Chavez Canyon and Pajarito ranches. It was in the hundred-degree range. At dinnertime we were told to come in and eat, and Cody came in after we did and he went to go get a glass of iced tea. He reached in and got a glass and filled it with iced tea, but when he stepped back and took a couple of drinks out of it, he reached in to fill it up some more. And Tryone told him, 'You can't have any more.' The other hands weren't limited to that.

"That day we were eating, and the meal was pinto beans, hamburger meat, and corn bread, and we served ourselves. Cody came over to serve himself. He had corn bread on his plate, and he went for a soup ladle to get some of that chili. Then he reached in for some more, and they told him, 'That's enough. You don't get any more.' Cody had to stand and eat in the kitchen. Everybody else was eatin' at the table."

Slim also spoke of another time about Cody being denied food. He said, "We were brandin' at a camp on the Pajarito, and this was hot, hard work. At lunch that day Cody had one peanut butter sandwich and a handful of potato chips and a hot Coke. Pilo and I had burritos and stuff. We slipped some to Cody. We were gonna take some cows to what they call the Deadman Pasture after that, and Cody was told to get the branding irons and stuff and get on the truck. He did that, and we had some cows in a different set of pens, and we were gonna take 'em. This was about a four-mile cattle drive.

"Cody and Marilea was comin' with me, and Cody got the stuff put up and was headin' for the truck. His dad said, 'Where are you goin'?' Cody said he was goin' to get a drink of water. 'No, you don't need a drink of water,' Paul said. 'Get on your horse right now.' Paul just jerked the gate open and let the cows loose.

"Both Cody and Marilea was pretty thirsty. I gave 'em some gum, and told 'em, 'We can drink when we get to that trough over there.' We drove the cattle across there, and Cody went to get a drink out of the trough and he didn't know how to drink out of there. So I showed him how to cheat the trough with a float and skim off the trough to get a drink. These troughs are big and you need to get right over the float. You brush the moss and stuff off 'em. Then you hit the float, and that lets fresh water come in. You just drink what's blowing up into the tank. You don't stick your face down into the trough.

"Those kids were pretty hard up that day. Marilea practically had heatstroke. She was completely white. We got her to wash her face and lay down in the shade. Cody was pretty close to the same. They (Paul and Pilo) was supposed to come out with the horse trailer and take us back. We sat there, waiting, and nothing came. So I said, 'Well, let's just go on back across.' We took that whole ride back across and there was Paul, sittin' in the shade."

Once again, on cross, the atmosphere became more contentious.

Grisham: Do you remember talking to authorities and telling them that part of the reason why you didn't want to talk to authorities about the abuse, was because you'd lose your job?

Britton: Yes, that had some to do with it.

Grisham: And you did lose your job.

Britton: Yes, ma'am.

Grisham Of the eight months you were there, how many months were the children off to school?

Britton: Off for the summertime, and then back to school.

Grisham: So, you were there two or three days a week, and all during that summer you saw Cody picking up rocks fifteen times?

Britton: Well, yes, ma'am.

Grisham   What were you doing that you saw him picking up rocks all afternoon?

Britton: I was working there too, fixing pick-ups or shoeing horses.

Grisham: All afternoon, ten to fifteen times?

Britton: Yes, ma'am.

Grisham: You've seen Tryone pick up rocks by hand too, haven't you?

Britton: Not that much.

Grisham: Where'd you see Tryone picking up rocks?

Britton: Around Donaldson's house.

Grisham: How many times were you actually all together working the cows that summer?

Britton: Well, when we were working them, we'd do it four or five days in a row. Gathering, branding, feeding, whatever.

Grisham: What days of the week did you work?

Britton: We got Saturday afternoon off, and Sunday, unless we were working stock. Those times we'd work right on through.

Grisham: You were let go when there was less stock on the ranch?

Britton: Yes, ma'am.

Grisham: You said you've seen people taken apart with a rope. What people did you see taken apart with a rope?

Britton: I've been a cowboy my whole life, and there's been instances where there'd be fights and someone would pick up a rope, and like that.

Grisham: (Demonstrates using a hay hook) Are you saying that someone my size, weighing ninety-eight pounds, that they couldn't grab a bale of hay and bump it up onto a trailer?

Britton: When you're talking bales of hay that would weigh eighty to eighty-five pounds, and they're moist, it's a hard thing to do.

Grisham: You'd pick up moist hay?

Britton: Yes, ma'am.

Grisham: What happens when you stack moist hay?

Britton: It'll burn sometimes.

Grisham: (Demonstrates how the haying on a trailer from the fields operates) "You're saying that Paul didn't accidentally pop Cody with the hay hook while the trailer was moving?

Britton: It was no accident.

Grisham: You know that for a fact?

Britton: When it happens more than once, it's no accident.

Grisham: Did you know Paul when he was foreman at the Five Mile Ranch?

Britton: No, ma'am.

Grisham: You didn't know him when he was foreman at the Cross D Ranch?

Britton: No, ma'am.

Grisham: All those afternoons Cody was out picking up rocks and didn't go into the house, there's a full shower in the barn, and there's water in the barn and refrigerator, correct?

Britton: Yes, ma'am.

Grisham: You ever see Marilea hit Cody?

Britton: Just in play.

Grisham: Never saw her smack him with gloves or hit him with a board?

Britton: No, ma'am.

Grisham: You never saw her do a single thing to this young man, did you?

Britton: No, not particularly. Just giggle at him if he got in trouble.

Grisham: Do you have any brothers or sisters?

Britton: Yes, ma'am.

Grisham: That kind of stuff go one when you were young?

Britton: Yes, ma'am.

Grisham How was Cody dressed when you were working cows?

Britton: He wore Levi's and long-sleeved shirts.

Grisham: Did he have chaps on?

Britton: Yes, ma'am.

Grisham: Gloves?

Britton: Yes, ma'am.

Grisham: Do you remember talking to Deputy Shepherd or Investigator Armstrong about this situation [of abuse]?

Britton: No, ma'am.

Grisham: Do you remember talking to anyone about this situation until your testimony today in court?

Britton: I tried to talk to the deputy sheriff down there in Lincoln. I gave him my phone number. He never called me.

Grisham: Did you ever talk to Dr. Christine Johnson?

Britton: Yes, ma'am.

Grisham: You never told Dr. Johnson about any cusswords, did you?

Britton: Yes, ma'am, I did.

Grisham: You never talked about a choking incident, did you?

Britton: Yes, ma'am, I did.

Grisham: You're absolutely sure you talked about that to her?

Britton: I'm pretty sure I did.

Mitchell on redirect asked Slim Britton, "Hitting Cody with gloves, boards, rocks, and a hay hook—were those accidents?"

Slim answered, "No, sir."

Almost every recess, when the jury was gone, brought on a new round of debates about what would be admitted into evidence and what wouldn't be. Sandra Grisham brought forth a motion about late-disclosed witnesses and continued to object about Joe Burchett being able to testify about material found on the ranch computer. She said all of that had no basis in fact.

One of the late-disclosed witnesses was Jim Forrester,

whom Sergeant Shepherd had finally been able to locate on the previous day. Through Forrester, Mitchell wanted to bring in about intergenerational abuse and the fact that Paul Posey's mom had killed Paul's dad and then committed suicide. The allegations about this were that Paul's dad had abused her, and she had had enough. Grisham objected that it was irrelevant and prejudicial. She told Judge Counts, "If we have to try a case, not just of Cody Posey versus the victims, but Cody Posey victim's parents, it's going to require us to put on much more testimony to counteract that. It is so removed that it can't possibly have any relevance. In order to disprove it, we're going to need another three days of testimony.

"And then there's the incidence of Jim Forrester saying he saw Paul take his belt off and whip Cody to the extent that he and another man, whose name he can't even remember, intervened—and this was fourteen years ago. So our objection is it's too remote to have any relevance in this case. Second to any relevance it could have, it is far outweighed by its prejudicial effect. He (Forrester) yelled, or Carla yelled, and Paul stopped. We haven't been able to run any criminal backgrounds on Mr. Forrester. It's just too remote."

Gary Mitchell argued that when Forrester supposedly saw the incident Cody was only about two years old: "It will show lack of control on Paul's part and very excessive punishment."

At this point Judge Counts chimed in and said he wanted to address Grisham's concerns about the late disclosure of defense witnesses. Grisham had a whole list of these and said, "We were not able to get ahold of Lawrence Gonzales over the weekend or Patrick Gonzales. We were able to get ahold of Mary Herrington. No one has been able to find a phone number for Sonia

McKnight [a person who knew Paul when he was younger] and there was no response to a phone call to Courtney Taylor. To all of this, Mitchell said that the prosecution had these witnesses' phone numbers for months, and he had given information about them all in good faith.

Grisham also had objections about certain things witnesses were scheduled to talk about, such as Mary Herrington speaking of Cody's isolation. Grisham said Herrington had not been on the ranch and didn't know for sure how isolated Cody was or was not. As far as Courtney Taylor went, her remark about Cody wanting to run away or live on the streets was hearsay, according to Grisham.

Mitchell responded that the issue of Cody's isolation would "go to show how a reasonable person would react to these situations. It is not irrelevant. Paul and Tryone were isolating him from the world. Whenever Cody befriended anybody, they cut off that contact."

Grisham shot back, "If that gets in, then the state wants to get in why Paul and Tryone didn't want those people calling Cody."

The timing of incidents also was a point of contention. Grisham said, "You can't say, for instance, that Cody was provoked on the day of the murders by Tryone saying she didn't like him three years before. And if that's entered, then is the court ruling that statements from Paul and Tryone about how much they loved him, and were concerned for him, going to be allowed to refute these statements about how much they hated him?"

Mitchell argued for the admission of different witnesses and stressed the things they had seen and heard about the abuse upon Cody. There was Sherry Gensler, who had been at Carla's funeral and said that Cody didn't want to go back to his dad; Lawrence Gonzales about a black eye; Patrick Gonzales about a black eye; Anthony Sanchez about bruises on arms; Courtney Taylor, who had encouraged Cody to run away when he was still in the fifth grade. Mitchell said, "Issues of provocation are always critical. Whether or not he was in imminent danger . . . it matters whether a person is imprisoned and is beaten. There were comments of dislike by Paul and Tryone that were outright hatred of Cody. Comments such as 'He's a worthless piece of shit' must be allowed to be put in by the defense.

"The state says Cody could have gone to agencies for help, but what happened when all past attempts got nowhere? He was totally boxed in. These witnesses called CYFD, principals, and teachers. They were concerned about what might happen. There was one meeting in Hondo Middle School where a parent will talk about how Paul stood up and talked about how worthless Cody was. He was so outraged he told Paul, 'This is no way to act about your child!'

"All information that Cody gave to teachers, friends, counselors, et cetera, goes to the hatred of these three others for him. If we were here trying a child abuse case, these statements would be in here, ringing out in the courtroom. If he was unable to escape from an attempted rape the night before, that goes to the issues we are talking about. Cody had said to some friends, 'I can't talk about it (the abuse). I'll get the hell beat out of me. Please don't say anything to the teachers.' Some teachers would not write him up for something because they knew what would happen.

"Cody finally talked to Counselor Nelson that he'd gotten hit by his father in the eye, instead of a softball.

This is a case where the family wanted him out of the way."

Grisham replied, "It's all classic hearsay. You can't kill somebody because they don't like you! If we're allowed to go into hearsay, we would bring up fabrications on Cody's part starting years before the events of July 5, 2004."

Judge Counts was unwilling to exclude the witnesses, except for Jim Forrester. He said that instead of a blanket denial, he would take objections as the trial resumed, and decide upon them one by one.

The testimony and objections and examination of Emily Nutt was just as contentious as that of Slim Britton had been. Mitchell got Nutt on direct to talk about Cody and his days of clowning at the church and being in the tournaments concerned with books of the Bible and Bible verses. Where it veered off track was when she got into an area where she heard conversations by Paul and Tryone, and once again Judge Counts had Mitchell and Grisham approach the bench. Mitchell told Judge Counts, "Emily Nutt had several conversations with Paul and Tryone about allowing Cody to participate in clowning. It was her understanding that Marilea had witnessed Cody arriving at school with a long-sleeved shirt, and then taking it off at school and dressing in a T-shirt. Then before being picked up by Tryone, he dressed back into a long-sleeved shirt. Marilea tattled on him. His punishment was that he could no longer participate in clowning and Bible drills. He was made to show up and not participate. Nutt tried to persuade Paul and Tryone to let Cody participate and for them to find some other means of punishment. She even went to the pastor of their church and made some phone calls that would have allowed Cody to participate in the Bible drills at state level. She got permission from them and again had a conversation with Paul and Tryone. Paul said, 'How would a bad boy being allowed to participate glorify God?' The last time Nutt saw Cody he was alone and there were visible signs that he was depressed. At that last time, there was talk about moving to a new ranch, and Marilea came up and said to Cody, 'Don't you tell them we're going! It's a secret!'"

Grisham responded, "What possible relevance does it have that Paul was changing jobs and going to the Don-aldson ranch and wanted to keep it a secret? All of the testimony is hearsay. I know the state is not going to be allowed to put on evidence as to what Paul and Tryone said Cody was doing during all this time. If I could put on all the comments that the victims said to others, I would be happy to stipulate, but I'm not going to be able to get in the problems Paul and Tryone were having with Cody and that they had discussed with other people. Cody had threatened them, so that they told others they had to lock up all their rifles. And if Marilea tattled on Cody, nowhere in the law is there an excuse for killing someone for tattling."

Mitchell responded, "The big issue in this case is to corroborate the testimony made by Cody. The corroboration is statements made as to the hatred of Cody by Marilea, Paul, and Tryone. They treated Cody differently than they treated Marilea. These three were acting as a group against him."

Judge Counts took it all in and said, "Well, we're dealing with three sets of statements. The changing of clothes at school, Paul's statement about 'the glory of God,' and Marilea and the secret."

In the end Judge Counts ruled that the statements

about changing the clothes wouldn't get in, but that the other two statements would.

There was one more argument that Mitchell wanted in, and it was about Marilea and the others not wanting Cody in their family. Mitchell even had knowledge of what was said.

Marilea: Do you know why Cody is living with us?

Nutt: No, honey, why is that?

Marilea: Because his mother just passed away, but we're not happy with him living with us.

Mitchell argued, "It's a verbal act, not hearsay. It shows that Cody is not wanted in that family."

Grisham replied, "Your Honor, then is it a verbal act that Tryone said, 'Cody threatened to kill us!' If this comes in, then everything comes in."

Mitchell: One of the crucial issues in this case is how Marilea viewed and treated Cody. She was part of this group against Cody. There's a huge amount of relevance in this statement.

Grisham: There's a huge amount of relevance in Tryone telling her mother that she and Paul had to lock up the guns because Cody threatened to kill them. And Marilea's not here to say she didn't say that, or explain about it.

Mitchell: This is one of the key parts of our case!

Judge: If it purports to Marilea's state of mind, then it might outweigh its prejudicial effect, but if it goes to state of mind of Paul and Tryone, then it's prejudicial because it's getting pretty far afield.

Grisham: The state of mind of the people who locked up those guns also shows state of mind.

In the end Judge Counts sustained the objection about these particular statements that Marilea had supposedly told Emily Nutt.

Brandon Harrington had some things to say about Carla's funeral that hadn't come out before. He started off by saying, "I was friends with Cody from the days at the Christian school, through third grade. I'd try to go over to Cody's house whenever Paul was at work. He put out a bad vibe. When Cody was over my house, he'd be like a regular kid. He was real quiet when Paul was around. One night I spent the night at their house and the next day we were out playing and Paul called Cody inside. He was in there for a period of time, and when Cody came back out, he was crying and emotionally upset.

"At the day of the funeral, me and Cody and a couple of other kids went to a swimming pool after the funeral. Cody said he didn't want to go back with his father. He was afraid of him. He wanted us to be on the lookout for his father so that he could go and hide if he came around."

Grisham said to Brandon on cross, "You seem to have

a remarkable memory for some details. What were you wearing at the funeral?"

Brandon answered, "I don't recall."

"How long did the funeral last?"

"I don't recall."

"Right after the funeral Cody went to the park with his dad."

"I didn't know that."

"Who else have you talked to about this?"

"Nobody."

"Did you talk to someone in Mr. Mitchell's office?"

"Yes, ma'am."

John McCallum, who worked for the Hondo Valley School District, admitted that the bus stop for the kids at the Hondo Valley School was right across the street from the school where the road from Chavez Canyon Ranch met Highway 70. It wouldn't have made any sense for Cody and Marilea to ride the bus to Hondo, because the nearest bus stop was across the street from the school.

Grisham said to McCallum, "Suppose I have a kid who is capable of making a 4.0 grade average. Would I be a bad parent if I said, 'School comes first. If you want to do extracurricular activities, you gotta get at least a 3.5 average. Would that be abusive?"

McCallum answered, "It might be unrealistic. I don't know if it would be abusive."

"Cody was capable of making a 4.0, wasn't he?"

"That's difficult to say. He was capable of making A's and B's."

Grisham wanted to know if what was acceptable for one child, gradewise, was not acceptable for another child, in the parents' minds. McCallum agreed that was acceptable.

Grisham said, "You never had any idea that either one of these children was being abused, did you?"

"No, ma'am."

"Never had it reported to you that Cody had bruises or a black eye?"

"No, ma'am."

"Never had a student report to you that Cody was being abused by his parents?"

"No."

"You never had any idea that either one of these children was being abused, did you?"

"No, ma'am."

"While Cody never did anything terrible, he was in your office a lot, wasn't he?"

"Mostly for infractions for talking in class or getting out of his seat."

"Cody ever tell you he was unhappy?"

"No, ma'am."

"Ever tell you he hated his sister?"

"No, he did not."

"If teachers saw indications of abuse, they are required to report it to the authorities. Isn't that right?"

"Yes, ma'am."

"You guys have training in that?"

"Yes, ma'am."

"Cody was smoking marijuana at one time?"

"I wasn't aware of that."

"Ever catch Gilbert Salcido smoking marijuana?"

"No, I didn't."

"Ever catch some kid named Robert from Albuquerque?"

"No."

"Paul pulled Cody out of Hondo and he said it was more disciplined at Capitan than at Hondo?"

"In his opinion, yes."

Mitchell was right back with a set of questions on redirect.

Mitchell: What was the racial makeup at Hondo schools?

McCallum: We were about 95 percent Hispanic.

Mitchell: Even though you never saw bruises on Cody, did you have concerns?

McCallum: I thought his parents were overly strict.

Mitchell: Is it unusual for abused children not to talk about it?

McCallum: No, it's not unusual at all.

Mitchell: In fact, it's common, isn't it?

McCallum: Yes, it's unusual for them to say anything to anybody.

Sandra Grisham was not friendly with Sherry Gensler (Cody's mother's cousin) at all, and launched into her questioning without her usual "Good morning" or "Hello." She asked Sherry if Carla had been staying at her house on several occasions, and if that's where Cody had discovered the LSD when he was eight years old. Sherry answered no, and that she wasn't even aware that Cody had taken acid when he was eight. Grisham wanted to know if Cody was playing at her house one time, fell down, and got a large scratch on his back. Sherry said that she had four kids of her own and she didn't know. Grisham asked if her kids fell down and got scrapes and scratches. Sherry answered that they didn't at the time, but one had received a broken arm.

When talking about the funeral for Carla, Sherry Gensler said, "Cody was upset from the funeral. It turned from being a sad upset to a mad upset. He kept saying, 'Mom said I never had to go with him again!' He kept saying, 'Don't let him take me! Don't let him take me! He beats me!' They left that day in the pickup and you could hear him yelling, 'Don't let him take me, Aunt Sherry. Don't let him take me, Aunt Sherry. Please!'"

This statement was very dramatic, but there was just one big problem with it. Cody had not left the funeral with Paul and Tryone after the funeral, according to most witnesses, including Officer Farmer.

Walter Gensler was Cody's second cousin, and he testified, "I saw bruises on Cody that he showed me. One time Paul hit Cody with a board across his back. He was probably eight then. Cody would go around and pick up sticks that were lying around the house. If there was one lying around anywhere, Paul would hit him and scatter the sticks and make Cody pick them up again.

"We went out to Five Mile Ranch and Paul had left him at the gate. It's out on the highway and Cody was red from being out there so long. He was dehydrated. That night we played and he was real happy. Then around seven-thirty P.M., Carla told him he needed to take a bath, but he didn't want to take off his shirt. Carla finally took off his shirt and he had bruises on his back and around his buttocks.

"I saw him with blood on him one time. He was picking up the sticks, but Paul didn't like the way he was doing it, so Paul hit him in the face with a closed fist. Cody spit up blood."

Grisham asked, "When Cody was hit across the back, was that the time he was taken to the hospital for photos?" Walter said that it was.

Grisham added, "To be fair, there weren't any bruises across his back, were there? They were on his butt?"

Walter replied, "Yes ma'am."

Then Grisham said, "You didn't really see Paul hit Cody with a board, did you?"

Gensler answered, "No, ma'am."

Jake Schmid was also raked over the coals by Grisham. She asked him if Marilea was the only one of his children who hadn't lived with him while growing up. Jake said that he'd been married before and he had a son named Steven.

Grisham stated, "You're suing Sam Donaldson, aren't you?"

"Yes."

"For how much?"

"I'm leaving that up to my lawyer."

"If Cody is found guilty for killing Marilea, you won't get any money from Sam Donaldson, will you?"

Mitchell jumped in and said, "Objection!"

Grisham responded, "Your Honor, it goes to bias."

Judge Counts replied, "It's calling for discussion between him and his lawyer."

Once again Grisham said, "It goes to bias," and Judge Counts overruled Mitchell's objection.

Jake answered, "That is not the reason I'm suing. I'm trying to get things changed."

"You knew about lawyers, and visitation rights, but you never went to a lawyer to enforce visitation rights?" Grisham asked.

"Correct, but it's almost impossible. You ask any father on my side of the deal, anywhere, and he'll tell you the same thing."

Mitchell was fairly steamed about the Sam Donaldson suit questioning by Grisham, and he asked Jake, "You're trying to get things changed. What do you mean by that?"

Jake said, "I'm trying to get some new laws passed. Try to get a way where some other kid like Cody won't slip through the cracks. He'll get the help he needs."

"You don't hold any animus toward Cody, do you?"

"No, I do not."

"You've been fair and up-front with anyone who wanted to talk to you, weren't you?"

"Yes," Jake replied.

"You knew there were problems, didn't you?"

"Yeah, we tried, but if anything it caused more problems for Cody."

"Your lawsuit with Sam Donaldson, does that have anything to do with the outcome of this case?" Mitchell probed.

"No, it won't make any difference one way or another. There are people who should have done something and didn't."

"It's not the money situation with you?"

"No, sir," Jake answered.

Grisham on recross asked, "You're not gonna turn down money, are you?"

"Of course not," Jake answered.

"And Mr. Donaldson's being sued for money, isn't he?"

"That's one way to make 'em wake up."

"Do you think Mr. Donaldson should have been sued to enforce your visitation rights?"

"I don't know what that has to do with anything. I wasn't referring to him on that. I was referring to teachers, counselors, and the sheriff's office."

"So you think Sam Donaldson should have done something that you didn't see and didn't do anything about?"

"Sam Donaldson doesn't have anything to do with that."

Cheryl Paul was on the stand to tell about the bruises on Cody's back and buttocks when he was taken to the hospital in Roswell. She said on direct, "One night Cody and Walter had been out playin', ate dinner, and were gettin' ready to take a bath and get ready for bed. His mom kept tellin' Cody to take a shower, and he said he didn't want to. 'I just had one last night,' he said. Carla told him, 'Cody, you been playin' and you need to take a shower.' After a few minutes of runnin' with him, she walked over and took off his shirt, and he had black-and-blue marks on his buttocks, and I'd say some on his back."

When shown hospital photos of the bruises and marks, Cheryl said, "I can't identify those photos, but I saw the way he looked in the hospital. They were like black-and-blue marks, and you could see where the board left marks on him."

After a round of witnesses testified about the black-and-blue marks, Verlin Posey was scheduled to be back on the stand. And the line of questioning was going to open up a whole new can of worms. Gary Mitchell wanted to get in evidence about Paul and Verlin being abused by their father when they were young, and even more than that, he wanted to have evidence presented that was dynamite. Mitchell wanted the jurors to hear that Paul and Verlin's mother had taken abuse for years, and then in an act of desperation killed Paul and Verlin's father, and then herself.

Chapter 15

Dark Secrets

Originally, Verlin Posey was back on the stand testifying about Paul, Tryone, Marliea, Cody, and the events that led up to July 5, 2004. Grisham wanted to know if Verlin ever heard any rumors about Cody having to do more work than normal ranch kids, including his own. Verlin once again said that Cody worked hard, but not more than other ranch kids. Grisham asked, "Did you ever see your brother do anything that would have justified him being killed?"

Mitchell objected, and before Verlin could answer, Grisham said, "Pass the witness."

Mitchell had a series of questions about organizations that it might be good for a child to be in. He asked Verlin, "Would it be good to be in the FFA?"

"Yes."

"'Knowledge Bowl'?"

"Yes."

"Football?"

"Yes."

"Basketball?"

"Yes."

"Would it be a fair assessment that Paul looked up to you?"

"I believe so."

"Would it be a fair statement that you wouldn't tolerate somebody beating a child?" Mitchell asked.

"I'm not gonna tolerate something like that."

"Even though you communicated by phone, it wasn't a situation where you visited your brother every weekend?"

"No," Verlin replied.

"Not some situation in which you observed on a day-to-day basis what was going on with Paul, Tryone, Marilea, and Cody?"

"No."

"On these ranches it's amazing if you get a break of a day or two?"

"Yes, sir. Nobody on a ranch ever gets caught up," Verlin answered,

"After Carla died, you wished to take Cody with you?"

"We offered."

And here is where Gary Mitchell intended to get into past history within the Posey family. Mitchell approached the judge, along with Sandra Grisham, and said, "I've been pretty reluctant about getting into abuse with Mr. Posey up here. His knowledge, knowing that his brother was abused as a child, [and] his knowledge, knowing that his mother was abused—that his mother killed his father and then committed suicide—I think the door has now been opened. I think it opened when the state brought Verlin up and talked about what a good father Paul was."

Grisham responded, "I think we can bring up that Verlin offered to take in the child and they would transition Cody [from Corliss Clees's family]. They were worried about Carla's family, however, not about abuse within Paul's family. It's irrelevant what Mr. Mitchell is now contending."

Judge Counts said, "One comment by Dr. Johnson did bring up about family genes, but no foundation has been laid. There hasn't been any expert testimony that would make that relevant."

Mitchell replied, "Paul spoke about this (his mother and father) with other ranchers. People have known about this for years."

Grisham was angry and responded, "This supposed knowledge is garbage! And there's a reporter now on Court TV saying, 'It was common knowledge that Paul was sleeping with his daughter.' It's garbage!"

Judge Counts said to Mitchell, "I'll give you an opportunity to offer proof, if we excuse the jury."

Mitchell replied, "I hate to make this a matter of court record, because as far as I know, Verlin Posey is a good man."

Nonetheless, the jury was excused for the weekend, and outside of their presence, Gary Mitchell started questioning Verlin Posey about his background. Verlin said that he was born in Ruidoso to Linda and Jay Posey. He was married to a woman named Shanda, and they had two boys and one girl. Before this questioning went very far, however, Grisham wanted the rest of the conversation to take place in chambers with no gallery or media present. Both Judge Counts and Mitchell agreed, and what was done next was between Counts, Mitchell, Grisham, and Verlin Posey.

From the outset it was evident that Gary Mitchell was not enjoying this. He did respect Verlin Posey and the questioning was difficult for both of them. It was learned that Paul and Verlin's mother did kill their father in February 1995 at their home near Roswell on the Diamond A Ranch. As far as the other questions went, however, Verlin did not agree that either he or Paul had been abused by their father.

> Mitchell: Is it true that Paul on more than one occasion was physically abused by your father?
> Verlin: No.
> Mitchell: Your mother on occasion was abused by your father?
> Verlin: No.
> Mitchell: Do you know Todd Proctor?
> Verlin: Yes.
> Mitchell: Do you know Mike Skeen?
> Verlin: Yes.
> Mitchell: Did you have any conversation with your brother that as an abused child, he would be doing the same thing to his son?
> Verlin: No.
> Mitchell: Do you know Sonia McKnight?
> Verlin: Yes.
> Mitchell: Was she a childhood friend of you and Paul?

Verlin: We went to Hondo schools at the same time.

Mitchell: You know Sandy Schmid?

Verlin: Yes.

Mitchell: Do you know Cecilia Nadine Peterson?

Verlin: Yes. She was my mom's sister.

Mitchell was trying to lay groundwork that there were people who would talk about Paul and Verlin's father having abused them and his wife, and it eventually led to a murder and suicide.

Mitchell said that Verlin had already testified that he wanted to take Cody in after Carla's death. He asked, "Isn't the real truth of the matter that your wife and family thought it would be best if Cody was there?"

Verlin replied, "First of all, I don't recall giving any reason to that. And second, that is not the reason."

"Then why did you want Cody at your house?"

"Because I knew that everything Cody had been through—losing his mother, at the time he had gone to live with his mother—and he did not want to live with my brother. I was offering anything I could do to make the reconciliation a little smoother. If Cody needed time to adjust to it, then maybe somebody outside the situation could talk to him about it. I was just offering anything I could do."

"Did Cody ever know about that?" Mitchell queried.

"I think Paul and Tryone told him."

"Would it surprise you if Cody didn't know anything about that until today?"

"Yes," Verlin answered.

"As you and Paul were growing up, especially before

graduation from high school, on what ranches did you guys live?"

"On the Slaughter Ranch, the old Fuller place, and at a house behind Hondo Valley School. We spent six years in the Hondo schools, and then went to Roswell High School."

Verlin was excused at this point, and Mitchell, Grisham, and Judge Counts stayed on in chambers to discuss the situation about alleged abuse by Paul and Verlin's father. Mitchell said, "Police officers, a paternal aunt, police files—all of these will speak of some pretty serious abuse on Paul, Verlin, and some abuse on his wife by Jay Posey. Sandy Schmid would testify that Paul on numerous occasions told her about being abused as a kid. He told her of his concerns about losing his temper with Cody. Paul told her, 'I'm afraid I'll be just like my dad.' He had difficulties dealing with his dad's homicide and mother's suicide. I can bring in psychiatrists who have done studies about these kinds of situations. A police report will tell about money being an issue at the time of the homicide/suicide. Most people felt it had come to a head for Mrs. Posey."

Grisham was just as adamant that none of this got in. She said, "It's way beyond the scope of direct. I spoke of events after 1997, so I wouldn't open any doors on this issue. Besides that, it is irrelevant."

Judge Counts responded, "The line of questions the respondent (Mitchell and Cody) proposes for the witness is beyond the scope of direct. To the respect to the offer of proof, the witness is providing the responses that support the respondent's theory of the case. I think it would be far more prejudicial than probative to allow counsel to ask all of these hot-button questions, only to have Mr. Posey say no. The objection as to this line of questioning to this witness is sustained. I haven't seen any doors open yet. I am very reluctant to have a trial about the murder/suicide of the senior Posey family."

Grisham wasn't done, however, and added, "I'm going to ask you to not let Mr. Mitchell slip anything in about intergenerational abuse. I don't want him asking those questions of my witness, so that he can set up something to rebut."

Mitchell responded, "Your Honor, I don't know how much more professional a lawyer can be by having us come in here into chambers. Let's face the facts, I could have gotten this stuff in front of a jury, and I might not be on your good side after I did it. It would cost me some money or something, but I haven't done this thing in some unprofessional manner. I've come in here and been up-front. When I tell somebody I'm gonna approach the bench, I do that. I may lose my mind in part of this trial, but doggone it, Sandy, I've been real fair on all of this!"

Judge Counts said to Grisham, "I cannot tell him (Mitchell) not to ask a question, when I don't know what preceded it. Who knows what doors might be opened by you? I can't rule on objections that might happen somewhere down the road. Mr. Mitchell has approached the bench when he's entered sensitive areas."

Then Judge Counts joked, "State's counsel has said that if I locked you all in this room, I could shorten this trial. So consider yourself locked."

At that point Mitchell said they needed to address the extent of the state's rebuttal case, since every day brought new information from witnesses. There were up to forty new (prosecution) witnesses that could be called, and Mitchell said he had no idea what they might say. "I have concerns if they are proper rebuttal witnesses, and I need to seek guidelines from the court."

Grisham replied, "About ninety-five percent of the incidents Cody introduced were brand-new to the state. He'd never brought those things up before. He says he was beaten about the face with fists since the time he was seven years old, and we're in the position of having to prove a negative. The only way those things can be disproved is to provide witnesses who will say they never saw a bruise, never saw a mark on his face, and that he was a happy kid.

"I want to put Terry Winkler on the stand to testify about the shooting incident in the truck. Winkler will say that he and Paul heard a shot. Paul jerked open the door, grabbed Cody, and said, 'Cody, Cody, are you all right? Did you shoot yourself?'

"Cody said that Paul grabbed him and threw him to the ground. That is not what Mr. Winkler will say. He will say that once Paul determined Cody was all right, he explained about automatic weapons and said, 'That's why I've told you there's no such thing as an unloaded gun.' Paul never cussed him out and never threw him to the ground.

"David Corn allegedly rescued Cody when Paul threw him into a pen of cattle that were squashing him against a fence. Corn will testify that did not happen that day. Little kids were on the fence, middle kids like Cody were in the pen, and older kids were on horseback that day. Nobody pushed Cody in there. The first time we heard about this was from Cody.

"We aren't entitled to reveal about any rebuttal witnesses, but as we learned of them, we told the defense. There will be witnesses like Sharon Barry, Art Ortega, of CYFD, and Norbert Sanchez, to say that there were no welfare checks from the sheriff's office about Cody. Gene Green, who will say there were no welfare checks on Cody from the Cloudcroft Police Department, and Officer Robert Farmer, who was at the funeral home, will speak of that. Farmer said Cody did not leave with his father, there was no sobbing, screaming Cody, and that Cody spent about twenty minutes with his dad at the funeral.

"Cathy Miller, at Cloudcroft, will testify that Marilea wasn't following Cody around at school, and a bus driver will say that she separated Cody from Erin Mc-Callahan on the school bus to Capitan because there was some inappropriate stuff going on between Cody and Erin."

Mitchell replied to all of this by saying, "Here's the problem—it's too late for the state to finally start investigating some of these incidents of abuse. We haven't had an incident of abuse that was a surprise to anybody. The state had ample time to check these things out, and what's happened in reality, we've found ourselves in trial and they knew all along what the defense was going to be."

Grisham responded, "The vast majority of what that child (Cody) disclosed on the stand—he didn't even disclose to his own experts, much less to the state. We had absolutely no way of investigating those incidents, until he was up there on the stand making those allegations. All that stuff was brand-new at trial."

Judge Counts said, "Well, I don't know that it's necessary to go through every one of these witnesses at this time. We can vacate a day for you (Mitchell) to investigate these people, but I'm not inclined to go through the list one by one now. I haven't seen all the stuff, so I don't know if some of this is a surprise. What can the defense

come up with—well, the state doesn't have to antici-
pate all of the defense's case, especially if it wasn't part
of their case in chief. The defense, however, does have
the right to contact these people. Once they have talked
to each one, they can decide if each is proper rebuttal to
the defense and whether or not there is due process."

Mitchell said that he wanted any notes from Dr. Myers
and Dr. Sosa. Grisham replied that Dr. Myers had just
flown into Albuquerque and she had picked him up at the
airport. Along those lines she also said that she wanted
to get in prior sexual activity that Cody had engaged in.
Grisham alleged that Cody was already sexually active,
and he couldn't have been as naive or as shocked as he
claimed about the supposed sexual encounter with
Tryone. Grisham said, "These witnesses can prove Cody
had sexual activity already with girls in the area. It goes
to show he was not isolated, and is in contravention to the
idea that he wasn't allowed any activity outside of school.
It also goes to prove he might have been downloading
pornographic material. It's relevant in many ways. As
much as Mr. Mitchell wishes this was a case against Paul
Posey, it's not. Paul Posey is dead, and Cody Posey isn't
the victim in this case, so that he can have protection
about any prior sexual activity."

Mitchell was, in fact, trying to utilize New Mexico
Shield Law, which protected a person from having to
reveal his prior sexual activity, but this shield law basically protected a witness or victim, not the accused.
Judge Counts said, "I can't rule on an action that hasn't
been made yet. As far as New Mexico Shield Law, I'll
rule on that when the motion gets made, and not before."

Judge Counts did, however, order Dr. Myers and Dr.
Sosa to hand over their notes about Cody to the defense.
Grisham agreed with this, and then as a parting shot

said, "You know what trouble we had getting notes from the defense experts. It's not like we've tried hiding stuff or playing games like the defense has."

When court finally resumed the next day, there were new problems. Juror number 3 had become ill, and Judge Counts wondered if that person needed to be excused. Mitchell said, "If he's sick, he's sick," but Grisham worried that if he stuck around, the person could infect the whole jury with whatever illness he had, and then they were in real trouble if a lot of jurors had to be excused.

Verlin Posey finally got back on the stand in front of the jurors to speak of the camping trip that he, his sons, Paul, and Cody had taken up into the Capitan Mountains. Verlin said they all had fun there, and that Paul was very patient in teaching the kids how to rappel. Verlin also said that Paul was very proud of Cody's roping abilities and that he thought Cody was turning into a good cowboy.

Verlin did admit that he saw less of Cody when Paul divorced Sandy and married Tryone, and he added, "We didn't live in each other's hip pocket. I just saw the family once in a while." Verlin knew that at one point Paul had given Carla custody of Cody, and Mitchell asked, "Were you aware that Paul disowned him?"

Grisham said, "Objection, it assumes facts not in evidence."

Judge Counts replied, "Overruled"; to which, Grisham responded, "Your Honor, it's false!"

Counts had Mitchell and Grisham approach, as often happened in the trial, and Mitchell said, "Paul disowned him so he wouldn't have to pay child support. There is an issue whether he signed it, but not whether it was written. Cody has testified that he was disowned."

Grisham shot back, "It's hearsay. Carla isn't here to testify to the document and neither is Paul. There is no foundation. There is no testimony that Carla filled it out or signed it."

Mitchell replied, "I beg to differ. Paul put it in writing, and Officer Farmer even had to go see an ADA to see what the document meant. It's part of the public record, and whether it was signed or not is not as important as how others perceived it. Cody has already testified that he was disinherited."

Judge Counts overruled Grisham once again, and Verlin answered, "I wasn't aware of the legal terms. I was aware of some kind of document. I was aware that some guns that were family heirlooms were not allowed to go with Cody."

The questioning once again turned to the last time Verlin had seen Cody, Paul, Tryone, and Marilea, on July 4, 2004. Verlin said, "I didn't see Cody by himself—my brother and I went over to the horse I was returning. We took the horse to the pen and let him loose. We went into the saddle house for a bit, and then returned to the group." Verlin testified that Cody was acting normally that day.

The next witness was Clayton "Clay" Posey, Verlin's son, and Cody's cousin. Clay was the same age as Cody. Clay recalled the camping trip with Paul and Cody. "We went hiking, we went rappeling, and played in the river. We had two tents—Paul and Sandy stayed in one tent, and Cody and I stayed in another. While he and I were alone in that tent, Cody never said anything bad about his dad."

Clay remembered other meetings with Cody and his

family. "We'd see Cody at our houses, at an anniversary, and wool growers meetings. Those meetings were at Ruidoso. The anniversary was also at Ruidoso, at the Museum of the Horse. We looked at stuff in the mu-seum, ate supper, and danced. I saw Cody and there was a girl there who wanted to dance with him. He acted okay."

Clay also spoke of the time he played on a basketball team for Corona School, and Cody was playing for the Hondo team. Clay said, "Hondo won the game, and Cody's parents and Marilea were there. We all talked after the game and Paul congratulated Cody for winning and also said that we'd both played good games."

Before the events of July 5, 2004, Clay said that he visited Cody and his family about every two months. He and Cody would play basketball out in the yard and they also shot pool on a pool table. "We would watch movies—things like comedies and John Wayne movies. We also jumped on a trampoline a lot at the Five Mile Ranch. I never saw Cody being afraid of his dad. I never saw Paul raise his hand to Cody."

Clay recalled seeing Cody and Paul on July 4, 2004, and said that he did not see Tryone and Marilea that day. Clay thought that he and his parents and siblings stayed at the Chavez Canyon Ranch for about an hour. "Everyone was standing around and talking. Cody showed us a new Leatherman tool he had just got. Paul had given it to him. We were all in a circle talking and I saw Paul and Cody together that day. Cody was acting normal and he visited with everybody. He wasn't scared or anything. He joked with his dad and it was all just normal stuff."

Dale English testified that he had known both Cody and Marilea.

Grisham: What kind of kid was Marilea?

English: She was a good kid. She was very shy. She was well-behaved and gifted.

Grisham: Are you required to report suspicions of abuse?

English: Yes, ma'am.

Grisham: Did you ever see Cody with a black eye?

English: No, ma'am.

Grisham: Did you see anything in his demeanor that would make you suspect he was being abused?

English: No, ma'am.

Grisham: Did you know Cody had found LSD in his mother's residence and taken it?

English: No, ma'am.

Grisham: Did you know Carla had drug problems and Cody was in counseling at the ages of four and five?

English: No, ma'am.

Teacher Brandon Devine also said he had a duty to report any signs of abuse, and didn't see any on Cody. Devine, however, admitted that Cody once came to class with a red mark near his eye, but claimed to have gotten it in a welding accident. Devine also saw Cody wearing T-shirts at school, which seemed to contradict that he always had to wear long-sleeved shirts.

Teacher Donna Crawford was asked by Grisham if she was ever contacted by a police investigator; to which, Crawford replied, "No, I wasn't contacted by anyone."

Crawford said that Marilea was a bright student, but just before going to Capitan, her grades had gotten worse, as well as those of Cody. Grisham asked about the pranks kids played on each other, and about some hiding Cody's belongings. Grisham asked, "Did you think Tryone was actually going to kill him for not having those items?"

Crawford responded, "No, lots of kids say that. It's just an expression."

Grisham wanted to know what Cody had been doing to get in trouble one time when he begged her not to tell his parents. She said that Cody had been getting up from his chair, joking, laughing, and disrupting the class.

Back to the topic of Marilea, Grisham asked if she ever saw Marilea hit Cody.

"No," Crawford responded.

"Ever hear her call him names?"

"No, ma'am."

This round of character witnesses was done, but there was an explosive issue just about to be presented that concerned computers and Internet porn. Before it was done, there would be accusations that not only had Cody been molested by his parents, but that Marilea had been as well.

Chapter 16

A Question of Incest

There were a few defense witnesses who alleged aspects of sexual misconduct among members of the Posey family, and the chief among these had been Pilo Vasquez. He said, "Marilea was a good girl—a queen of the house all the time. Paul and Tryone spoke very well about her. I don't know if there was a problem or not, but on one occasion I was working out around El Pajarito. I went to a road, and there was a house on the other side. I went around the house and I didn't see Paul's truck when I first went there. So I got up there and the door was kind of open, because the houses up there don't have locks on the doors. Paul and Marilea were there, and when I went in, there was something going on. Paul said, 'Pilo, see what I have here.' He had some kind of cut or scratch. Paul said, 'Marilea kicked me because we were wrestling.'"

Pilo wasn't sure if it had been more than just wrestling. He thought the whole situation wasn't right. He didn't believe that Paul and his stepdaughter should have been engaging in that kind of physical contact.

After those comments, the whole issue of the ranch office computer and father/daughter incest sites and mother/son incest sites was visited. To address the validity of this issue, the prosecution called Sergeant Robert Shepherd to the stand to lay a foundation. Shepherd spoke of Agent Norman Rhodes and himself seizing three computers from the Posey residence on July 8, 2004, at around 7:00 P.M. Eventually Jack Henderson, an investigator with the district attorney's office, looked at the various computers and analyzed their contents.

Henderson had specialized in forensic computer examinations, data recovery and analysis, and had taken classes at a white-collar-crime center. Henderson was a certified forensic computer examiner, and, by 2006, had testified in nearly one hundred court cases about computers. In his process with the Posey computers, Henderson photographed the towers, inside and out, removed the hard drives, and used EnCase, which mirrored exactly what had been on the computers' hard drives. Through EnCase he could discover information as to when the computers had been used and the boot sequence. The system dates and times were important—they showed if the date and time were set correctly on the computers, and when someone had accessed a certain Web site or made entries on the hard drive.

Henderson connected each computer to a hardware write blocker so that Windows wouldn't start a link to access other drives. This ensured that the drive was not altered in any way. Then he used EnCase Forensics–Version 3 to create an image of the hard drive. Henderson sorted the files, looking for pornography sites in this instance. He checked dates and times when the system was used, and noticed that on the ranch house computer, the time was set to eastern standard time, rather than New Mexico mountain time. So if the computer said a certain file had been accessed at 8:00 P.M., for instance, it had actually been accessed at the ranch house at 6:00 P.M., mountain time.

Henderson used some keywords on these computers, and he noted that neither Cody's nor Marilea's computers had been hooked up to the Internet. The main office computer, however, had been connected to the Internet and the hours someone had searched porn sites were not consistent with what he usually saw in this regard. In most of his previous cases, porn sites had been accessed in the evening, but on this computer, someone had been looking at porn sites in the middle of the night.

Henderson said, "Internet Explorer will cache some programs that have been accessed before, so they wouldn't have to be downloaded again. Redirects normally don't have dates and times, but in this case there were some that did. In fact, there were a lot, and that was unusual. I'd never seen that many before. It made me feel that those files might have been corrupted one way or another. I believe there was some damage to those files, and I didn't feel that the times and dates were reliable.

"System times and dates can be altered. For instance, I could change the time and say that I had written something to the hard drive at five this evening. (It was earlier than that when Henderson was testifying.) It is easily changed on Windows 98 like that one. You cannot tell if the user did that or not."

Janice Schryer, a co-prosecutor, asked, "Can you or anyone search for something and end up not being where you thought you'd be?" (In other words, stumble upon an incest site by mistake.) Henderson said that was possible, and then he added that he had concerns about all the information on the computer as to reliability of times and dates.

"I also had concerns that the computer had been left unattended for a period of time between the murders and the arrest of Cody Posey. That computer could have been changed by design or inadvertently, and all we would be left with is altered evidence. The office computer was actually turned on and running on July 8, 2004. The computer in Cody's room had last been accessed on July 7, 2004."

Henderson wasn't coming right out and saying it, but he was alluding to the fact that someone had been using those computers between the time of the murders and Cody's arrest. That person could have deleted files, added files, done all sorts of mischief with times and dates and the information stored on the computers.

Defense attorney Rose objected and said, "I just called this witness as a foundation witness. It's improper to impeach my witness (Cody)."

Judge Counts agreed and said, "This line of questioning is more suitable for rebuttal. Objection sustained."

Rose wanted to know when Henderson had first seen the computers, and Henderson said he received them on July 14, 2004. He had received them from Sergeant Shepherd and done analysis on them later. Henderson said he wrote a report about the computers and didn't state at the time that he had seen any problems with the computers. Later he spent three weeks analyzing various aspects of the hard drives, and did more analyzing in the last weeks of December 2005.

Rose wanted to know if it was possible that a law enforcement individual could have altered the files on the office computer on July 7, 2005, and Henderson answered it was impossible to say who had done it. Rose asked him, "If you had concerns about dates and times on this computer, could you talk to other experts in the field about this?"

Henderson answered, "Yes."

Rose queried, "Did you do that?"

Henderson said, "No, I didn't have the time."

> Rose: You're aware that this computer evidence is important to both sides in this case?
>
> Henderson: Yes, sir.
>
> Rose: It's a pretty serious case?
>
> Henderson: Yes.
>
> Rose: Do you agree that incest porn sites were viewed on that computer?
>
> Henderson: I have no doubt that incest sites were viewed.
>
> Rose: Somebody was searching for those sites?
>
> Henderson: Yes, the key word is somebody.

Schryer opened up a whole new can of worms when she noted that the office computer had been at Chavez Canyon Ranch since 1999, and the Poseys had not moved there and had access to it until 2001. She asked Henderson if porn sites had been viewed on that computer going back to 1999, and he said yes. Rose however, asked if those had been incest porn sites, and Henderson said no. He agreed that incest sites had been viewed starting in 2001, after the Poseys had moved into the residence.

The next witness on the computer issue was Joseph Burchett, the owner of a computer store in Ruidoso, and initially he was spoken to outside the presence of the jury. Burchett did repair and installation of computers, reloaded machines, and recovered information. He often used EnCase 5—a newer program of EnCase than Henderson had used. Burchett had gone to the New Mexico School of Mines, and had a bachelor's degree in computer science. On the request of Gary Mitchell's office, Burchett had begun an analyzation of the Posey residence computers.

Burchett got the information on DVD discs, read Henderson's reports, and said that Henderson had done a good job. Burchett added, however, that he did not have the same problems as Henderson did about dates and times. When he became aware of Henderson's problems, he and Henderson had a conference, and Burchett ran some more tests. Burchett accessed the porn incest sites and said once again that he had no problem about times and dates. He went through the files, history, and "cookies," and had some concerns about redirects on temporary files stored on the office computer. So he did additional testing. Like Henderson, Burchett said that a redirect is a generated page that doesn't store the times and dates. Wanting to see if Henderson's EnCase 3 had a history of problems, Burchett did some research and found that there had been some bugs in EnCase 3 software. The research showed that the main problem concerned redirects.

* * *

Burchett now became like a Ping-Pong Ball, batted back and forth between the defense and prosecution. At stake was whether Paul or Tryone had viewed incest sites, and then tried to force Cody into having sex with Tryone. For the defense that was a key factor in Cody losing control on July 5, 2004.

Schryer wanted to know if Burchett had actually checked Henderson's software to see if it did have problems, and Burchett admitted that he hadn't, he had only used a similar version. Schryer wanted to know what forensic training he had. Burchett answered none. She also got him to admit he wasn't a full-time computer expert, and that he was a fruit orchard manager in Hondo, as well as a computer store owner.

Schryer asked, "How many forensic analyses have you done?" Burchett said he hadn't done any before. She wanted to know what official organizations he belonged to, and he said none. "You've never been qualified as an expert, have you?" she said.

"No." Burchett answered.

"Can you tell us who did those searches for incest on the ranch computer?"

"No, I cannot," he answered.

At this point Schryer wanted Burchett's testimony to be excluded, and Judge Counts looked up case law and said that Schryer had not yet met standards, according to *Alberto* v. *New Mexico*. Schryer brought the whole reliability of the ranch office computer into question because someone had accessed it after Paul, Tryone, and Marilea were already dead. The chain of custody had been broken and files had been accessed by an unknown person.

"Questions of times and dates are unreliable, and those times and dates cannot be put forth before a jury," Schryer said.

Rose shot back about *Deloto* v. *New Mexico*, wherein a computer program that used animation to show what happened at a crime scene was allowed, and in the present case it wasn't the defense who had seized the Posey family computers, it was the state. He asked if the prosecution was now saying that their own evidence wasn't reliable. "This computer is important. The hard-drive evidence shows relevant information. We're not generating evidence, we're simply showing evidence that is there. This kind of information is routinely brought in by the state in child molestation cases. The searches on the computer for the incest sites were when Marilea and Cody were at school or sleeping. The only ones who could have done that were Paul and Tryone. It's critical to corroborate what Cody said about the events of Paul and Tryone on the night before the killing, and not just a figment of his imagination."

Schryer argued, "Burchett only checked what Henderson gave him. He never checked the actual computers—"

Judge Counts broke in, "Are you saying that Henderson corrupted those files?"

Schryer answered, "No, I'm saying we don't know who accessed files on July seventh and eighth. Slim Britton had a key to the gate and house. We don't know when and what he did there. There was no law enforcement on-site for a period of time."

Judge Counts replied, "I don't think this is a hearsay issue. As far as chain of custody goes—that does go to weight. The court, however, will not suppress the evidence due to chain of custody. The jury will be given an opportunity to decide if Mr. Burchett or Mr. Henderson is more reliable."

* * *

When Burchett testified again, with the jurors present, he said that he had spent sixty hours looking at information connected to the computers. Marilea's computer didn't have a modem, and Cody's hadn't accessed the Internet since 1999. The real computer in question was the one that had been in the ranch house office. Burchett searched that one to see if there was a history of the files, and he looked at "cookies," URL cache files, and regular cache files.

With a search engine Burchett was able to go back and see what keywords had been used, and noted that pornography photos had been cached. Burchett used keywords like, "incest, swinger, wife, daughter, and son." Porno sites had been visited on the office ranch computer since 2001, and incest sites since 2002. That was a time period when Paul did have access to the computer.

Burchett said about the viewing of porn material, "It was reoccuring over a decent amount of time from 2002 through 2004. I could show that it was intentionally downloaded. The person had to use certain keywords and they searched on Google and AOL Search."

Burchett brought in copies of what had been searched, and these became Defense Exhibit N. Among this material were things searched on Google that concerned adult stories, online writing, and fictional incest. Another Google search was about father/daughter incest and contained images. There were free incest stories from an AOL Search, a search for "sunbathing daughter," "drunken wife pics," wife swimming search, "sexy wife photo album," "wife in a skimpy bikini," and "wife naturalist pics."

Once again there was an objection from Schryer, saying no one could tell who had visited those sites, and besides, there were no times and dates attached to them. Rose countered, "All of this goes to back up Cody's story about July 4, 2004. We have a right to present all the evidence."

Judge Counts responded, "Well, since there were no incest Web sites visited before 2002, there is a reasonable inference that those things came in since 2002. But without dates and times, then there is no foundation."

Rose got Burchett to testify that all his searches of material before 2001, when the Poseys moved into the residence, showed that the office computer had been used to access news sites, but not porn sites. Rose once again asked that this be admitted, but Schryer said she wanted to voir dire Burchett first, and she was allowed to do so.

Schryer: Isn't it true that earlier sites can be overwritten?
Burchett: They can be.
Schryer: Some of those sites can expire?
Burchett: They can.
Schryer: So you can't say for sure that there wasn't porn before 2001?
Burchett: Not in any of the records I could find.

Despite Schryer's objection, Judge Counts allowed the evidence in, and Rose got Burchett to testify that whoever had been viewing incest Web sites had also been viewing ranch property for sale in New Mexico. Rose asked a rhetorical question—who would be most likely to be viewing porn and ranch property for sale, and, in essence, answered his own question by saying that of course it was Paul Posey, not Cody Posey.

Now came the matter of just how many pornographic images the jurors were going to be able to view. There were at least 160 images attached to the keywords of "incest" and "daughter," alone. Rose wanted to get at least some in, and asked Burchett about image #40—an image about mothers and young sons. There were sites on rape, and images attached to that as well. Even though rape was not the primary topic of searches—incest was— there were still stories and images about rape.

So back and forth Burchett went—answering questions by both the prosecution and defense.

Schryer: You were raised in the Hondo Valley. How many of the key people in this case do you know?

Burchett: None.

Schryer: Is your father an ag teacher at Hondo?

Burchett: Yes.

Schryer Your office is in Mr. Mitchell's building in Ruidoso?

Burchett: Yes.

Schryer: Defense Exhibit N is a very hefty document. There are some four thousand entries in it, the vast majority with no dates and times. If the DA has a concern about the accuracy of the data, that would be a reasonable concern?

Burchett: Yes.

Other defense items came up, such as Defense Exhibit P, which showed that with the time subtracted from eastern standard time, some incest was viewed at 5:35 A.M., and Burchett admitted that Cody was not at school at 5:35 A.M. Defense Exhibit O was about a porn site viewed on a Friday, and Cody did not have school on Fridays. Some porn sites were viewed on Sundays when Cody could have accessed them.

Porn and incest weren't the only points of contention about the computers—so were the topic of murder and searches about murder. There had been a story going around that Cody had been interested in the Menendez brothers, who had killed their parents, claimed to have been abused as children, and then got even by murdering them.

To get at this issue, and try to refute it, Rose asked Burchett if the keywords "Menendez brothers" had come up on any Web site. Burchett said he had looked for that and came up with no hits. As far as the word "murder," Burchett said, "That had come up, but they were old sites and had been searched for by Sam Donaldson."

This murder topic was another one hotly debated by Schryer and Rose. Cody had said earlier in testimony that he had never looked up on the Internet about the Menendez brothers, about murder, or about the law. As far as computers went, he said his dad had made him write letters twice on the office computer, but never allowed him to use the Internet. The letters had been about letting some ranch hands go. Cody said there was a password to that computer and he didn't know what the password was.

Schryer, however, said that Internet or not, Cody had written something about murder on his own computer. This brought a new round of arguments—Rose said that he had not brought up information about Cody's computer, so Schryer could not get into specifics now. Rose claimed, "I did not open the door to Cody's computer."

Schryer shot back, "The defense brought up stuff about what was and wasn't dated, so that should go for

Cody's computer as well. Cody did search about the Menendez brothers."

Judge Counts asked, "This is something off the Internet? If so, there is testimony that Cody's computer hasn't been hooked up to the Internet since 1999. This is not relevant because Cody, nor anyone else in his family, accessed the Internet from that computer."

All of the computer stuff about pornography and incest had raised some serious questions in one juror's mind, in a very damaging way. This juror apparently had come to some kind of conclusion about Paul, Marilea, and incest, and had sent a note to the lawyers and judge asking about this matter. Schryer was furious and said, "The state wants no further allegations of abuse between Paul and Marilea! One juror has convicted Paul of sexual abuse of Marilea. How did she find this out? Supposedly from computer evidence, and it should be stricken. It is extremely clear that a question by that juror is about this."

At this point Rose chimed in and said, "We encourage the jurors to ask questions. The juror asked on one piece of paper about this. The court can instruct them (the jurors) about the materiality of a question. This juror has not decided yet. The state may be offended by the question, but there have been plenty of trials where the defense has been offended by a certain question. There is no basis for striking that juror. We object strenuously to striking that juror. As all of this relates to the computer testimony—the computer testimony is very important and we've been all through this already."

The prosecution wasn't buying the fact that the juror in question hadn't made up his or her mind and definitely wanted this person kicked off the jury, stating,

"This is the same juror who I've brought to the court's attention before."

Judge Counts replied, "I've been monitoring the jury closely. I haven't noticed any disruptive behavior. I didn't notice that the juror has acted improperly. I don't feel that by merely asking the question, that juror has acted improperly in prejudging evidence. The motion to have the juror removed is denied."

As with other witnesses, the testimony of Steven Chaves became more contentious in the cross-examination, rather than on direct. Chaves was in the military during the trial, so his testimony was read in court by a reader taking the part of Chaves as he had responded to Sandra Grisham's questions over the telephone.

Grisham had asked Chaves, "You didn't have any classes with Cody, did you?"

Chaves replied, "No, I just saw him in the hallways."

"When you spoke with Investigator Armstrong, you didn't tell her about any cusswords from Paul and Tryone?"

"I should have, ma'am," Chaves responded.

"Paul was a good guy to work for?"

"Yes, he was real nice to me."

"Did you work with any other ranch hands on the ranch?" Grisham posed.

"Slim and Pilo."

"Was Paul real nice to everyone except Cody?"

"Yes, ma'am," Chaves answered.

"How about Tryone? Was she real nice to everybody but Cody?"

"Yes, ma'am."

"Do you remember her saying anything about

Sam Donaldson wanting to put turf in where there were rocks?"

"No, she just wanted the big rocks out of there to make it look nice."

"You said that Cody was one of the brightest fourteen-year-olds you'd ever met?"

"Yes, ma'am. He was very smart. As far as ranch work went, he knew more than I did. I learned a lot from him. I was seventeen at the time and he was fourteen," Chaves remarked.

"Paul didn't like him hanging out with the Salcido boys, did he?"

"Yes, ma'am. Paul didn't speak very highly of them. Paul said he didn't like Cody hanging out with them because of drugs. That, and he didn't think they were a good influence."

"He didn't say he didn't want Cody hanging out with them because they were Hispanic?"

"No, ma'am."

"He approved of you?" Grisham queried.

"Yes, he respected me and my dad."

"And your dad is Hispanic, I assume?"

"Yes, ma'am."

"Was Paul a hard worker?"

"Paul was a very hard worker," Chaves replied.

"And Marilea?"

"She worked a lot harder than most girls her age."

"On the rock pile incident, did Tryone say to Cody, 'If you think you can do a better job, maybe you should be the parent?'"

"Yes, ma'am. She actually said that quite a bit. I remember her cussing and making a big scene, though."

"On the hay incident, had Paul originally been on the ground, and Cody up on the truck?"

"Yes, ma'am."

"And Cody hit Paul with a bale of hay?"

"Yes, he accidentally hit his dad with a bale of hay."

"How do you know it was an accident?" Grisham inquired.

"Because when you throw a hay bale down on the ground, it rolls and goes crazy. You have no control of where it goes. It bounced and rolled and hit Paul."

"Were you ever up on the trailer and you threw bales off on the ground, and they rolled and hit someone?"

"Yes, ma'am. I accidentally hit Paul too. It almost knocked him down."

"You never told anybody in authority that you thought Cody was being abused, did you?"

"No, ma'am."

"Did you know it's the law in New Mexico that if you suspect a child is being abused, you have to report it?"

"I wasn't aware of that," Chaves answered.

"Did you ever think it was serious enough, you should tell someone?"

"Well, I thought that growing up on a ranch—it's always a hard life. Parents are always really strict with their kids. There were times I didn't know what to think."

On redirect Mitchell asked Chaves, "You grew up on a ranch, and did you think that kind of treatment by Paul on Cody was appropriate?"

Chaves answered, "No, sir. But I grew up on a farm. It's a little bit different. Some of my buddies who grew up on ranches, they had a hard life."

Mitchell asked him about the hay incident, and Chaves said, "I knew that Paul was doing it on purpose, because he would look at me, give me a little grin, and then drop a hay bale on Cody. Then he would just throw them over to where Pilo was. Because Cody was almost directly below us, and while Cody was bent over, Paul would drop one on his head or back."

Mitchell wanted to know what kind of cursing Paul and Tryone had done toward Cody. Chaves said, "Um, they called him 'fuckin' idiot' most of the time."

If Steven Chaves was basically pro-Cody, both Terry Winkler and David Corn were not. With them, it was Mitchell who zeroed in with questions on cross-examination. Mitchell asked Winkler, "You say that you were over at the Chavez Canyon Ranch a lot. You actually sold the feed to Sam Donaldson, not Mr. Posey, correct?" Winkler said that was true.

"You sell feed on a commission basis?"

"Yes, sir."

"In Lincoln County and Chaves County, these absentee owners don't always stay at the ranches, correct?"

"Yes, sir."

"When you're dealing with ranch managers, they're the only ones making the accounting?" Mitchell queried.

"Right."

"So it's important for you to get along with these ranch managers?"

"Yes."

"You deal with hundreds of head of cattle on a drylot basis?" Mitchell asked.

"Yes, sir."

"A drylot basis is penned cattle and feed goes to them because they're getting ready for slaughter or just growing them?"

"Yes, sir," Winkler answered.

"How often do you get out to a ranch?"

"I'm at these ranches all through the year. I'm there with every delivery. I try to take care of my customers like I'd like to be taken care of. So I'd get out to a ranch about every six weeks."

"You weren't there when Slim Britton was talking about an incident with Cody, or when Pilo did?"

"I don't know what you're talking about," Winkler said.

"That's because you don't know the dates, correct?"

"I don't know what events you're talking about."

"You never saw an incident where Cody needed punishment, did you?" Mitchell queried.

"He got straightened out a time or two. We had about seven hundred sheep in a pen, and Cody was supposed to be watchin' a gate. He was watchin' birds instead. Paul grabbed him by the arm and said, 'You watch what you're doin' here!' But by no stretch of the imagination could you call it abuse."

"You made a good commission to the ranches you sold to where Paul was working?"

"No more than the commission that I made on other ranches," Winkler replied.

"I didn't ask you if you made any more on other ranches, did I?"

"Yes."

Grisham jumped back in on redirect and asked Winkler, "Are you getting up here and lying to these folks because you made a good commission?"

Winkler answered, "No, ma'am."

* * *

On cross-examination with David Corn, Mitchell asked, "There were times when Paul and Cody worked calves when the Corn brothers were not around, correct?"

Corn said, "There could have been branding when me or my brothers weren't there."

"You weren't on that ranch on a day-to-day basis, were you?"

Corn said that he wasn't.

"You didn't look in the ranch house to see if any holes had been patched in the wall, did you?"

Corn said that he hadn't.

Mitchell asked, "If Cody was being abused outside of your view, you wouldn't know about it at all, would you?"

Corn said that he would not have known.

Up to this point the testimony had been about incidents and allegations of abuse and the importance of the ranch office computer. Now, however, it was going to get into the very mind-set of Cody on July 5, 2004, by doctors Johnson, Cave, Myers, and Sosa, and whether he had planned the murders in cold blood or had merely snapped in a rage beyond reason and control.

Chapter 17

Mind Games

The "psyches" were definitely a key part of the defense and prosecution cases for and against Cody Posey. There was never a doubt that Cody had killed Paul, Tryone, and Marilea—so the main question the jurors were going to have to struggle with was *why?* Had it been a cold-blooded murder, justifiable homicide, or a loss of mental control and the ability to reason.

The first psychiatrist on the stand was Dr. Christine Johnson, and she was an advocate of the defense side in the matter. Mitchell had Johnson spell out all her expert qualifications, and then asked her, "How can we attempt to determine if the child at the time of the incident—what the child was suffering from in the way of mental disorders?"

Johnson replied, "Psychologists try to find out by listening to the self-report of the person, but self-reports have their limitations. So we then turn to other sources, such as friends and family members. Often what is still going on can help you determine what happened then, especially if they are suffering from chronic conditions. Ideally, you can find information right before the time of the incident. That way you can confirm or not the information from the self-report."

Mitchell asked, "On the morning of July 5, 2004, do you have an opinion if Cody was suffering from a mental disease or disorder?"

Johnson answered, "I believe he was suffering from depression and symptoms of stress disorders. Possibly a combination of post-traumatic stress disorder and an adjustment disorder."

Mitchell wanted to know, "Do you have an opinion what occurred that morning affected Cody's ability to reason?"

Grisham jumped in with an objection, wanting to know what portion of the morning Mitchell was talking about. So he rephrased his question: "Do you have an opinion as to circumstances that might have led up to extreme emotions?"

Once again Grisham objected, saying that she wanted to pin down an exact time on July 5, 2004, because there were legal questions that were very time specific and could mean the difference between first-degree, second-degree, or manslaughter verdicts.

So Mitchell tried a third time: "Do you have an opinion if those things affected his ability to reason?"

Johnson replied, "I believe his emotional condition at that time would have impaired or gotten in the way of his ability to reason."

Mitchell asked, "When the homicides occurred, did Cody experience a temporary loss of self-control?"

"I believe that his control was reduced. It was impaired."

"Would that be as to all three of the victims of homicide?"

"Yes."

"Do you have an opinion that his mental disorder affected his decision to take away the life of another?"

"I believe it impaired his judgment in making that decision."

Mitchell asked, "Can disorders we've spoken of be in the family genes and passed down through a family's history?"

It was surprising that Grisham did not object to this question.

Johnson replied, "Depression might run in Cody's family. And trauma and abuse are an intergenerational condition. It seemed to have passed down from father to son."

Mitchell said, "As it relates to children, do we have to talk about them differently than in adults about reason and loss of control?"

Johnson replied, "Yes, I think that with a child, you're starting out with impaired abilities, at least compared to adults. You're starting out with someone whose judgment is immature. Kids have emotional influences and poor self-control. Adolescents are operating with influences that make them less mature, no matter how bright they are. Influences will often make them act in ways that show less than good judgment."

"Did you see Cody Posey as any different than any other adolescents of ages thirteen or fourteen?"

"Cody is bright, but socially and emotionally, he was less emotionally mature. Part of what he's been struggling with has made him emotionally less mature. His emotions have gone underground."

Mitchell asked, "In Cody Posey, in your evaluation,

were there actions or situations in Cody's life that would lead to extreme emotions?"

Johnson said, "Yes. I saw depression before the killings. A mood disturbance that has been described as labile. He was becoming less able to control his emotions. Things were becoming more stressful. Cody was struggling to feel good about himself and to prove himself to his father. He was struggling to get his father's acceptance. Cody was in a struggle for his life. He was trying to gain approval of his worth. He was losing control of his anger. It had always been overcontrolled. He began to erupt. As he began to erupt more, things were becoming scarier and more heated in the house.

"Cody had made a home for himself in Hondo School. That's where his friends were and his girlfriend. He was taken out of the school, and it was unexpected. It was a huge source of stress. His depression increased after that. He went to a new school, and adjusted, as he always had. He put a good face on it, but he was feeling the loss. When school was out for the summer—well, he believed that part of the trade-off would be that things would get better. He thought he would be able to get his driver's license and play football in the next year. But football was taken away from him after he got to Capitan. It was another indication for him that things would not get better. The abusive situation escalated and he was cut off from his friends. He was isolated and becoming more helpless. In his words, 'Summer was always a prison without bars.' School had always been his safe haven. He was reaching a point of despair that summer."

Mitchell wanted to know if abuse generated fear in abused children, and Dr. Johnson said, "Yes, it's a classic response to that kind of abuse. It's a feeling that it could happen again at any time, so that you feel you live in a world of danger."

"Was Cody Posey, in 2003 and 2004, in a very dangerous situation?"

Before Johnson could reply, Grisham objected that the question called for speculation, and Judge Counts agreed.

Mitchell countered with, "You described escalating abuse—how did that affect Cody on the morning of July 5, 2004?"

Johnson said, "I believe that every day during that summer, he was becoming more despairing. He was more on alert for the next awful encounter."

Mitchell asked, "Hypothetically, if he was being abused verbally and physically by both parental figures in the home, would that have exacerbated the situation and his ability to cope with it?"

Johnson said, "Yes, if it's from both, then there's not a prayer for help from the other parent. It's a double whammy. It exacerbates hopelessness."

"What if the child had been able to attain no assistance from a sibling, close in age?"

"The isolation would be extreme. The sense of being hopeless and helpless was exacerbated."

"At the time you did the evaluation, you did a provisional finding of sexual abuse. At that time you had available the statement of Cody Posey and a videotape of the investigation. Did you have material other than that?"

"Not until yesterday."

"With additional information, and visits to pornographic sites, hypothetically, if a child has received severe abuse—emotionally, physically, and verbally—and received it from both parental figures, and the sibling has hypothetically spied on him, and we have some major sexual abuse, how does that affect his reason and maintenance of self-control?" Mitchell queried.

"I think it would add to the stress, confusion, and emotional distress. Things had gone to another level. Judgment would be harmed even further."

"Should those emotions just go away at the drop of a hat? Or should those emotions just erode over time?"

"For someone not dealing with them, I don't think they just erode. In this situation, where someone who detaches and tries to avoid them, adding further to it adds to the problem."

Mitchell asked, "If you're unable to escape from the abusive situation—is the danger always imminent?"

Johnson replied, "That's the nature of chronic abuse. It feels like it's always imminent."

There was a break and then Grisham had her chance at Dr. Johnson. And as it would be for both sides, when questioning "opposition witnesses," the real fireworks and battleground of court proceedings occurred.

Grisham started off by saying that psychology was a "soft science," not a "hard science," and she had Dr. Johnson explain that to the jurors. Johnson said, "It's because the nature of inner life, which is the subject of psychology, is difficult to pin down like would be done for a blood test, for instance."

Grisham asked, "Basically, we have to deal with opinions"; to which, Johnson agreed.

Grisham said, "You met with Cody ten different times. About how long did you talk each time?"

"From an hour to a couple of hours."

"You talked to Cody on September 7, 2004, and Cody told you that school authorities wanted to put him in a gifted program, but his dad wouldn't let him, isn't that correct?"

"Yes."

"But in your evaluation he fell below the gifted program, didn't he?"

"Yes."

"Did he tell you on that same day, 'I owed my dad and stepmom for what they did to me'?"

"Yes."

Mitchell soon objected, because it was obvious that Grisham was going to use Cody's own words, which he had expressed to Dr. Johnson, against him. On approach Mitchell told Judge Counts, "If they try to use it as an impeachment, this is improper through this witness."

Grisham countered, "It goes to the jury for mental issues. There is no issue as to what Cody did. He took a gun and shot them. The issue in this case is his mental state. We have to be able to combat the defense."

Judge Counts thought about it, and overruled the defense objection.

Grisham went on with Johnson: "Cody told you the abuse started about two years ago, because he started getting good at stuff?"

Johnson said, "Yes, his perception was it started about two years ago."

"Did he say that his dad always wanted what was best for him, but he could never tell?"

"He said his father wanted what was best for him, but he could never tell what his father wanted."

"He told you he started thinking about what he was going to do. He told you it wasn't the right thing to do (kill them), but it was like looking at a cartoon?"

"Yes, he said it was like a haze. It was like looking at a cartoon."

"You asked him when did it start looking like a cartoon, and he said, right when he did it. Right when he started to pull the trigger, didn't he?"

"Yes."

"Speaking about abuse, he said that one year a kid tripped him, so he turned around and socked him?"

"Yes."

"Then he said a couple of years ago, a kid was messing around with him, so he threw him into a drum set?"

"Yes."

"Did you find out later that he's gotten into ten fights since being arrested?"

Mitchell was up and objecting, but Grisham said, "I think aggression and getting into fights is relevant to his mental condition."

Mitchell responded, "I think there's a time and place for this, but it isn't now."

Judge Counts overruled the objection, and Johnson answered, "The last I recall is eight fights."

"Did Cody tell you right before he killed them, he was thinking about his alternatives?"

"I don't think he told me that he was thinking about it at the time. I think he said that he'd thought about it before."

This was very important—legally. If Cody had thought about this at all before pulling the trigger, it could mean the difference between first-degree and second-degree murder. Any forethought, rather than just blind action, made a huge difference.

"And when you say before, how much before?"

"I'm not sure."

"Right before he did it, did he think he could call CYFD or call friends or run away, or even think, 'I can just live with it'?"

"Right now, I cannot put that at a particular time."

"If he had thought about it before, and expressed that to a fellow student, would that affect any of your diagnosis?"

"No," Johnson stated.

"So he said that day, he snapped?"

"Yes."

"He said, 'I thought of it as a way to end my problems, to get rid of my problems. The best way to get what was happening to stop'?"

"Yes."

"He said, 'I remembered there was a gun handy. This was bullshit. Why keep living a life I don't want to live?'"

"Yes."

"So, is he describing thinking to you, before committing the acts?" Grisham inquired.

"Yes."

"Did he describe his thought processes happening after he snapped?"

"No, I wouldn't necessarily say it was in a continuous timeline."

"Did he tell you at any time he was really mad about having to clean the corrals that morning?"

"Yes," Johnson answered.

"You have any reason to believe he wasn't telling you the truth when he said that to you?"

"No."

"Did he tell you he loved fires and he thought they were fascinating?" Grisham asked.

"I believe I asked him about fires. He said he hadn't set any, but that he loved fires and thought they were fascinating."

"He didn't tell you about getting into trouble after starting a fire at a camping trip?"

"No."

"He told you he was only wasted one time on alcohol?" Grisham queried.

"Yes."

"He told you that Paul and Tryone didn't have an alcohol problem?"

"Yes."

"Did he tell you about a time when he smart-assed Tryone, and his dad grabbed his hair, turned him around, and Cody socked his dad?"

"Yes," Johnson answered.

"That precipitated one of the incidents where his dad was on top of him and said, 'Quit before I hurt you,' didn't it?"

"No, that was a different one. Cody described hitting his dad for the first time in the chin. He described it as moderately hard, and his dad dragged him into the living room. His dad swung and missed and Cody hit him. And they got into a fistfight in the living room," Johnson stated.

"Did Cody say he always thought it would be cool to be a cop or an assassin?"

"Yes."

"Did he ever tell you he lost his mind?"

"I don't ever remember him telling me those words."

"Just to be sure, Doctor, you're not testifying to a reasonable degree of psychological certainty or probability that Cody was unable to form a specific intent to kill that day, are you?"

"No."

Grisham said, "Assume a hypothetical, that Cody told Dr. Myers he thought of calling CYFD, calling his friends, this and that. Then he decided those things hadn't worked, so he would try this plan. That's an indication that he is thinking, correct?"

"Yes."

"And his actions tell you he was thinking that morning, don't they?"

"Yes."

"Assume as a hypothetical, he got the only weapon that wasn't locked up in a gun safe, he's thinking when he got that weapon, is he not?"

"Yes."

"When he takes the snake shot out, because quote, 'I didn't think it would do the job,' that's indicative of some thinking and some intent, isn't it?" Grisham asked.

"Yes."

"When he uses gloves, tucks the gun in the back of his pants so the others couldn't see it, when he saw Marilea and his dad outside underneath the bumper of the truck, he decided to pass them by and go inside the house first. His thought was 'If I don't shoot Tryone first, she'll call 911.' Correct?"

"Yes," Johnson replied.

"He exchanges a few words with Tryone before killing her, after he pulls the hammer back to shoot a second time, he said, quote, 'It was just to make sure that I got her.' He covers his mom with a blanket so the others wouldn't see her as they ran into the house. When he ran to the kitchen, he hid behind the refrigerator, lying in wait for the other two to come in. He shoots Marilea, quote, 'So she wouldn't tell or anything.' People on psychotic breaks don't think about covering up their crimes, do they?"

Johnson responded, "It's not impossible."

Grisham went down a list of actions Cody took after the killings—dragging the bodies out of the house, getting a backhoe, putting the bodies in a manure pile, covering them up with enough manure to make it look natural. Grisham also said that the only time Cody showed fear that day was when he nearly flipped the backhoe. Johnson disagreed and said Cody did express that he was afraid earlier that day.

Grisham asked, "Does someone who is afraid go up to someone else and say, 'I do a better job than you, because you never do it!' Is that indicative of someone who is afraid of his father, saying something like that?"

"Sometimes that is exactly what it is."

"Fear?"

"Fear, and an attempt to deal with fear. It can be a response we call 'counterphobic.' When you confront what you're afraid of as a way to deny that you're afraid."

"Can it also be a smart-aleck kid just bad-mouthing his dad?"

"Yes."

Grisham went on with her list of things that Cody had thought to do after the killings—changing his clothes to hide evidence, breaking a window to try and make it look like some stranger had entered the house, throwing the gun and shells into the river, keeping the ammo box because it might float. Grisham said, "Cody is quoted as saying, 'I tried to throw people off, because I didn't want to go to jail for life.' Doctor, I'd like you to look and see if there are any words where Cody said to you, 'I was afraid that morning.'"

Johnson replied, "He might not have used those exact words, but it's possible that there was detachment—disassociation."

Grisham said, "So it's possible that he was very emotional that morning, but unemotional that afternoon?"

"Yes."

"Is that a sign of psychotic traits?"

"Not necessarily."

"The next few days Cody went swimming with his friends, played basketball, smoked dope—you wouldn't think that would be consistent with someone who hasn't developed a conscience?"

"It could be that."

"On page six of your notes from September 9, 2004, Cody said, 'I don't know why I thought those things would have been the right thing to do (the killings). I just thought it would have worked.' In that same interview he said, 'My dad told me to go out and clean the corral. I hated it. He knew I hated it. So that's what set me off. I was pissed, but I can't remember at what level. I knew killing was wrong, but I didn't think about it being wrong until afterward. I privately felt right. Being justified. But I knew others wouldn't agree, so I took steps to hide things.'"

Grisham went on with other aspects of the days of July 2004, such as the fact that Cody had said there was nothing in the first days of July that caused him to cry. He said, "There were no tears in the week before the killing." He described his thoughts, "None of my other plans worked, possibly this one might."

Grisham went on to talk about Erin McCallahan and Cody. Cody said that people had falsely accused him of punching Erin in the arm when he got mad at her. In fact, Cody called Erin his girlfriend at Capitan, but he was also trying to stay in touch with Brenda Lucero and even writing letters to a girl named Teresa. Grisham was getting at the fact, that in her opinion, Cody was an opportunist, unconcerned for these girls' feelings.

Grisham brought up that Cody said he had smoked dope at least twelve times with Gilbert Salcido. The reason he did it, he said, "I thought it was a cool thing to do."

Grisham asked, "Do you think it was fair for Paul and Tryone to be concerned about that?"

Johnson answered, "Yes."

Grisham said, "Is it possible that Paul and Tryone were thinking of changing high schools, not to be mean to Cody, but because they thought he shouldn't be hanging out and smoking dope with those kids?"

Johnson answered, "Yes."

Grisham now got into aspects of Carla and Cody. She said that many times Carla had promised to pick up Cody for visitations, and didn't show up to get him. "He had his bags packed and she didn't show up. What kind of effect does that have on a child who is packed and ready to go?"

Johnson answered, "It can be devastating."

"When they say they are going to send you presents, and never do?"

"Yes."

"Is prime time for bonding between the ages of six months and three years?"

"Probably the first year."

"If there is a mom who isn't totally there because of drugs or alcohol problems, can that be devastating for a child?"

"Yes."

"Assume there's testimony that Paul and Carla took Cody to counseling because of problems developed because of his mom."

Johnson replied, "I don't assume that a problem with his mom would be the only reason they would take him to counseling. A doctor said it was ADHD as well."

Grisham said, "The family (Paul, Tryone, Cody, and Marilea) played board games almost every night after dinner. That's not consistent with an abusive family, is it?"

"It's not inconsistent with an abusive family."

"Is there anything in the literature on abuse that talks about abusive families that sit down to dinner together and then play board games?"

Johnson replied, "You could view it as a situation of control."

Then Grisham got into the issue of depression and Zoloft. She said, "Dr. DiMata prescribed Zoloft for Cody, but didn't recommend counseling. Wouldn't most doctors recommend counseling if there was a serious problem?"

Johnson couldn't say why Dr. DiMata had not recommended counseling.

As far as Dr. Johnson's own testing of Cody, Grisham said, "You did a Rorschach test and some responses are reflectors—in other words, things that stand out. Cody gave three of these. These responses would suggest a self-inflating response and someone who is starting to show narcissistic traits?"

Johnson answered, "It could be, but it looked to me as a defense against low feelings."

Grisham said that on validity tests Cody showed signs of constantly lying.

Johnson replied, "It could have been a cry for help."

On the Million Adolescent Clinical Inventory (MACI) test, Grisham said Cody showed signs of exaggeration of emotional problems and signs of self-pity. On another test he showed signs of a person with marked oppositional tendencies—in other words, someone who constantly thought he was in the right, and argued or fought with others. On the trauma symptoms checklist, he did not have an elevated score of sexual distress. Cody had shown poor anger control, signs of grandiose self-worth, and gotten into fights with others.

Grisham asked, "Did Cody have serious criminal behavior?"

Johnson said, "There wasn't a pattern, just one event."

"Does it get more serious than murder?"

"No."

There was a long break, and then Grisham was right back, with vigorous questioning of Dr. Johnson. Johnson did point out that all of the referrals of abuse to agencies had come to naught. The CYFD referral, the spanking on his back and buttocks, which had led to a hospital visit, the fact of having no lunch money for two weeks, the social worker going out to 5 Mile Ranch, the talk with Mr. Nelson—none of these had helped Cody, and, in fact, may have made things worse for him.

Grisham said, "Isn't it true that most abusers keep their kids away from school, instead of trying to make sure that they're there every day?"

Johnson replied, "I don't know if that's true."

"In a lot of cases, don't abusers keep kids home from school so that bruises will heal before they're sent back?"

"That makes sense."

"As for kids isolating themselves in their rooms, isn't that pretty typical of a teenager?"

"Kids isolate themselves for different reasons."

"Do abused kids usually articulate that they've lied, cheated, stolen, and done illegal drugs?"

"They could, if that was the expectation of the adult," Johnson answered.

"Do you think it's arbitrary to treat kids differently, based on their different behavior?"

"Not necessarily."

"Almost everyone is depressed at some time?"

"Yes."

"How many go out and murder people because of depression?" Grisham announced.

Mitchell jumped in with an objection, and it was sustained.

Grisham wanted to know, "Do you have an opinion as to whether Cody was sane or insane on the morning of July 5, 2004?"

Once again there was an objection, that this was beyond the scope, and this objection was sustained as well.

After Grisham was done with this round, Mitchell asked more questions of Dr. Johnson. Mitchell said, "Do abused children tell you of every instance of abuse?"

Johnson answered, "I believe abused children do not want to tell of every instance of abuse and would rather avoid talking about abuse."

"Do you find it difficult as a doctor to try and get them to give you that information?"

"In the course of intervention, kids start talking more about it. Cody did not want to talk to me at all in the beginning."

"Did you go out and talk to other people who had seen this child abused, such as Slim Britton?"

"Yes."

"Was using a hay hook on Cody, abuse?"

"Yes."

"When you were asked, was Cody thinking—when you talk about impaired judgment, what does that have to do with thinking about something?" Mitchell asked.

"Thinking does not equal a rational, well-judged decision. With someone who is overwhelmed by emotions, it distorts the quality of thinking. Their judgment is impaired."

"So, if one was in fear, and thinks about a way of opening a door or window to flee, does that indicate that they are not thinking?"

"No."

"Does it do away with the fear that they have?"

"No."

"Which one controls at those times—thinking or the emotion?"

"I think it's more likely that the emotion impairs and erodes the thinking."

"For example, sometimes people can drive long distances and not recall what they did as they drove down the road?"

"It happens."

"When we talk about the events that arouse strong emotion, are we talking about the ability to exercise judgment?"

"Yes. Judgment suffers, not necessarily reasoning. Judgment is a controlling factor in our behavior," Johnson explained.

"Cody talked about being extremely angry that morning. Can that anger cause a temporary loss of self-control?"

"Yes."

Mitchell wanted to know if Cody in his statement to Shepherd and Armstrong might not have told them the whole truth. Grisham objected and Judge Counts had Mitchell and Grisham approach.

Counts asked Mitchell, "Where are you going with this?"

Mitchell responded, "Children who reflect upon an event may not give an accurate accounting of an event."

Grisham responded, "Dr. Johnson cannot vouch for the credibility of that. Mr. Mitchell is trying to say that

Cody was trying to please the officers, so he gave them answers they wanted to hear."

Judge Counts replied, "I'm not sure what he's going to say, so let's go on."

Mitchell asked, "Do children on occasion try to please adults with their answers?" and Johnson said, "Yes." Mitchell then asked, "If you ask a child to reflect back upon a traumatic event, can you tell what is a reflection and what actually occurred?"

Johnson replied that sometimes events were very highly emotional and a person might not have a clear recall of them. Sometimes a person would try to please others by reconstructing the events in the way he thinks the person wants to hear.

Mitchell wanted to know if Cody said on more than one occasion that he was in a haze on the morning of July 5, 2004, and Johnson said that Cody had given her that information.

Mitchell noted that Cody had spoken of seeing the events of the killings as if they were a cartoon, and he asked what Cody meant by that. Johnson replied, "He said it was like a cartoon, things weren't the same." Asked if Cody had told her about Tryone hitting him, Johnson said, "Yes, he talked of an incident where she climbed on top of him, punching him."

"Did you learn that Cody had a real love for Hondo school?"

"Yes, he loved Hondo school. He called the people there his family."

Mitchell asked, "Did Cody ever tell you he was thinking of self-defense?"

In a disgusted voice, Grisham objected. "Oh, Your Honor! He cannot insert self-serving statements from Cody! They are hearsay."

Mitchell shot back, "I have the right to examine this witness, and have her use her notes."

Judge Counts took some time to look at the rules of law and said that Mitchell's question was beyond hearsay, but Grisham countered, "This absolutely does not take it out of the hearsay rule. I have the rules of law book on my desk."

This topic went around and around until Mitchell went in a different direction, wanting to know about Cody's results on a Rorschach test. Johnson said, "His results were consistent with those of people who are capable of dealing with life's problems in a flexible way, as opposed to impulsively. He had an ability to stay in touch with reality. In regard to weaknesses he showed angry and oppositional tendencies that suggest underlying anger. This is a result consistent with very low self-esteem, and at the same time an unrealistic tendency to think very highly of himself. Taken together in my mind, it appears to have been a defensive need. Cody's behavior was consistent with need for attention."

Dr. Johnson finally stepped down from the stand, but even then, she was not dismissed, but, rather, subject to recall. Both Mitchell and Grisham knew that Johnson was going to be a very important factor in Cody's trial. All of the other psychiatrists had used her findings as a starting point for their own evaluations.

If Dr. Johnson was basically pro-Cody, it could be said that Dr. Susan Cave was even more so. She had testified in various courts on the average of once a month for the previous five years. She wasn't just a defense witness—in 2004, she had testified three times for the prosecution, and overall she had testified for the prosecution forty-five times.

Dr. Cave had traveled to the Bernalillo County Juvenile Detention Center when she had interviewed Cody. She talked with him about his past history and the killings, and administered a psychiatric test on him. Dr. Cave basically gave answers about Cody's mental state that were beneficial for the defense during direct by Mitchell. And once again, the tougher questions came on cross-examination.

Grisham wanted to know, "Did you rely on any expert or study when you said that kids don't think like adults until they are at least sixteen?" Cave said she relied upon her own knowledge of this.

Grisham said, "You agreed with Dr. Johnson's diagnosis of Cody, but to be fair, she didn't diagnose him with post-traumatic stress disorder, did she?"

Dr. Cave said, "I don't disagree with her, I think we just see things a little differently."

"Cody wasn't diagnosed with ADHD at school, was he?"

"I think it was a consideration."

"You're not testifying that because of a mental condition or defect, Cody Posey was unable to form specific intent on the day in question, are you?"

"No, I'm not."

"In fact, many of his actions that morning showed his ability to show intent, and indeed showed that he did?"

"Yes, they can be interpreted that way."

"Taking snake shot out of a pistol and reloading it with other ammunition so as to kill, can that be interpreted in another way?"

"No, not that action."

"Is there another way of interpreting passing by his

dad and Marilea, so he could shoot his mom first so she couldn't call 911?"

"We don't know how much the attempted sexual assault the night before had an impact on that. Maybe he went after her first for that reason. I think his emotions were very complex."

"Do you think he shot her in the head, a kill shot, and then shot her again because she was still moving, has any interpretation except an intent to kill?"

"No, probably not."

Grisham started going down the list of things Cody did after the killings, and also a list of things he had complained about as abuse.

Grisham asked about Cody's attempts to cover up the crime scene.

Cave said, "They showed poor judgment and adolescent thinking."

"Meaningless chores he talked about, such as the rocks, they wouldn't be meaningless if they were in the horse pens, would they?"

"No, there was probably a reason for that."

"And stacking rocks up along a wire fence to keep predators from grabbing lambs, that probably had a purpose as well?"

"I have no knowledge in that field."

Grisham said, "Much of what you based your analysis on derived from Cody's statements?"

Cave answered, "Much more than that. There's well over a thousand pages of reports in this case that I read."

"Yes," Grisham replied, "but if Cody was being untruthful for much of what he told you, would it affect your opinion?"

Cave replied, "Possibly. I'd have to see what it was."

* * *

On redirect Mitchell shored up Cave's earlier statements. He asked her, "What happens to children when we have them reflect on a traumatic event?"

Cave said, "They're likely to become very emotional."

"As a psychologist, when you have children reflect back on a traumatic event, what do you have to be aware of?"

"You have to remember that memory is not perfect. That children's recollections of events change over time. There have been a lot of memory studies."

Mitchell asked, "About the ability to kill, if I attempt to defend myself from somebody who seeks to cause me great bodily harm or even death, can I have an intent to kill?"

Grisham objected, "That goes to an issue not before the court."

Mitchell replied, "That goes to the issue directly before the court!"

Judge Counts overruled the objection, and Dr. Cave said, "You could form the intent to kill in the service of protecting yourself."

Mitchell queried, "Do you have an opinion in your diagnosis whether Cody was acting out of fear and anger that morning?"

"Yes. It's my opinion that he was overwhelmed by fear and anger and by the sense he didn't know what was going to happen next."

"Can we control those overwhelming emotions?"

"You might be able to. You could also lose control. It's a common human experience."

Mitchell asked, "Is rape a violent act?"

Grisham objected once again, saying, "There is no testimony before this court about rape! Even from Cody

Posey. I'm going to ask that Mr. Mitchell not use that word again."

The judge sustained the objection, and Mitchell rephrased his question. "Let me use a more technical term—is an attempted rape a violent act?"

Cave responded, "Yes."

Mitchell wanted to know, "Have you dealt with victims of such acts, and what happens when they later see the perpetrators of those acts?"

"Yes. It's a very disturbing experience. There is an emotional reaction. A very simple way to look at this offense is—Cody didn't like these people, they were mean to him, and he wanted to kill them. That's the most simple way to look at these incidents. But as a forensic psychologist, I see the world in a more complex way. And I think these acts have to be viewed in the entirety of their context. The family dynamics, the family history. This boy and his personal history. It was much more a complex and dynamic situation."

Grisham took one last shot at Dr. Cave. She said, "You cannot testify to a psychological certainty that Cody Posey lost control over his actions on the morning of July 5, 2004, can you?"

Cave responded, "No, I think I can. I think he was not in full control of himself."

"That was not my question. Did he lose control? Could he have chosen not to load the bullets into that gun?"

Cave replied, "I think if he had any other exit open to him, I think he would have chosen that."

Grisham said, "Doctor! Could he have chosen not to put those bullets into that gun?"

Cave said, "I'm not sure."

Chapter 18

A Different Mirror

Even before Dr. Myers, a psychiatric witness for the prosecution, uttered one word, both Gary Mitchell and Sandra Grisham were battling over what jurors would hear him say. Mitchell moved that Dr. Myers not be able to talk about Cody's prior sexual activity with girls, since it didn't involve anything that had to do with his father, stepmother, or stepsister. Mitchell said that Cody's case came under the New Mexico Rape Shield Law, which prohibited talk of a victim's prior sexual activity. In this case Mitchell was contending that Cody was the victim of an intended rape.

Grisham argued that the shield law did not apply in this case, because Cody was not the victim. Paul, Tryone, and Marilea were the victims in the case. She said, "This is the State of New Mexico *against* Cody Posey, *not* the State of New Mexico against Paul Posey, Tryone Posey, and Marilea Schmid." Grisham said that Cody had used girls for oral sex and that he had showed his sexual maturity at the age of fourteen. Grisham went on to say that these girls had not been Cody's girl-friends, so these were casual sexual encounters. She said that Dr. Myers would show that it went to Cody's personality—a personality that used other people, especially underage girls.

Grisham argued, "The defense's theory of the case goes to the alleged sexual contact of Tryone and Cody on the night before the murders. The state's theory of the case is that Cody Posey was showing psychopathic tendencies. We have test results that show that. We have his actions that show that, and we have him having oral sex with three underage girls. There is also testimony before the court that a great deal of porn was downloaded. This goes to show an inference that Cody Posey was downloading that porn. There is evidence before the court that Tryone's pants were undone and pulled down and her bra was not just pulled up, but also undone. I think it also goes to an inference that Cody was the one who was sexually preoccupied in this case, not Paul. Any kid who knows something about computers could have gone back and reset the time and dates on the computer. All of this is highly relevant to the case."

Mitchell just as strongly argued, "I've been dealing with the Rape Shield Act ever since it came into existence. The whole thing is designed to protect an individual and particularly children. If this doctor is going to get up on the stand and talk about a junior-high kid having sex with another junior-high student, then he's living in a world that we're not living in. If we're talking about petting or kissing, it doesn't point to psychosexual behavior—if in fact it ever occurred. This hasn't been acceptable for admission for a number of years, especially as it relates to children."

Grisham countered, "How many times did we hear about Cody's isolation? How many times did we hear that he was psychosexually immature? The Rape Shield Law doesn't apply. We're not saying anything about Cody's consent."

Judge Counts turned to Mitchell and asked, "Let's say the state was prosecuting somebody for rape. Are you saying the state could be barred from bringing in a rapist's past sexual history?"

Mitchell replied, "Yes, without a nexus in the state of New Mexico where it relates to that. Whoever seeks to present that evidence must do so in a timely manner before the court. What the doctor asked Cody about sexual activities with other junior-high students has absolutely nothing to do with incest or mother/son relationships. What Cody did is classical adolescent sexual behavior. No matter who the person is, we don't get into their prior sexual past, especially when they are a victim. We are talking about a minor child. Sex amongst teenagers is not illegal. The state is trying to say we've got some kind of psychopath here, but even the DSM-IV disagrees with that. They're just trying to say he's a lying psychopath. They're trying to get in everything they can, from carrying a knife in his pocket in the third grade to this stuff. We don't allow it in any other case, so why are we suddenly going to allow it in Cody Posey's case? We protect children day in and day out in this state, and I've heard Sandra Grisham arguing for these exact same points. Defense attorneys don't even try to get into this stuff anymore, 99.9 percent of the time, because we know it's totally inadmissible. How does a sexual experience by this child, no matter how naive, relate to adults' abuse of a child?"

Grisham was right back with, "Mr. Mitchell wants to

talk about the Rape Shield Act, but I've become intimately aware of the Rape Shield Act. It does not apply to defendants. It applies to victims. In this case we're showing personality, maturity, and lack of isolation. All of which are relevant in this case."

Judge Counts took some time and looked up New Mexico case law on the matter. He said, "Evidence of a victim's past conduct shall not be admitted. We don't find ourselves in that situation. The Rape Shield Act does not apply in this situation. As far as the relevance issue, that's subject to the testimony of the psychologist, and I can't rule on that at this point."

Mitchell was still upset, however, and spoke up. "Because the state has tried so hard to defraud the jury into thinking this is some kind of children's court case—"

Before he got any further, Grisham broke in. "I'm going to object to Mr. Mitchell's phrasing! This is a children's court. Cody is being tried as a youthful offender. There is no attempt by the state to defraud the jury!"

Mitchell wasn't to be swayed, however, and said, "As a child Cody needs to be protected. Cody Posey is a victim of that sexual assault. Let me point out something that I feared. The doctor in his evaluation refers about the veracity of certain evidence. Whether it's Cody's testimony or other witnesses' testimony. Especially as it relates to abuse. In the state of New Mexico, experts commenting on testimony that has come in as direct evidence is improper. I would move to limit that he not be allowed to do that. This doctor's evaluation reads more like a closing argument. Particularly as it comments on Cody's veracity. At this juncture we ask the court to order the doctor not to comment on the veracity of the evidence. I fear that in this case we are bordering upon that time in the trial, when the state would like to have a mistrial by this stuff, and it would be dangerously close to the wire. The doctor would get up there and say whatever he wants, and the defense couldn't do much about it, because he'd cloak it by saying he's a psychiatrist who has examined this child."

Grisham was immediately irate about being accused of wanting a mistrial. She said, "Dr. Myers knows not to say that Cody is lying. However, Mr. Mitchell's psychologists went on and on and on that they believed Cody was sexually abused, they believed Cody was physically abused, they believed Cody was fighting for his life and his identity as a man. When you diagnose someone as sexually abused, and Cody is the only source for that information, you are commenting on his veracity. When Dr. Myers does not diagnose him as sexually abused, he's entitled to say why. He won't say Cody is lying, but he may say from a psychologist's viewpoint, 'This behavior doesn't make any sense.' He's perfectly entitled to explain his diagnosis.

"When you attempt to explain psychopathy, you have to relate about prior lies. And there are prior lies that have been presented in this court. Cody himself in his confession said one thing, and then later changed the story. Cody's psychologist talked about him as lying to his family. I believe that when there are significant points which are not true, then that is admissible. The testimony of Dr. Johnson and Dr. Cave was replete with instances of them commenting on his veracity. And the reason for this is, Cody left no witnesses at that ranch as to what happened. Everything they (the psychologists) say he said, that he had been sexually abused, that he was afraid, and that it was building and building, and that this was the high point of the abuse—they are commenting on the veracity of testimony. If the jury believes Cody, they are free to disregard the testimony of Dr. Myers. He's not saying he's a human lie detector. He's saying that lying is important in deciding what someone's psychological makeup is. The court can caution jurors on this. We need to be able to rebut the evidence of Dr. Johnson and Dr. Cave with psychological evidence of our own."

Judge Counts decided, "What I've heard is that the state will not be asking an expert to comment directly on testimony and its veracity. If the child's counsel thinks a line has been crossed, they can object."

Finally, after all of that, Dr. Wade Myers was allowed on the stand, and he would try to relate a mirror image of Cody's thought processes and mental health over the years. Myers's testimony would have starts, stops, time-outs, and bump along in an even more erratic manner than the testimony of Dr. Johnson and Dr. Cave. Myers started by telling Grisham and jurors that he had done a psychosexual report with Cody and found out what Cody's sexual life, sexual practices, and sexual preferences had been. Cody told Myers that he'd had two girl-friends in his life, and that he'd dated Brenda Lucero from January 2004 until his arrest. When he'd gone to Capitan, he'd picked up Erin McCallahan as a girlfriend, but he never really dropped Brenda. Cody said that neither girl knew of the other's existence. Cody also related that he hadn't had sexual contact with either one of these girls except for kissing. He hadn't made any sexual advances toward Brenda because he loved her and didn't want her to think he was just going with her to gain sexual favors. As far as other unnamed girls went, Cody said he'd had sexual contact with them in the form of oral sex. They had both given each other oral sex, and these were casual encounters.

Of this psychosexual report Dr. Myers said, "It gave me an indication of how Cody relates to others. In and of itself, it didn't suggest psychopathy, but when you're rating the items on the youth version, impersonal sexual activities are one thing in my opinion that would be reflective of that."

Dr. Myers also took a delinquency/violence history from Cody, and discovered the most notable area was some fights at school. In one fight a boy had taken Cody's hat, and Cody got into a fight with him. Another time a boy shot a rubber band and almost hit Cody in the eye, and Cody got into a fight with that boy. Then Cody said he was in a group at school known as the Rockers and Skaters. The Rockers and Skaters got into a brawl with the jocks at school, but Cody said he never gave anyone serious injuries, nor did he receive any serious injuries in these fights.

Cody spoke of his legal history and denied any kind of antisocial behavior. Cody said he hadn't participated in any cruelty to animals, fire setting, or stealing. He had skipped school a few times, but was not a constant truant. As far as religious history went, Cody said he wasn't going to church at the present time, and didn't even bring up about his years in the Baptist Church when the family lived near Cloudcroft, nor the clowning program at the church.

Dr. Myers took a mental status exam of Cody. Myers looked at Cody's appearance, mood, movements, facial reflections, and checked for delusional thinking, hallucinations, anxiety, attention, and ability to calculate and speak. The test revealed that Cody was polite and cooperative, well-spoken, had good attention and memory, and, overall, his cognitive functioning was intact.

On the third visit with Dr. Myers, Cody had seemed more nervous because of his upcoming trial. Dr. Myers did a digit span test, which was a repetition of numbers to see how well a person's memory functioned. Cody did above average on the test. Myers did another test to check for visual motor speed, organizing and planning, logic and anticipation. Cody did very well on these tests until near the end, when he seemed to lose focus.

There was a controlled oral word test, where, for instance, a person would say every word they could think of starting with the letter *P*. Cody did well on this. There was a fifteen-item memory test, to see if someone was faking problems about memory. Fifteen numbers, symbols, and letters were used, and most people, even with some brain damage, will do well. Cody got all fifteen correct, so there was no indication that he was trying to fake memory problems.

There was a Children's Depression Inventory to show emotional and physical symptoms, such as low energy and bad sleeping habits. Cody scored within the average range. Dr. Myers ran a nonadaptive personality test on Cody, which gauged signs of possible personality disorder. Cody showed some tendencies of a negative temperament. People with a high score were generally dissatisfied with life and themselves. Cody did show signs of being annoyed easily and he became angry at small provocations. Cody scored a 97 percent—which meant that he scored higher than 97 percent of the norm.

As far as personality disorders went, Dr. Myers assessed Cody as having problems with controlling anger, unstable in his relationships with people, and tended to look at people as being either all good or all bad.

On the Rotter Incomplete Sentence Test—Adolescent Version, Cody had some interesting things to say. He said he hadn't lived up to his potential, and that his dad had been "mean to me, but taught me things as well."

As with the others, Dr. Myers would lay out a format that was in line with what the prosecution wanted to present, since he was a prosecution witness. It was on cross-examination, redirect, and everything that followed, that the questioning would become more heated and provocative. One of the first rounds of this was over Cody's understanding of what oral sex meant. Mitchell laid forth a contention that Cody thought "French-kissing" was oral sex. Dr. Myers didn't have his notes with him, which tended to muddy the waters further, but he said that Cody definitely meant oral sex as being each one of them had their lips on the other's genital region. Cody had told Myers, "She did it to me, and I did it to her."

Mitchell still contended that this was not substantive evidence, and that the prosecution was trying to get this evidence in via the back door. Mitchell said, "It's a neat trick. I have to give them credit for that."

Grisham shot back, "Mr. Mitchell is the one who decided to bring up a psychological defense, and I'm allowed to rebut it. This is not hearsay. The obtaining of this kind of material is not unique."

Once the issue was about Zoloft and depression, Grisham maintained that Zoloft had essentially cured Cody of his depression, so he couldn't cite that as a reason for the killings on July 5, 2004. Tryone had even said about the Zoloft, "I'm thrilled about the way it's worked." Mitchell claimed all of this was hearsay, and the judge agreed, sustaining an objection.

The issue of Cody's depression was also touched upon by the words of Gilbert Salcido. Gilbert had told Dr. Myers that Cody seemed to be very happy on the days he had spent over at the Salcido residence in July 2004. "He was happy and smiling. He ate five hot dogs," Salcido said.

Dr. Myers also said he had looked at hundreds of family photographs in which Cody was in the photos. Myers said, "Pictures showed him with a lot of different family members doing different things at parks, family gatherings, working on the ranch, a school dance, camping, and at an aquarium. Almost uniformly, he seemed to be a happy child with smiles on his face. Usually, if a child is clinically depressed, you can get a sense of it from photographs such as these. I didn't see that. And there were never any bruises, black eyes, casts, bandages, or anything like that in the photographs. I didn't feel that his depression had anything to do with the events of July 5, 2004."

Dr. Myers discussed the "safe house" interview Cody had done with Sergeant Shepherd and Investigator Armstrong on July 7, 2004, at the CYFD office. Myers related, "One of the things I was trying to determine was if Cody had an argument that morning, and had his father struck him. It's hard to say. In the first part of the interview, Cody said he had an argument in the kitchen, and that his father didn't hit him. Then by the third version, there was an argument in the corral, and his father did strike him."

This line of testimony brought an immediate objection

from Mitchell, followed by an approach to the bench. It was a moment that made everything hang in the balance. Mitchell had contended for a long time that Dr. Myers would cross the line and say that Cody had been lying in his testimony. According to Mitchell, Dr. Myers had no right to do that in front of a jury, and by saying Cody had changed his stories at the CYFD interview, Dr. Myers was saying that Cody had been lying.

Mitchell told Judge Counts, "I move for a mistrial with prejudice! The very thing we tried to avoid being put forth has happened. These expert witnesses cannot get up here and try to impeach Cody. There are no ethics involved here. This is blatant misconduct!"

Grisham argued, "This is utter nonsense! The diagnosis that this child is showing psychopathic traits by constantly lying is perfectly ethical."

The jury was sent out on a long break, while Judge Counts listened to audiotapes of what Dr. Myers had just said. Grisham must have known the trial had reached a precipice from which it might tip over into a mistrial, and all the long days of testimony would be down the drain. She argued vehemently, "Testimony has been before the jury in the 'safe house' interview. Dr. Myers's diagnosis is that he did not find Cody to be suffering from a mental disease or defect that would have prevented him from forming an intent to kill. Cody didn't have a substantial disorder. I'm not going to ask if Cody Posey was a liar. Dr. Myers is just going to take the events of the incident as told by Cody, and relate that the events are so bizarre, especially about the alleged sexual assault, as to make no sense. Dr. Myers will talk about them in terms of psychiatry. We've heard all week by the other doctors that Cody was an abused child, and they took that story of sexual abuse and said it was true, and then based their evidence on that. All of that is indirect testimony as to the credibility by the doctors. It is Dr. Myers's contention that it was traits of psychopathy, and not depression or PTSD, that led to the events of July 5, 2004.

"Also, he'll talk about the veracity of a witness's statements about dropping forty-pound bales of hay on a person's head and what that would do to a person. Myers is a medical doctor, as well as a psychiatrist. There is plenty of evidence before this jury that Cody had been lying during the 'safe house' interview. He was telling one story, stopped, and then said, 'Oh well, I might as well tell you the truth.'"

Judge Counts had a key question, and it concerned the fight Cody supposedly had with his father on the morning of July 5, 2004. "Isn't that a direct question about his credibility?"

Grisham answered, "Dr. Cave and Dr. Johnson found Cody to be credible, but the amount of testimony about abuse by others than Cody is minuscule. As to the main witnesses—Cody killed them all. The vast majority of abuse is claimed by Cody. From the others it's only a squished finger, hitting on the back with a rope, spanked on the buttocks. Those few things weren't the basis of the defense doctors' findings of abuse. They had to base their diagnosis on what Cody said. They based their findings of sexual abuse on what Cody said. Cody was the only witness to that alleged event. I'm not going to have the doctor say Cody is lying, but I am going to have him point out what is important to determine whether or not he was hit that morning, whether or not that hit was the precipitating event to loss of control, and everything that has been testified to by Mr. Mitchell's experts. I cannot be constrained in rebutting that. Without this,

Mr. Mitchell gets to go to the jury and say, 'These were horrible, horrible people and they deserved to die. So let my client off.'"

Mitchell was just as worked up as Grisham and fired back, "Let me point out, a doctor who uses the term 'predatory form of violence'—that's deliberate murder. They wish the doctor to talk like that. Not to be facetious, but I'd tell him to come out here, get a law degree, get licensed in New Mexico, and go to work for the DA's office and give a closing argument. That's essentially what he's doing!

"And about the sexual abuse, they're going to talk about clinical credibility as if we're in some Ford test warehouse and we've watched it and observed it all. It's going to boil down to—Dr. Myers is going to say, 'It stretches incredulity to think Cody would stand and be burned twice by a torch.' He's using language that isn't direct, but he's calling Cody a liar. No offense to the doctor, but I can tell he doesn't know beans about welding.

"Also, about the supposed infrequent abuse of Cody, and whether Cody is exaggerating about the abuse to help his case—I don't want a mistrial, I don't want to go through this again. It's not like they haven't been amply warned by the defense about this kind of conduct. But this psychiatrist doesn't qualify as an expert at predicting the unknown. There's no great lie detector test in his head. Gee whiz, we've gone off into another realm here! My point under case law is simple—it's one thing if you're commenting about whether this can be classified as clinical depression. It's completely wrong to stand up here and say, 'I'm a psychiatrist from Florida, and this boy is sittin' over here and making all this stuff up to help his defense.'"

Grisham argued, "Dr. Cave and Dr. Johnson explained

about the change of stories because abused children are initially reluctant to tell the truth about abuse. I am just as adamant to put on a rebuttal that this is consistent with psychopathic traits. Predatory versus impulsive and emotional is the difference between psychiatry and the law."

Judge Counts told Mitchell and Grisham, "All right, I understand the arguments." Then he called for a recess so that he could study case law. What hung in the balance was whether the trial would proceed at all.

After the break Judge Counts came back and told Mitchell and Grisham, "The jury is to decide if the defense is telling the truth. The state has been careful to preface their remarks, and what Dr. Myers was saying is that he was trying to determine if there was a fight between Cody and his father that morning. That is the heart of the case and what the jury must decide. To the respect of the testimony of Dr. Cave and Dr. Johnson— if the jury decides to deny what Cody said, then they can decide those diagnoses are incorrect. That is different than an expert witness getting up and saying, 'I'm going to tell you whether this incident occurred or not.' That is a psychological lie detector test, which the Supreme Court has rejected. Had Dr. Myers got past saying he was trying to determine that, and got all the way to a conclusion that it had not occurred, that would have been grounds for a mistrial. Mr. Mitchell spoke up before that train wreck occurred. I am going to caution counsel—if you elicit testimony from your psychiatrist where he purports to say what did or did not happen, that will result in a mistrial of this case."

Grisham knew everything she said from that point on to Dr. Myers would be like walking on eggshells. To not say enough would allow Dr. Johnson and Dr. Cave to have the last word about Cody's state of mind on the morning of July 5, 2004. To say too much, and have Dr. Myers in essence say that Cody was lying about all the abuse, would cause a mistrial. Grisham told Judge Counts, "I need further guidance."

Counts responded, "Dr. Myers can tell us what his diagnosis was. Johnson and Cave were not deciding whether Cody's remarks were true or not, but that is the issue here."

Grisham still wasn't sure how far she could go with all of this, and asked, "Can he testify to counter Dr. Cave? What can he testify to as his basis for his diagnosis, and be within the court's ruling? I need to rebut their testimony, but the last thing the state wants is a mistrial. I'm simply looking for guidance. And there's another area—Cody's takes on abuse got more pervasive as time went on, and then he exploded them on the stand. I want to be able to ask my expert about psychopathic traits, one of which is lying."

Judge Counts replied, "As I see it, one way of looking at it was Cody was in a safe environment, so he opened up and disclosed more. I think it is reasonable for the state to say it is reasonable that he lied to expand his story."

Grisham replied, "Can I then go to say that it is consistent with psychopathic traits?"

Judge Counts responded, "I think you can. All of this goes indirectly to Cody's veracity. But the doctor cannot say, 'I sat down to determine whether or not this happened.' If he says that, the top of my head is going to fly off!"

Grisham said, "I will caution him about that."

Judge Counts agreed that all of this was a difficult

area, but he couldn't give any better advice than he'd already given. Grisham agreed and said, "I'm walking on eggshells now. I'm not arguing with the court, I just want to ask Dr. Myers about the sexual abuse issue and ask him why he didn't diagnose the child as being a sexually abused victim. His reasons as a psychiatrist. He's not going to say the child lied, he's going to say, 'I found things inconsistent with what Cody was telling me.' I think it is extremely important for the state's case from a psychological standpoint. I mean, it doesn't make sense to burn someone if you want them to have an erection. Dr. Myers will speak to the fact that he's never seen allegations like this before. Otherwise, it muzzles my psychologist."

Mitchell wasn't through getting his two cents in, however, and said, "The state has pushed this to the nth degree. We have this doctor up here claiming he's never seen this kind of thing, yet everybody knows that rape is an assault. It's battery. It's not just some kind of sexual act done out of love and affection. This doctor intends to talk about things such as 'atypical, stretching credulity, bizarre.' I've been objecting to this all along. We in this country only allow judges and juries to make decisions in matters of law. We don't allow politicians, psychiatrists, and lawyers to make those kinds of decisions, but that's exactly what we're getting into here. God, the state just keeps bringing this stuff and bringing this stuff!"

Grisham shot back, "Doctors can state opinions. He can say my studies show that this would be extraordinarily atypical. He has the knowledge to state that opinion. It is a direct rebuttal of Dr. Cave and Dr. Johnson. They were constantly saying, 'I believe Cody.'"

Judge Counts agreed and said, "The state says they are going to avoid questions that reflect directly on the truthfulness of Cody Posey. The doctor can testify that the incidents are so different than you would expect, that they are not the norm."

Grisham replied, "Thank you. I think I have sufficient guidance."

After that long break the jury was brought back in and the questioning of Dr. Myers proceeded. Grisham asked him what his opinion was about Cody's "safe house" interview with Shepherd and Armstrong. Myers answered, "One of the issues was looking to see if Cody understood right from wrong at the time of the crimes. I found numerous instances of his behavior which would point to the fact that he did understand right from wrong. Things like putting the gun in the back of his pants when he went into the house on the way to shoot Tryone. The alibi he wrote down. The hiding of the bodies. The disposal of the weapon. Acting cool, calm, and collected when he met teacher Todd Proctor at the store and had a three- to five minute conversation with him after the murders. Shooting Marilea so she couldn't tell anyone else about what he had done. His plan to escape to Mexico. All of that was understanding the wrongfulness of his behavior."

Moving to the incidents about the bales of hay being dumped on Cody from a truck, Myers said, "I think it would have caused serious neck injuries or head injuries if that would have happened."

Now Grisham moved toward tricky ground, asking about the alleged sexual assault on the night of July 4. Even Dr. Myers chose his words very carefully when answering her questions. He said, "One of the first things in the 'safe house' interview—Cody was asked had anyone ever made him do anything he didn't want to do. And he said no. But then he added, 'I was made to go to Capitan High School.' He never mentioned sexual abuse."

Grisham asked, "You've studied sexual predators over the years. Was there anything about Cody's allegation?"

Myers answered, "You have to look at the allegations, and then look at the person who claims to be the victim of sexual abuse, to see how those factors interact. One of the things that struck me was that Cody in the past had acted pretty aggressively when his father tried to fix the back of his collar. I would rank watching a metal rod being heated up in front of you for twenty-five to even sixty seconds as being far more threatening and something you'd want to escape from than just having your hair pulled. Based on what I know about Cody's personality, it would be unusual for him to stand there and watch what happens, not just once, but twice, knowing that the burn was going to come. I think there was clear evidence of emotional abuse, and I think in the past he was abused by his father, but based on information I received, I didn't believe that physical abuse was still a clinical issue for Cody."

Grisham said, "Dr. Cave and Dr. Johnson said Cody felt safer as time went on, so he told of more incidents and more violent ones. Do you have an opinion on that?"

Dr. Myers now chose his words very carefully. As Judge Counts had said, if Myers called Cody a liar on the stand, "The top of my head is going to come off!" So Myers replied in very measured tones, "My response to that would be that I could give an alternative explanation. When in a youth or juvenile detention center, it wouldn't be unexpected if someone gave renditions of events that would help their case or decrease the amount of consequences they might get for their actions."

Grisham wanted to know if Cody had indeed been walking on eggshells in the months before the killings, and Myers responded, "I didn't think he was walking on eggshells. His parents might have been walking on eggshells. The more his father tried to restrict him and put limitations on him, the more Cody would rebel. It was an escalating conflict between them."

Grisham said, "We heard that Cody back-talked to his dad on the morning of the murders. One of the other doctors said that was counterphobic."

Myers replied, "That is an example of defense. It's like saying, 'I'm better than you.' It's part of his personality. He was rebelling against authority."

"What is your opinion of Cody's mental state at the time of the murders?"

"I think from a psychiatric standpoint—I found he had signs of a disturbed personality that had some psychopathic features. I thought those were his personality factors that played directly into the crimes."

"Did Cody Posey suffer from a mental condition on July 5, 2004, which would have caused him to not be able to form an intent to kill?"

Myers said emphatically, "He did not have a mental disorder."

Grisham asked, "Was Cody Posey able to weigh his choices that morning?"

Myers said, "Yes, in fact, he told me he did weigh his choices before he acted. He said he considered four things—whether to call CYFD, whether to call his teachers, whether to run away, or whether to just live with it."

"In your opinion, did Cody Posey have any uncontrollable impulses that day?"

"No, in my opinion he did not. There was a deliberate plan."

"Can a person who is fourteen years and nine months old form a specific intent to kill?"

"Yes, they can."

"Do you have an opinion whether Cody Posey was in fear of death or great bodily harm from Paul Posey on July 5, 2004?"

"My opinion was he was not in fear. Had he acted in fear, I would have expected a different result to the crime. I think it would have just been against his father and it would have happened very quickly. I think he would not have killed his stepmother or his stepsister. This was very different from that. The theme he related was that he was feeling mad, not fear that morning."

"Do you have an opinion as to whether Cody Posey lost his mind that morning?"

"My opinion is, he did not lose his mind."

Mitchell on cross was not pleased about where Dr. Myers had taken his answers, and he spoke to him in a fairly sarcastic tone. He often did not call him Dr. Myers, or Mr. Myers, but rather called him "Doc."

Mitchell started out by saying, "Well, Doc, why don't you tell me how much you expect to be paid for your testimony?"

Myers replied, "My rate is two hundred fifty dollars an hour."

"How much do we owe you?"

Myers responded, "I don't know, I haven't tallied it up."

Mitchell said, "How about giving us a rough estimate."

"This is my seventh day, and we've capped it off at two thousand a day. So it's about fourteen thousand, to this point. And that includes my report, which is kind of in rough form."

"The report you've been testifying to is in rough form?"

"Yes."

"So it's not even in final form?"

Grisham objected to this question, but it was overruled.

Myers answered, "Yes, because I've been given additional information since I've been here."

At this point Mitchell started bringing up names of people who had testified as to abuse being heaped upon Cody by Paul and Tryone. Mitchell wanted to know if Myers heard the statements from these various people. Mitchell went down the list of people one by one: Steven Chaves, Slim Britton, Pilo Vasquez, Emily Nutt, Brandon Devine, William Brust Jr., Eli Salcido, Leo Salcido, Rita Lucero, Alicia Chaves, Bryan Aragon, Sherry and Walter Gensler, Anthony Sanchez, and John McCallum. Of all these, Dr. Myers said he was aware of Steven Chaves, Slim Britton, and Pilo Vasquez.

When Mitchell brought up about the hay hook incident, Grisham wanted to approach, and said to the judge, "We may start getting into credibility and then it goes to veracity, which could cause a mistrial."

Judge Counts said, "The credibility issue cuts both ways."

Mitchell decided to press on, taking the risk that he might be opening doors that had remained closed up to this point. Mitchell brought up the incident where Paul had supposedly placed a hay hook near Cody's crotch and said that if he popped the clutch of the pickup one more time, he would jerk off Cody's balls.

Myers responded, "In December of 2005, I had Cody describe every incident of abuse. He did not describe a hay hook incident."

Mitchell asked Myers about other incidents of abuse, as told by other people besides Cody. Myers said that he had not heard Slim Britton talking about a hay hook to Cody's hand or Paul hitting Cody with a lariat. When Mitchell brought up about Cody being roped and dragged across a corral, Grisham piped up and said, "Cody brought all that stuff up, and Dr. Myers didn't have a chance to review that information. His reports were in December and January. We're going to get into credibility again and Mr. Mitchell is in danger at this point of causing a mistrial."

Judge Counts said, "I thought Mr. Mitchell was asking if he considered it. If the answer is no, then he didn't consider it."

Grisham responded, "Mr. Mitchell is trying to be like Wile E. Coyote and get into the very issue I wasn't allowed to do. Then I'll have to come back and ask Dr. Myers why he didn't consider it, and then we get right into the issues that can cause a mistrial."

Judge Counts replied, "It seems to me that Dr. Myers has been giving different answers than that. And I've been keeping in mind what you've been speaking about. You can come back and ask why he didn't consider them. If he didn't hear about them, then that is the reason."

Mitchell chimed in, "I have a right to ask the expert what he considered, and what he didn't, to make his reports. If Pilo, Slim, and others don't get in with their statements, then it sounds like Cody is making all of this up."

Grisham wasn't backing off. "Once this opens up, Dr. Myers is going to have to say he thought Cody was lying on the stand. If I ask him why he didn't consider them, he's going to say, 'Because I believed Cody was a psychopathic liar.'"

At this point both Grisham and Mitchell were getting heated in their arguments. Both of them knew it was a key issue whether the jury thought that Cody was lying about the abuse or not. Judge Counts also knew this was a legal minefield. He said, "I don't see anything improper with Mr. Mitchell saying, 'Had you heard about Slim Britton's version of this? Or have you heard about Cody's version of this?' And Dr. Myers can answer yes or no. Mr. Mitchell isn't asking, 'Is this the gospel truth?' He's just asking, 'Did you take it into consideration?'"

Grisham wouldn't give up, however, and said, "That leaves the question in the jurors' minds, 'Gee, golly, if he had considered it, then maybe his report would have been different.' And once I ask him why he didn't consider it, he's going to say it was unbelievable. 'This kid was lying.' This is the problem. Or he'll leave the impression, which Mr. Mitchell wants, that he rejected it because I paid him a lot of money, and not based on any fact that Cody is a pathological liar. It is incredibly unfair to repeat all of Cody's claims, without allowing me to rebut them."

Judge Counts responded, "If the question is—was Dr. Myers aware of these statements being made, and did he use that in the totality of his report, then that doesn't open the door."

Grisham, however, wasn't satisfied with where things stood. She argued and argued her point, until Judge Counts had the jurors take a recess so the questions could be discussed more openly, rather than in hushed voices during an approach.

* * *

Once Myers was back on the stand, Mitchell again asked him a litany of questions about what had gone into his report and if he'd considered what Paul and Tryone thought about Brenda Lucero, Hispanics in general, whether Cody had to wear long-sleeved shirts on hot days, what Cody had said at his mother's funeral, and what Doyle Baker had said. The constant theme was: "Did you take this into account?" Sometimes Myers had, and at other times he hadn't.

Mitchell also got into the fact that Cody didn't see any of the money he got from SSI for his mother's death. The money went into Paul's account. All Cody got, according to him, was a measly $20 a month for all the work he did. Over and over again, Mitchell did not call him Dr. Myers, instead he called him "Doc."

Mitchell asked, "Cody can't remember certain things about his mom's death, because it is hard to think about?"

Myers agreed and answered, "There were many nights he cried himself to sleep and had nightmares. He still has dreams that she is alive and they have good times together, but then he wakes up and she is dead and this makes him sad."

Mitchell asked, "You're not of the view that certain children are born bad, are you?"

Myers replied, "No, but they may be born with genes that may give them a greater chance of psychopathy."

Mitchell said, "Doc, you are an authority on Zoloft and have written about its possible side effects. You have testified in one case about a side effect of Zoloft?"

Myers said he had, and as with many drugs there was always a possibility of side effects. But he added, "You can't talk about the possible side effects on every drug, or nobody would even take an aspirin."

"Yes, but Cody was increased from twenty-five milligrams to fifty milligrams on Zoloft?"

Myers replied that Zoloft had no bearing on the case.

Mitchell wanted to know if Cody had fears about being around his dad, and Myers replied that Cody was a chronic worrier.

Mitchell had been talking for so long, that his voice almost seemed to be wearing down at this point. He touched once again about how Cody defined "oral sex." Mitchell contended that Cody thought it meant French-kissing, but Myers said, "No, Cody said he had oral sex three times, and he had an orgasm each time."

Mitchell responded, "The other day, outside the hearing of the jury, you didn't recall that information about defining oral sex, but today you do recall he said that?"

Myers replied, "I don't remember you asking me the other day if he had climaxed. If you had, I would have told you."

"Doc, Cody told you even though he had been offered intercourse, he refused that?"

"Yes."

"And, in addition, you had talked to him about kissing and foreplay?"

"Yes, but I just wrote down very choppy notes."

"He particularly liked Brenda Lucero, isn't that right? Because she was modest and beautiful and he thought he was in heaven when she was around?"

"Yes, that's what he said."

"He thought it was important that she didn't care what other people thought about him?"

"Yes, because for a while, she still told him after he was arrested that she liked him, and she would wait for him."

"I appreciate that you said that you explained oral sex

to Cody, but would it surprise you that he didn't know what oral sex meant until he talked to you?"

"I'm not sure how to respond to that."

"In all fairness, your notes don't reflect anything about orgasms, do they?"

"No, they don't."

It was hard to tell who would wear down first— Mitchell, Dr. Myers, or the jury. Quite often Mitchell used the phrase "Doc, did you consider?" when talking about friends, family, and ranch hands that knew Cody. And the financial situation really irked Mitchell. Cody had practically worked like a slave on the various ranches for a pittance. Mitchell asked, "Do you think a man like Sam Donaldson could afford to pay a young man who was doing the work of another man? Working ten hours a day?"

Myers replied, "I'd have to speculate about Sam Donaldson's finances, but I assume he's pretty well off. Even so, there was no insistence by Paul that his son be paid a fair wage."

Mitchell said, "In the hypothetical, do you think it would be demeaning to a young adolescent that his family would not even stand up and ask that he be paid a fair wage?"

Myers said, "From what I've read, this was a family with a lot of pride. I can't see Paul going to Mr. Donaldson and asking for that money. As far as I could see, Mr. Posey was very hardworking and in that sense was a role model for Cody. I think he was trying to help him build character."

"Well, Doc, don't you think it would build character

if you had a father who defends your work every now and then?"

"There's many instances where his father defended his work. Even Cody said he was glad his father taught him certain things."

"Doctor, that's not my point. In any other business in this country, if a child did that work, it would be in violation of child labor laws. But his father didn't even stand up for him. I'm sure Sam Donaldson is a generous man. Paul should have said, 'Could you please pay Cody a decent wage?' Isn't the point that his father would do that?"

Myers said, "My understanding is that a job is highly valued here. I don't know if I could conceive of Paul doing that. I think he was appreciative of having a job."

Switching gears, Mitchell wanted to know if on the incomplete-sentence test, one of the things that stood out was that Cody wanted to be loved. Myers said, "Yes, but he filled this out when he was incarcerated and no longer had a family to love him."

Mitchell asked if it would surprise Dr. Myers if there were witnesses who said Cody felt that way long before the killings. Myers replied, "Cody said he felt loved by his father. I think he felt loved by his sister."

In a bitter voice Mitchell responded, "In all fairness, Doctor, did I speak about his sister?"

Myers retorted, "You were speaking about love from the family."

Mitchell said, "Didn't you have a certain mind-set when you went down to interview this child?"

"No, I went there with an open mind. I was going to see about his maturity, his mental state at the time of the offenses, and risk assessment."

"So today you're saying you didn't go down there

with a certain mind-set to make a report that would be beneficial to the state's theory?"

"No, I didn't."

"Doctor, don't you have the reputation as the expert they can call on, particularly in Florida, if the government needs someone to oppose other psychologists and psychiatrists?"

"I do a fair amount of criminal forensic work for both the defense and state."

It had been a long, grueling session for Mitchell with Dr. Myers, and Grisham took a last stab at him to refute some of the things that Mitchell had been contending.

Grisham:	Who gets the money we're paying you?
Myers:	All of it goes to the University of South Florida.
Grisham:	Does the University of South Florida care which side you come down on, on this?
Myers:	No.
Grisham:	Did Cody tell you about being roped and pulled thirty feet before being able to turn over?
Myers:	No, he did not.
Grisham:	Would you expect some teacher would have noticed something besides just a black eye if he was continuously being punched and beaten?
Myers:	Yes, I would. Cody or any child isn't a cartoon character who could just

bounce back from having forty-pound bales of hay dropped on his head, or pushed out of a moving car without physical injuries. It's not possible.

Grisham: You don't think Zoloft was a factor in these murders?

Myers   No, you don't take Zoloft and go out and rob a bank, for instance.

Grisham On cross you spoke of emotional abuse to Cody.

Myers: Between 2000 and 2004, I found three instances of emotional abuse in Tryone's journal.

Grisham: You read Cody's journal, did you see anything in there about abuse?

Myers: There was not one entry about being physically abused.

Grisham: Whatever happened to Cody in the past, would you agree he was not suffering from a mental disease or mental condition on July 5, 2004?

Myers: No, he was not.

Chapter 19

Flying Sparks

There was a break between the testimony of psychiatrists for the state with a stream of witnesses speaking about other aspects of Cody's life and schooling. Even these people brought forth a round of discussions between the defense and prosecution as to who should be able to testify, and who should be excluded. Tim Rose said that Charlene "Charlie" Cooper had been disclosed late, and shouldn't be able to testify, since the defense witness Emily Nutt had already been permanently excused and couldn't be called back to refute anything Cooper said.

Judge Counts asked Rose, "Have you interviewed this Cooper?"

Rose replied, "We have an investigator out trying to find her. I don't even know what the heck she's going to testify to. We've had an inadequate time to prepare."

The prosecution came back with, "You want to talk about a surprise! Ms. Nutt refused to talk to us. We had no idea what she was going to say before she got on the stand. We're entitled to put on our case. We are allowed to rebut Ms. Nutt. Besides, these are not case-in-chief witnesses, they are rebuttal witnesses."

Rose replied, "Ms. Nutt wouldn't talk to the prosecution because Grisham had said to Nutt, 'Don't you know in this state, not to report child abuse is a crime?' So she felt threatened by her."

Judge Counts eventually said, "The motion to exclude Ms. Cooper is denied. I don't think the rules of discovery have been violated. You have brought up the hearsay rule, so if you think something is objectionable, you have to bring up an objection at that time."

Charlie Cooper eventually testified about the fact she never saw any problems in the Posey family, and that she didn't believe that Paul or Tryone had abused Cody. She also testified to the fact that she had not seen either Paul or Tryone treating Cody differently than they treated Marilea.

Laura Christiansen testified as a prosecution witness that she lived in Carrizozo and drove a school bus for the Capitan School District. Her route took her from Capitan, through the small town of Lincoln, and as far as Hondo. In the spring of 2004, Christiansen had thirty-five kids who rode on her bus, and among these were Cody and Marilea. She recalled that Cody and Marilea sat near the back of the bus within a few seats of each other.

Rather than saying that Cody had been quiet and couldn't talk to others on the bus, as he had related, Christiansen said that he was often talking to friends. Christiansen recalled, "He acted like the other kids. He didn't do anything on the bus that stuck out. Cody was normal. He would talk and joke, and I never saw Cody hesitate about getting back into his parents' vehicle at the end of the day."

Janice Schryer next asked various police chiefs and county sheriffs if they had any "welfare checks" on abuse of Cody that had been called into their offices. Sheriff Norbert Sanchez, of Otero County, said there were no reports made concerning any instances of abuse between 1999 and 2002, and Police Chief Gene Green, of Cloudcroft, said the same about his department. So did Sheriff Tom Sullivan, of Lincoln County. Sullivan explained that when someone called the sheriff's office with a complaint, there was a call sheet made about it and an officer would be dispatched to the caller. There was a dispatch log listing every call that came into the office, and he had searched the logs to see if the name Posey ever was listed. Sullivan said, "We searched everything, clear back to 2001 when the Poseys first came to Chavez Canyon Ranch, and there was no record of any calls about Cody Posey."

The prosecution asked Cloudcroft Middle School teacher Carrie Lewis about Cody when he was in her language arts class (basically, the structure and use of English). Lewis had contacted the Posey family because Cody was turning in his homework late, or not turning it in at all, and the quality of his work was very poor. Lewis set up a conference to see what could be done about it, and Paul and Tryone came in to see her, along with Cody. Lewis recalled of this conference that "Paul and Tryone said they wanted Cody to do his best. They had high expectations of him. There were no bad words from them about Cody."

Two other conferences were scheduled as well, because Cody was not improving. In the winter of Cody's sixth-grade year, the discussion began to turn

toward keeping Cody from advancing to the seventh
grade, because his language skills were so poor. Eventually that is exactly what happened.

The prosecution asked Lewis about how Cody had
been after his mother had died, and how Lewis had reacted to that situation. Lewis said, "I let the child dic-
tate what they needed in a case like that. I didn't hover
around them. I kind of let them take the lead if they
need something extra. I don't remember if he ever saw
the school counselor about that."

There were arguments about photos of Cody that the
prosecution wanted to present. It was a big issue, because most of the photos were going to show Cody
looking happy and smiling, even around his dad and
Tryone.

Mitchell argued, "In all the school photos—of course
he's not going to have black eyes or bruises. And of
course he's going to be putting on a front around his
parents. I wonder if the state has a single photograph
of Cody when family members are not present? We're
creating an absurdity with these photographs. The state
of New Mexico routinely prosecutes child abuse cases
where they realize people are not going to have photographs of people abusing their children. I've yet to see
someone come in here with photos of them abusing
their child. Don't we have hundreds of photographs
where it seems to show they were one big happy family?
Sure we do. But is that supposed to refute evidence of
abuse? I suggest to the court these photos are inadmissible. If the court does allow some photos in, I would
like the amount limited. There is no reason to show
twenty or thirty photographs of the same event.

"A few photographs are taken of Cody's time with Carla, and some photographs with Sandy. The interesting thing about the rest of the photographs with Paul and Tryone and Marilea—they seem to have been taken at the following locations—Fun Trackers in Ruidoso, Carlsbad Caverns, and with either Cody's uncle or grandparents. There is always someone else in the photo with Cody.

"My objection is—the defense has not alleged child abuse in the presence of step-grandparents or a step-uncle. We allege that there was abuse when others weren't around. The key to photographs is that they are just a millisecond point in time. They are not all-encompassing. In addition, we didn't allege that there was child abuse when the photos were taken. These photos do not rebut anything that the defense brought up. They're limited to a very short period of time when no abuse was alleged to have taken place. If the prosecution has photographs of the times Slim was speaking of, or Cody was speaking of, or at the times that any of the other witnesses were talking about, that would be a different ball game. But that is not the situation here. It seems to me that what the state is going to attempt to do is come up here and show photographs of limited periods of time when Cody's family was being visited by relatives, or when he was being taken by his stepmom Sandy. And they are going to show photographs of Marilea and the family smiling and that sort of thing."

Grisham replied, "The state has five different albums we found in the house. Two of them were marked, 'Cody.' None of them were marked, 'Marilea.' The defense has alleged preferential treatment for Marilea, and the existence of the album disputes that argument. *State of New Mexico* versus *Simonson* says that the prosecution is entitled to refute false impressions given to the jury by the defendant through rebuttal testimony. Mr. Mitchell says they are just milliseconds. Yes, they are, they are just little snippets of time that go from the age of seven forward. These are little, tiny statements from the graves of three people to contest the allegations in the child's case that he was abused three to five times a week, and sometimes three to five times a day.

"The allegations of abuse in this case have mushroomed. The state does not contend that these photographs would have been admissible in our case in chief, but once Cody Posey took the stand, and the psychologists took the stand and said he was suffering from pervasive despair, that he had depression and Cody said he was abused, then they are relevant. Mr. Mitchell wants to come before this court and say that somehow these photographs were taken in between the signs of abuse. Your Honor, the testimony from our psychiatrist, and the one to come, is, you don't turn depression on and off. The psychiatrists will say that is apparent in these photographs. We have happy, smiling, cheerful children being treated equally. There are no bruises on Cody's arms or bruises on his face. No black eyes. Every one of those small snippets of time goes to dispute the false impression that the defendant made during his case, that he was being abused at least two to three times a week. The court has heard how those allegations of abuse have mushroomed from maybe ten in the taped interview at the safe house to literally thousands by the time we get to trial.

"Those photos show both Cody and Marilea at the same time, both doing chores. They are not being treated differently. Even one photo shows Cody throwing a flake of hay over a fence, while we can see Marilea's arm with a flake of hay she's putting into a corral.

We have pictures of Marilea with a barrel, and Cody right there. We have pictures of the 'Fiesta Dance'—they show that these two kids were not being treated differently and that Cody was not being isolated. He was not kept down on the ranch with no exposure to anyone. We have photos of Cody at a birthday party at the age of seven. Pictures of Cody on a fence, watching sheep, with no bruises on his face. Pictures of Cody on a trampoline, pictures from Verlin and Shanda Posey, showing Cody right there, and Paul with his hands on Cody's shoulders. This is supposed to be his abusive, horrible father? That tiny piece of evidence goes to rebut that his father hated his son.

"Here's one with Tryone, with her arm around Cody. Pictures of Cody's bedroom that he said was stripped of everything except a mattress and a sheet. Here's Cody on a camping trip. Cody with his arms around his sister, Marilea, who was supposed to be a spy, who he didn't like. Pictures of a loving couple who were supposed to have used a blowtorch to make their son have sex with them. Pictures of Cody, who was supposed to be so terrified of water that he couldn't stand putting his head underwater. We have pictures of him playing Marco Polo in a swimming pool with his head underwater. These pictures put a lie to Cody saying that he was abused two or three times a week. Mr. Mitchell knows how important these pictures are, which is the reason he's trying to keep them from the jury."

Mitchell responded, "If it was okay to prove a negative of the great violence done to children in sexual abuse type cases, in which people took videos of numerous family outings, whether it was fathers who abused children, or great leaders who abused children—we could have found thousands of photographs showing happy moments in the lives of these victims. To suggest in any fashion that parents who are abusing their child are going to take photographs of that is ludicrous. I point out to the court that the utilization of this type of evidence doesn't reflect at all what is going on. It stretches the imagination to the breaking point!"

Grisham replied, "Mr. Mitchell well knows there aren't photos of kids who are abused two or three times a week. He makes my argument for me. There aren't any photos of when Cody was with the Clees family or Sandy. Every single one of these photos shows that this child was treated just the same as his sister. They were treated as a family unit. I'm not saying these are photos of the days he was abused. I'm saying these photos show that he did not have marks on his face and arms. They would have been there if his testimony is to be believed. The parents did not choose when the school photographer is there. They didn't say to themselves, 'Whoops, we better not hit him about the face for the next two weeks.' They didn't choose times when people would come over. If he was abused two or three times a week, there would have been marks. There were no marks, no isolation, and that's what the pictures show."

Judge Counts thought about all this and said, "I think the photographs may be relevant. There was testimony that Cody was ostracized. Three against one. They may be relevant to show that at least in that time frame, that was not the case. The photos from school don't go to rebutting anything. The court will agree that showing four or five albums of family photos is cumulative. I don't need five hundred pictures of a trip to Carlsbad. The state may show two photos of each event."

* * *

Art Ortega, a social worker for CYFD, had gone out to the 5 Mile Ranch when the Poseys lived there to check up on Cody. There had been a report filed by Sandy that both Paul and Tryone were calling him names, such as "faggot" and "pussy boy" and other derogatory epithets.

Schryer asked Ortega if the interview with Cody had been done about forty feet away from his parents, and Ortega said yes. Mitchell asked on cross, "Because this child was bright and quick to smile, everyone assumed that everything was okay?" Ortega responded, "After talking with him, he seemed to be okay."

Mitchell added, "I'm not being critical of you. You guys work hard, are underpaid, and there's not enough of you. It's a tough chore to go out there and do it all by yourself. In an avalanche of child abuse cases in New Mexico, this one got a pretty low priority, didn't it?"

Ortega replied, "I wouldn't say we prioritize them that way, but we look at the facts to make a conclusion."

Mitchell asked, "The truth of the matter in New Mexico—you guys have to look at all the neglect cases where a child is not getting enough food, water, clothing, and shelter, and if they are living in filthy conditions. Correct?"

"Yes, sir."

"I'm not exaggerating when I get up here and say there is far too much for CYFD to do, because the state legislature fails to fund this thing?"

Ortega said, "Yes, sir."

On redirect Schryer came back with, "Were you satisfied with the amount of time you spent with Cody?"

Ortega replied, "Yes, ma'am."

"Did you see any signs of Cody not being truthful with you?"

"No, ma'am."

"Do you do your job to the very best of your ability?"
"Yes, ma'am."

If the judicial sparring between Grisham and Mitchell
had been intense, that only seemed to intensify once
psychiatrist Juan Sosa got on the stand—then the sparks
really began to fly. Sosa ran through a litany of instances
about Cody, which he had noted in his evaluation,
which upheld the prosecution's view of things concerning Cody's state of mind on July 5, 2004. Sosa even
went further than that, by proclaiming that Cody had
been showing psychopathic traits by that year. Dr. Sosa
couldn't come right out and say that Cody was a psychopath, because no one under the age of eighteen may
be described in those terms in a court of law in New
Mexico, but Sosa could definitely put into the jurors'
minds that Cody might be a very dangerous individual
if allowed to go free. Sosa was also adamant that Cody
had not been abused to such an extent that it destroyed
his ability to form an intent to kill on July 5, 2004.

Mitchell came out swinging on cross, and once again
his common theme, as it had been with Dr. Myers, was
"did you consider?" He wanted to know if Sosa considered statements made by Sandy as to abuse. Sosa
replied that he couldn't quote her directly, but that he
had spoken with her.

"Doctor, I want to know if you can recall who persons
such as Emily Nutt are?" Mitchell asked.

"I can remember her name," Sosa said.

"Can you remember what she said?"

"I read the statements," Sosa responded; to which,

Mitchell said, "That's the problem, she didn't give a written statement."

Dr. Sosa admitted that he'd read about much of the testimony that had already taken place in trial on the Internet, and Sosa added, "One of the things that was glaring to me was that hardly any of the individuals (those who had been on the witness stand) reported it to anybody. Whatever their suspicions of abuse, they didn't report it."

Mitchell shot back, "The fact that they didn't report it doesn't mean it didn't occur, does it?"

"Well, sure," Sosa replied. "You can't prove it one way or the other."

Mitchell wanted to know if Sosa had interviewed Pilo Vasquez, and Sosa said that he had over the phone.

"Pilo reported things to you that he didn't even say in this courtroom, didn't he?"

"Yes, he did."

"He reported some very traumatic things that happened on that ranch, didn't he?"

"He described many things," Sosa answered.

"Do you recall Steven Chaves?"

"Yes."

"He described a rock-to-the-back incident, a pair of pliers used on Cody's finger, a slap that was so hard it knocked a cowboy hat off Cody's head. All Cody had done was ask to use a wheelbarrow. Chavez described—"

Before Mitchell could go any further, Grisham objected and said, "Mr. Mitchell is repeating all of his evidence in the case. He doesn't have to regurgitate all of the evidence of the last two weeks!"

This was overruled and Mitchell went on with other names, such as Shara Paul and Helen Porter. Sosa said he didn't recall Porter and that Mitchell had an advantage over him, since he had notes and Sosa didn't, on the stand. Mitchell replied, "Well, Doctor, you don't want me to do this from memory, do you?"

Sosa quipped, "You're asking me to do it, Mr. Mitchell. That's pretty hard."

Some people in the courtroom laughed at this response, but Mitchell was not amused. He said, "You can consider your notes if you brought them."

Sosa admitted, "I don't have them with me."

Mitchell then said, "You can look at my notes if you want to," and when he handed them to Sosa, the psychiatrist said in surprise, "These are my notes!"

At this point Grisham announced, "I probably have a thousand pages of discovery. I can enter it all into testimony if you want me to. I will stipulate Mr. Sosa didn't consider anything in trial except the testimony of Cody Posey and the two doctors (Johnson and Cave)."

Mitchell wasn't pleased with Grisham butting in and said testily, "Your Honor, if I may continue the examination!"

Judge Counts replied, "I'm not certain I heard an objection."

When Mitchell's next question was about computers, Grisham objected again, and Judge Counts said, "Let's take a recess."

To which, Mitchell said very loudly, with a tone of disgust, "Good idea!"

As the jury filed out, someone from the gallery said, "Whew!" They were obviously commenting on Sandra Grisham and Gary Mitchell, who were now becoming more assertive and appeared to have reached some new plateau of irritability.

Outside the presence of the jury, Grisham told Judge Counts, "I have carefully stayed away from anything that has to do with computers. Mr. Mitchell is headed somewhere he doesn't want to go. Both Dr. Sosa and Dr. Myers looked at the computer sites, and they think it's much more likely Cody accessed those computer sites of pornography. I want to go there. I don't think Mr. Mitchell wants to go there. And besides, it wasn't introduced on direct."

Mitchell replied, "Well, I don't disagree with any of that, Judge. Imagine that. But I'll move on to a different subject, anyway." After he said this, he heaved a big sigh.

Once testimony began again, Mitchell asked Sosa, "Did you ever indicate that Cody was cruel to animals?"

"No."

"Ever been in trouble with the juvenile justice system?"

"No."

"Suspended from school?"

"No."

"Member of a gang?"

"No."

"Did he stay out at night?"

"No."

"Set fires?"

"One person said he once set a fire."

"Destroy property?"

Sosa brought up the incident when Cody had fired a pistol into a vehicle's dashboard, and Mitchell told him that had been an accident.

Dr. Sosa did comment about Cody and school—that

Cody had been manipulative at times, so that others would feel sorry for him. "He would try to make Paul and Tryone seem worse than they were," Sosa said.

Mitchell asked about methods in breaking a horse that Pilo and Slim had used, as opposed to Paul Posey. When this came up, Grisham said in disgust, "May we approach?"

She was momentarily cut off by Judge Counts, who had other things to contend with at the moment, and he was mad. Someone in the gallery had been talking during testimony. Counts said, "I want to remind the gallery they are not to talk. I've heard reports from the jury that they've heard talking from the gallery. I'll absolutely clear the room if it happens again!"

Once Judge Counts had that out of the way, Grisham continued, "Now Mr. Mitchell is trying to get this in, and it wasn't on direct."

Mitchell replied, "It was brought up about cruelty to animals. You can't sit there and crucify this child with so-called feelings of grandiosity, when he protected animals from the brutality of his father. I can bring in all sorts of evidence of cruelty to animals by his father. It was a constant on that ranch, and a constant between Cody and his father."

Grisham argued, "Anybody who has worked with horses knows that Paul was not cruel to his horses. All of this is far more prejudicial than probative. This is a ridiculous attempt to get in animal cruelty by his father."

Mitchell battled back, "It has to do with the protection of animals, and not thinking you're better than someone else (as had been claimed by Sosa about Cody). This is a critical factor. The doctor brought up that argument. Sosa spent a long time on grandiose feelings and callousness."

Grisham replied, "The court already ruled on this matter as hearsay. Cody may not have been cruel to animals, but he shot three people in the head!"

Mitchell wasn't giving up. "I feel I'm right on this, but maybe there's a way out of this. Let me ask this witness—'Doctor, when you considered grandiose feelings in an argument between a son and a father, if the child sought to protect an animal, would that matter?'"

Judge Counts finally said, "I think Mr. Mitchell is entitled to examine the basis of his reasoning for grandiosity. But I'm not going to allow in all the hearsay."

After the arguments Mitchell asked Sosa, "In regard to grandiosity, what if there is a legitimate reason for the child to disagree with the parent?"

Sosa replied, "That happens with adolescents, and parents give them some leeway."

"So, do we still consider the child to have grandiose feelings if he has a legitimate reason?"

"I would have had to been there. I wouldn't tell my father I was a better cowboy than him, if I wasn't."

"So I'll ask a hypothetical question—if the father does something in particular that causes a problem, and the child disagrees, that is not grandiose, is it?"

"No, but you asked it in a very nice way. But with Cody, it escalated, and he said his father called him a smart-ass. It then escalated into physical hitting. I mean, according to Cody, he lied many times and said many things that aggravated the situation at home. We don't know the tone he used that day."

Mitchell said, "Doc, Cody told his dad, 'I can break a horse better than you.'"

Sosa replied, "Well, for an old cowboy, and you know that culture, that's pretty tough. His father responded in a very negative way."

> Mitchell: You know from Pilo and Slim, Cody received some kind of blow from his dad many times, but just walked away?
>
> Sosa: Pilo was interesting. He told me a lot of cowboys didn't like Paul, because he wouldn't take advice from them, and—

Before Sosa could go any further, Grisham jumped in before the psychiatrist said something more that she wanted the jurors to hear. Grisham exclaimed, "Now we're getting into hearsay. I'm going to object as nonresponsive." In effect, she had just reproved her own witness.

Judge Counts agreed and said the response was not responsive.

> Mitchell: Isn't it correct that children who have been abused will attempt to stay away from the abuser?
>
> Sosa: Yes, but there are others who will try to emulate the abuser. They will try pleasing them.
>
> Mitchell: They will try their best to please the abuser?

Sosa: At some points, yes. At some points they will be very confrontive. Many of them will do things that get them into more trouble.

Mitchell: In regard to an abused child, if that parent seeks to have the child show no emotion, and a child is attempting to please the abuser, the child will show no emotion, isn't that correct?

Sosa: It's possible.

Mitchell: What if the abuser tells the child, "Don't be a wimp?"

Sosa: That's ranch life, Mr. Mitchell. Those cowboys want their boys to be men.

Mitchell: (With a disgusted tone of voice) "Well, Doc, that doesn't mean we should allow them to beat their children, does it?

Sosa: I didn't say that.

Mitchell: I know that you didn't, Doc, but the fact that this was ranch life doesn't excuse abuse, does it?

Sosa: No, but it happens.

Mitchell wanted to know if abused children tried to find safe places, and Sosa said that they did. Then Mitchell asked where an abused child might go to find that, and Sosa answered, "It can range from a very real physical place to an imaginary one."

Mitchell wondered if for adolescent children, to be accepted and loved was an extremely strong emotion. Sosa responded, "It is supposed to be for most children who are aware of the importance of social recognition and status. Growing up with peer groups is important at that stage."

Mitchell asked, "The idea of thinking that words don't hurt, that's nonsense, isn't it?"

Sosa agreed. "Oh, words hurt!"

"Especially if you refer to them with some type of vulgarity?"

"Yes."

Mitchell wanted to know if Cody used words appropriately, and Sosa said, "Yes, he has a great knowledge of language. He is well read. He uses grammar correctly. In fact, he makes for pretty good reading. I read his testimony in the courtroom and it sounded better than yours."

Sandra Grisham and a lot of the gallery cracked up at this, and even Mitchell laughed.

Sosa followed up with, "Sorry about that, Mr. Mitchell."

To which, Mitchell replied, "Oh, a little levity in this trial would probably help us all. You even made me blush, Doctor. But getting back to serious stuff, isn't it correct when you discussed Marilea with Cody, the word 'fear' was something you suggested to him?"

Sosa said yes.

Mitchell asked, "In your discussions with Cody about alternatives, weren't the alternatives brought up by you? Weren't you the one who said, 'Why didn't you call CYFD? Why didn't you call a friend or teacher?'"

Sosa replied, "I think I brought that up. He initiated it, though. When he described fear with Marilea, he described what he saw in her face."

"Are you aware that after the loss of his mother, that on more than one occasion, Cody was told by his dad to suck it up and stop crying?"

"Yes."

"The fact that the child doesn't necessarily cry, or show great emotion, doesn't mean he has flat effect, does it?"

Sosa replied, "If you take it one event at a time, we can have flat events in our lives. The problem here is, even in the testimony in this courtroom, he was flat. He was very personable with me, but he was very flat with me. The only time I saw Cody wipe his eyes is when there was a reference to the loss of his mother. Looking at Dr. Johnson's report, for example, and Dr. Myers's report, they didn't describe a great deal of emotion. Fear, intensity, et cetera, weren't there."

Mitchell asked, "The way we learn about emotions and the expression of emotions—we learn that from the ones around us?"

"Yes, sir. We learn what is acceptable and what isn't. It all depends on what's going on at the time."

Mitchell wanted to know if culture played a part in expressing emotions, and Sosa stated, "It has a lot to do with it. For example, there is a great deal of differences between the Indians, Anglos, and Hispanics I see."

Mitchell wanted to know how much Dr. Sosa was charging the state of New Mexico, and he said $1,200 per day.

Grisham asked on redirect if Sosa was going to be paid, no matter what his evaluation of Cody was. Sosa said that was so. Then Grisham questioned if she had asked Sosa to come down one way or another in his evaluation. Sosa replied, "No, you asked if I wanted to do it. I say what I see and what I think."

Grisham asked, "The last time you testified is when

my husband hired you, and you testified for the other side, correct?"

"Yes, ma'am."

"Is your opinion for sale?"

Sosa answered, "My time is, my opinion isn't."

Grisham said, "On July 5, 2004, is it still your opinion Cody was not suffering from a mental condition or disorder?"

Sosa replied, "It is my opinion that there is no evidence that he was suffering from a mental illness that incapacitated him from making a decision on that date."

"He was capable of forming an intent to kill?"

"Yes, ma'am."

Chapter 20

Verdict

Some of the most emotional testimony for Paul, Tryone, and Marilea came from Verlin's wife, Shanda, and Tryone's mother, Leona. Shanda testified that she never heard Paul or Tryone calling Cody names and she hadn't seen any bruises or marks on his face while visiting Paul, Tryone, Cody, and Marilea at the various ranches where they had lived. Grisham asked Shanda about several photos, and let the jurors see the photos in question. Some photos concerned a camping trip to the Capitan Mountains with Paul, Sandy, and Cody, as well as Verlin, Shanda, and her son Clayton. Shanda once again said that Paul had treated both boys well on the camping trip and she didn't have any concerns about leaving Clayton with Paul.

Shanda related that Cody was excited when he learned that he and his dad would be moving to the 5 Mile Ranch from East Grand Plains. Cody liked the idea of living on a ranch and being a cowboy. Shanda said that she and her family visited Paul, Cody, Tryone, and Marilea on the 5 Mile Ranch at least eight times over the years. "I never had concerns about Cody there. I never had a feeling that there were any problems on that ranch. I have photos of Cody at Easter, hunting for eggs on the ranch. There were no problems, and I was around Cody when he was alone at various times.

"Jake and Sandy Schmid visited us once on the Roadrunner Ranch, where we lived, and Cody was with them. They had an ice chest full of beer and—"

Mitchell objected at this point and wanted to know where this was going. Grisham told Judge Counts, "They showed up with alcohol and were under the influence. Sandy has said on the stand that she doesn't remember this incident, and I want to show that Shanda does."

Mitchell replied, "This is hearsay and irrelevant. This has nothing to do with the present case."

Judge Counts responded, "I guess it goes to the credibility of Sandy. It has minuscule relevance, but I'll allow a couple of questions."

When asked the same set of questions, Shanda said, "Jake and Sandy had Cody and Marilea that weekend. When they arrived, they had a cooler of beer and they both were drunk. I passed that on to Paul."

Shanda then related, "We moved from the Roadrunner Ranch to Feliz Ranch, about thirty miles south of Roswell. Paul, Tryone, and the kids helped us move. We left my two-year-old daughter with Paul and Tryone at one point, and I never had any worries about that."

Shanda recalled that she and Verlin helped Paul, Tryone, Cody, and Marilea move to the Cross D Ranch, near Weed. She said that Clayton and Cody would go out and play basketball or play in Cody's room. She saw Cody's bedroom and described a chest of drawers, a bed with a red metal headboard, nightstands, several pictures on a wall, and a guitar in his room. She said it was not stripped down to just a mattress and sheet, as Cody had claimed. In fact, she had a photo of Cody sitting on the bed with the red metal headboard.

Shanda spoke of Cody coming to visit on her daughter's fourth birthday at the Feliz Ranch. Shanda recalled, "He was fine—normal and happy. There were no bruises. We also saw him and his family at the Joneses' anniversary party in Ruidoso. I had a discussion with him there about the museum. He explained that he had been to the Museum of the Horse many times and wasn't interested in it."

This was important from the prosecution's point of view because it tended to refute the idea that Cody had been isolated on the ranches and never allowed to go anywhere. The same was true for photos that showed Cody at a water park, Carlsbad Caverns, and other places.

As far as other activities, there were photos that showed both Cody and Marilea working on a ranch, and Cody and Marilea together at various activities. In one photo Cody had his arm around Marilea, contesting the idea that he couldn't stand to have her near him.

Mitchell asked on cross if any of the photos brought into trial were taken when Paul and Tryone were not around. Shanda said she wasn't sure.

On the stand Leona Basham recalled that she had first met Cody in 1998. She and her husband saw Paul, Tryone, Cody, and Marilea about every three or four months. Leona had photos of Cody on a bike, and photos of Marilea and Cody together. Leona related that Cody and Marilea were treated the same way. Leona said, "We considered Cody to be our grandson. We didn't treat the kids differently. There's one photo that shows the kids with hand puppets that we gave them."

Asked about Cody's room at the Cross D Ranch, Leona talked about his bed being covered with a bedspread that her mother had made. "Tryone gave it to Cody, and there was a bed in that room."

Leona described photos of Cody at their home when they lived in Albuquerque, at the Albuquerque Zoo, on various ranches, at Carlsbad Caverns, at an amusement park in Ruidoso, and in Jacksboro, Texas. One of the more important photos, as far as Grisham was concerned, was that of Cody in a swimming pool. Grisham said, "He claimed to be afraid of water, but there he is in the photo. Cody went underwater with no problem. He and Marilea would play Marco Polo in the swimming pool."

Leona recalled, "The last time I saw Cody was on June 10, 2004, at our house. The last time I saw Tryone and Marilea was on July 4, 2004, and they were helping me with a garage sale. That's the last time I saw them alive. I never saw my daughter hit him or beat him. I never heard her cuss at him. I never heard her cuss at anyone. Tryone had the feeling that Cody resented her from the beginning, but she never treated Marilea or Cody any different."

Mitchell had few questions for Leona, but one touched on the fact that almost all of the photos showed Cody when other people were around. Mitchell contended that Cody smiled for the camera because he felt obligated to do so.

Steven Kennedy testified, "My little sister was Marilea. I knew Paul since about 2001. We would meet the family at the ranch and Cody and Marilea would be playing in the yard. We came by unannounced and I had the most contact with them in the last year and a half of Marilea's life. At the time I was doing work for a road crew on the highway, and lived in a mobile home not far from the Chavez Canyon Ranch gate. I never saw any physical abuse on Cody at that time. I didn't hear Paul or Tryone calling him names, or see any fights. I went up to see them a couple of times a month. Most of the time it was in the evening, and Cody and Marilea would be playing video games. Cody never expressed any problems to me.

"For the most part, Cody and Marilea had a brother/sister relationship. I took Marilea alone with me once in June of 2004. She didn't say anything bad about Cody. Paul and Tryone would brag about Marilea and Cody. Tryone was great. I never had any problems with her."

Kennedy had one more chilling thing to say on direct. "I went out shooting with Paul and Cody one time. We were all shooting into a bank. Cody was a pretty good shot."

Mitchell asked Kennedy on cross if he would take trips up to the Posey residence for only a little while during the day. Kennedy said he stayed there and visited for about an hour.

After Kennedy spoke, Mitchell wanted to get a few more defense witnesses on the stand. Grisham was adamant that Jim Forrester would not be one of them. Grisham said, "It's just a blatant attempt to get in something that the court has already ruled cannot be admitted. And as far as Dr. Susan Cave coming back on the stand to testify some more, she's already testified in this case.

Other than coming up and testifying that her diagnosis is right, and theirs is wrong, she has nothing to add."

Mitchell disagreed and said, "Dr. Cave is not to be re-called simply to state her opinion, but to talk about whether it's proper to diagnose a child with psychopathic traits. It's a direct rebuttal of what the two state's experts have said."

There was also an argument over whether Elvira Lerma and Mike Skeen would be given a chance to testify. Mitchell said, "Elvira Lerma is the ex-wife of Mr. Lerma, who worked on the farm near the Chavez Canyon Ranch. Her children were the children Cody was playing with in the summer of 2004 at a time when Cody said that his father came up and was upset that he was playing with Hispanic kids.

"She would testify that she herself observed an incident where Paul was on horseback, Cody rode up to him because he said he missed a ewe down by the river, and Paul roped him off his horse. She says Cody got back up on his horse and went after the ewe. Another time, she'll testify, Cody was too small and couldn't throw a hay bale up to where her husband was working. Paul went over to hit Cody with an open fist, and she was driving a pickup at the time, saw him, drove up fast, and Paul stopped.

"In another incident she describes a time with Tryone at school. Tryone and Marilea were watching Cody's actions throughout the day at school. The reason it comes in at this stage—it's new discovery. She rebuts a constant barrage of the state's psychologists and photos that Cody wasn't abused. She's an eyewitness to it. She also witnessed the racism involved.

"Mike Skeen witnessed an incident in June 2004 in which he drove by the field where his son, Clint Skeen, was working. Mike and his older son, Taylor, were present and they stopped to visit Clint. Paul, Marilea, and Cody drove up. The children went out to the field to work, and Mike and Paul were visiting. Mike inquired about the children, and Paul bragged to him that he had hit Cody and knocked him down in that field. Paul said, 'I saw Cody talking to the Lerma kids. I drove up and called Cody over.' Paul told Mr. Skeen that he hauled off and hit Cody with an open fist. Cody started to cry and Paul told Cody to stand up and take it like a man. And because he was still crying, Paul hit him again. This was a quote from Paul to Mike Skeen, who was a neighboring rancher.

"We would like to recall Slim Britton because of what happened yesterday when I was inquiring of Dr. Sosa about the horse. And Slim will testify that in fact Paul, on more than one occasion, was abusive to his livestock. What Paul, was doing was uncalled for. They (Slim and Pilo) tried to teach Cody to be gentler with horses. Dr. Sosa brought up where Cody spoke back to his father. These were two grown men who were trying to teach Cody a better way."

By this point Grisham was very passionate in her arguments against everything Mitchell had just said. She told Judge Counts, "Mr. Mitchell is trying three dead people who cannot speak for themselves. This is outrageous! They can't defend themselves! It's been on national TV, him saying all of this stuff. The state feels it has been severely circumscribed in its rebuttal. Mr. Mitchell had his chance to put on his case in chief, so that the state could rebut it. And by the way, Elvira Lerma was nowhere around during this alleged incident with her kids. It's not even close to proper surrebuttal. It's just saying, 'Oh, we found some new witnesses, so now we want to put them on. And we have some old witnesses with new stories.'

"If Slim Britton gets to come back on, then we can bring Steven Kennedy back and have him tell how Slim Britton was given a well-bred horse to take care of, and when it left him, it was thin, malnourished, and covered with welts. This is supposedly the wonderful rancher who tried to teach Cody the proper way to deal with horses?"

Judge Counts noted all the different issues at hand and said, "Well, the primary thrust of the Elvira Lerma situation was that Paul Posey was a racist. That is not relevant to the issues before us. That part is excluded. The part where she drove up and saw Paul with a closed fist, and somehow she may have stopped him from hitting Cody, that is excluded. The incident with the ewe, where Cody was supposedly roped and dragged some distance—I think this incident doesn't provide anything from the state's rebuttal, so it is excluded."

At this point Mitchell chimed in and said, "Your Honor, I seldom do this, but part of the problem here is Dr. Myers went through a list of abuse incidents and said that Cody was basically lying. One of the incidents was Cody being roped and dragged. We can't have the psychologists come in and say this child is lying and not be able to rebut that. There is, in essence, another witness out there who indicates that it did occur."

Grisham replied, "If Dr. Myers had sat up there and said Cody was lying, there would have been a mistrial. But that is not what Dr. Myers said."

Judge Counts responded, "I'll take this under advisement." Then he added, "As for Jim Forrester, based on everything the jury heard so far about abuse, going back to that incident is not particularly probative. State's objection to him testifying is sustained. Slim Britton is coming back. If Mr. Mitchell keeps his questions to a narrow issue, I'm not going to disallow that."

There were a few more questions coming from both the prosecution and defense, and then it was time for Judge Counts to rule on whether the jurors could decide if Cody's actions had been precipitated by a lifetime of abuse, and that he had a "reasonable" fear for his life on the morning of July 5, 2004. If the jurors found this to be true, then they had to acquit Cody of the charges.

Judge Counts also ruled, despite objections from the prosecution, that the jurors could find Cody guilty of lesser charges than first-degree murder, such as second-degree murder or manslaughter. Counts even agreed with the defense claim that "Marilea was a potential abettor of the parents," and the jurors could take that into consideration.

Closing arguments were basically a recitation of "facts" about Cody and the killings, as seen through the eyes of the prosecution and defense. Janice Schryer told the jurors, "Cody Posey and his defense team have tried to create tales of abuse to pile more and more manure atop of Paul, Tryone, and Marilea, and to negate any responsibility he might have had to take for his own actions."

Gary Mitchell asked the jurors, "How much do we ask of a fourteen-year-old child when none of us would have tolerated a tenth of that? We wouldn't be here if it weren't for abuse." Mitchell produced a hay hook and spoke of Paul jabbing it at Cody's groin. Mitchell said, "Do you think a single male in this courthouse would tolerate me coming up to him and putting this next to his testicles?" Speaking of the alleged sexual molestation on the night of July 4, 2004, by Paul and Tryone upon Cody, Mitchell said, "We go to a whole different world when we get to that conduct. How much can we ask of a child?"

In response, during her closing, Sandra Grisham proclaimed, "How much can we ask of a child? How about one simple thing? 'Thou shalt not kill'!"

When Grisham began to mock the alleged sexual assault—referring to using a blowtorch upon Cody to somehow make him have an erection—Corliss Clees stormed out of the courtroom.

Grisham projected photos of Paul, Tryone, and Marilea on the wall and said, "Your job as jurors is to judge the facts and then apply the law. The reason your job is not nearly as difficult is because Cody Posey gave you the facts. Who had the gun that morning? Who was armed? Who was lying in wait? Cody Posey. Every single act he took proves to you this was not some unconsidered, rash decision. He thought about it and he thought about what he had to do to get away with it. He was caught, but that does not mean he was not thinking."

The jury of seven women and five men deliberated for four hours on Monday, before going home, and returned on Tuesday morning for more deliberation. This went on all day, until 6:15 P.M., February 7, 2006, when the jurors announced they had a verdict. By 6:40 P.M., the gallery of the courtroom was packed to capacity. A double line of sheriff's deputies flanked the courtroom aisle, to quell any disturbances once the verdict was read. At 6:42 P.M., Cody Posey, wearing a dark suit and white shirt, entered the courtroom and sat down at the defense table next to his attorney Gary Mitchell. As soon as Judge Counts entered through a side door, Cody lowered his head and appeared to be praying.

At 6:44 P.M., the jury was ready to pronounce its verdict upon Cody, and their findings were handed over to Judge Counts, who read that the jury found Cody Posey guilty of voluntary manslaughter in the death of his father, Paul; guilty of second-degree murder in the death of his stepmother, Tryone, and guilty of first-degree murder in the death of his stepsister, Marilea Schmid. Cody lowered his head and began to cry as Mitchell embraced him. In the gallery Cody's aunt Corliss Clees dropped to the courtroom floor and began sobbing. An ambulance was called for.

After Judge Counts thanked the jurors for doing their civic duty in a difficult case, both District Attorney Scot Key and defense attorney Gary Mitchell spoke to reporters outside the courtroom. Key commended both Janice Schryer and Sandra Grisham, "for not succumbing to emotion, sympathy, or buying in to the abuse defense. It's hard to be happy about a verdict when three people lay dead in graves, and a fourteen-year-old boy admittedly killed them. We're satisfied with the judgment and consideration of an Otero County jury that thoughtfully looked at all of the massive amounts of evidence, to find the verdicts that they did."

Mitchell, on the other hand, said, "You wonder when we will start taking care of our children in New Mexico. You wonder how long we adults will continue to hold these children to much higher standards and expect them to suffer much more than what we would suffer as adults, and to tolerate much more than we would tolerate as adults. All the adults stood by and this happened and nobody stopped it. And so many knew. So now we adults put all the guilt on Cody Posey, and we, the state of New Mexico, now ask that we send him away. Forever."

Gary Mitchell had one shot to keep that from happening. Within thirty days there would be a sentencing hearing, and one man—and only one man—would hold Cody Posey's fate within his hands. That man was Judge Waylon Counts, and it would be the defense and prosecution that would have to convince him whether Cody was amenable to treatment as a child, or whether he should be put away in prison for the rest of his life.

Chapter 21

People for Cody

At the beginning of the trial, the courtroom gallery had been pretty evenly divided between family members supporting Cody, and those against him, but as news spread of the proceedings, the gallery became filled more and more by Cody supporters—ordinary people from the region who felt strongly enough about the case to disrupt their lives and attend the trial. Emanuella Grinberg, a reporter for Court TV, spoke with some of these people and they ranged from all age groups and social backgrounds. Janice Bolton, sixty-three, claimed to have been emotionally and physically abused by her own parents, and told Grinberg, "I think it's so sad what happened to that boy. I just hope the judge is lenient with him."

Shirley Godwin, a friend of Corliss Clees's, said, "My heart absolutely breaks for that boy. We knew it had to be bad, but I never dreamed they would go this far."

Slim Britton told Grinberg that from what he saw of

the abuse toward Cody, he was not surprised that the boy had killed his family. Britton said, "When the word 'manslaughter' came out (for Paul), I was a little relieved. But when 'murder' came out, I was crushed. I don't believe it was that."

Even Gary Mitchell weighed in, saying, "When you beat a dog again and again and again, do you really expect it's never going to bite back? This boy never had a chance. He never had a childhood. He never had a family to love him. This jury could have given that to him, and I now fear he'll never have any of that."

In point of fact, there were many jurors who, after the verdict, became pro-Cody. They felt they had been restrained in how they could vote by the structure of the law and jury instructions. Alternate juror Carol Gareau-Rasco, who was not part of the voting process about guilt, said that she felt the verdicts might have been different if the jurors had known what the sentences could be. But during the guilt phase they were not to take into account anything about sentencing. Gareau-Rasco said, "When it comes to the law and sentencing, I think there's a certain moral obligation that we have when deciding the verdicts." She added that she would have voted for manslaughter on all three counts. As the days progressed, six jurors would eventually sign their names to a letter to Judge Counts, asking for leniency for Cody.

After the verdicts came in, not everyone was sorry about the results. Verlin Posey told Grinberg, "I had the feeling that this might be the way it (the verdicts) went, because of all the lies by Cody. I'm not happy, but I can live with it. At least he's not free. Even if they're true, and my brother was abusive, then my brother was entitled to his day in court. Cody made himself jury and executioner that day."

Robert Williams, a defense contractor at nearby Holloman Air Force Base, said, "Cody had a choice that day, as all abused kids do. He could have risen above the situation and decided not to follow the same path, but he made the wrong decision."

For the most part, however, the tide of sentiment in the surrounding area was running very high for Cody. An organization was created called "People for Cody Posey," and it had a wide range of supporters, including Carol Gareau-Rasco; Pat Patterson, juror in the case; Cristol Williams, alternate juror; Bobbi Bartlett, who called herself a "legal eagle"; Gloria Garcia, of Alamogordo; Nancy Briggs, of Roswell; and Neanie Allee, who said she was from the "middle of nowhere." The advocates weren't just from New Mexico, or the West—there was Vickie Hatton, of Louisiana; Deborah Corsello, of New Jersey; Diane Troedson, of Minnesota; Stephanie Benson, of Illinois; Pastor Bob Marcaurelle, of South Carolina; and Laura Martin, of Ontario, Canada. There were advocates from as far away as the United Kingdom and South Africa. Cody Posey was starting to become a worldwide phenomenon.

Typical in some ways of all of them was Rosemarie Ferrara, who lived and worked in Alamogordo. In fact, the place where she worked was only a few doors down from the courthouse. Rosemarie had never been politically active, but the Cody Posey case had struck her to the core. She felt that she had to do something, even if she was just an ordinary citizen. She became active with "People for Cody Posey" and also wrote letters to the editor of the region's newspapers, was vocal around town of her support for Cody, and accessed the Internet for Cody.

Rosemarie said later, "Heartfelt is probably a good description of my thoughts with regard to this case. It actually hurts my heart to think of all this." Rosemarie responded to a "Letter to the Editor" submitted by a man named Pete Esquibel Jr., who believed Cody should be sentenced to life in prison as an adult.

Rosemarie replied, *If you had known that six or seven evaluations of Cody by experts showed no evidence of psychopathy, as alleged by the prosecution and that indeed the only one that did was brought forth by the prosecution, I assume you would have considered that there may be something odd going on. If you had read the online petition with over 3,000 signatures and responses from people across the globe, many who have described the terror and pain they endured at the hands of abusers, I imagine you would have been hesitant to describe the situation Cody was in as "killing someone when you are angry," and more likely describe it as an act of self-preservation and defense. I think if you had realized that many of the stories on that online petition were from people right here in your town, you would have been less callous in reducing torture and abuse to mere parental punishment. I am assuming you have led a perfectly normal life and that like me and so many others, your parents were mature adults that desired to discipline their children instead of destroying them, and that you were not a victim of the kind of abuse in so many of the hundreds of letters Judge Counts has received."*

An e-mail message by Rosemarie related:

Imagine being hit over and over again with rocks the size of a softball or being struck by hay bales in the back of the head and getting a black eye as a result of being hit with a closed fist. What does it feel like to get your fingers squeezed together with a set of pliers? Picture getting hit with a 2x4, hit with a lariat, stuck with a hay hook on your hand cutting it open, and being threatened with the use of it on your genitals. Imagine being roped and dragged or experiencing water and food deprivation. Imagine all of these things happening not to you, but to your ten to fourteen year old son or brother.

Do you wonder how you might try to get out of it if you know your abuser was your father, that you were stranded on a secluded ranch, that the people you thought could help you proved over and over again that it was "none of their business" how people disciplined their kids. Do you think you might feel that even if you were able to get help that the beatings you received would increase if you got sent back to the same home?

I am going way out on a limb sending this e-mail to hundreds of people who may never even speak to me again because of it, but I am willing to take that risk. Some of you may be rolling your eyes because you were included in the petition request that I sent you the other day. If someone had the chance to save your child's life and yet walked away, how would you feel? Yes, for those of you who are saying that the stepsister involved did not have anyone helping her, I am not going to argue with you. But none of this would have occurred if this boy had not experienced the abuse and torture at the hand of Delbert Paul Posey. Cody did try to go the right routes. He did try to get help from the police, teachers, CYFD, etc. A child's life is at stake here, while some who don't know the details may pass judgement right away. If I change the opinions of even a few, it will be worth it. No matter how you feel about the case, please consider trying to help get him sentenced as a child not an adult. He was fourteen years old and acted out of desperation in this situation. He needs to be able to get help, not more abuse in our adult prison system.

Please read and sign the online petition, "Mercy for Cody Posey." In the last few days, this petition has been signed by over 900 people across the world, and many of them right here in Alamogordo. Again, I am not afraid of the backlash I may receive if there is someway I can help.

Rosemarie did get backlash from some people. A woman named Liz wrote an angry e-mail to her, stating, The boy should get the death penalty just like the three other people he murdered! Let me know what I need to do to cancel my membership with [an organization with which Rosemarie was affiliated].

Rosemarie was civil and polite in her letters and opinions, compared to the raucous invectives written by others in the area. One of the most outspoken and scathing was routinely on the Mountain Mail Country Web site. Michael Morris, who ran a daily column on the trial while it was in session, was harsh in his criticisms of Sandra Grisham, Dr. Wade Myers and Dr. Juan Sosa. About Janice Schryer, he wrote, Whoever first said, "Don't come to a battle of wits unarmed," must have known 12th District prosecutor Janice B. Schryer. He compared her style in court to that of a cartoon character— Scooby-Doo. He called the team of Schryer and Grisham "the bitter, ugly gals." Of Dr. Myers he wrote: Grisham is trying hard to keep her witness from looking like the shill liar and fraud I told you he was weeks ago. Myers does not treat kids—he helps imprison them. His fame is as a shrink who has sent more insane and retarded people to execution than any other. Morris called Myers a "two-bit-renta-doc."

Morris saved his real anger and contempt for Dr. Juan Sosa. Morris wrote, If you thought Juan Sosa was a reprehensible individual the last time we visited him, brother, are you in for a dose now. Morris described Sosa as "Juan Mengele," "incompetent," "with the insane ravings of a madman." Morris even cooked up a scathingly clever photo of Dr. Sosa, holding a sign that read, WILL TESTIFY FOR FOOD.

There were plenty of others in the area who also demonized Grisham, Myers, and Sosa as the unholy trio. But there was also a "silent" community on the other side of the issue. They may not have been a "silent majority," but they were out there in the counties of Lincoln, Otero, and Chaves. A reporter noted that these people didn't honk their horns for Cody, didn't hold signs and walk around the courthouse, and didn't sign petitions, but they were hoping that Cody Posey would be sentenced as an adult by Judge Waylon Counts.

Cody's supporters, however, were much more vocal and active, and there were plenty of them in the area. On February 19, 2006, they ran a full-page ad in the *Alamogordo Daily News,* seeking mercy and leniency for Cody. One petition by now had nearly two thousand names upon it, with people from forty-seven different states, Canada, Germany, Poland, France, Japan, Sweden, and Australia. Not only petitions were being signed, but Gary Mitchell had received over three hundred letters of support from well-wishers. Mitchell said, "This is shocking—the number of letters we've received from people who were also abused is incredible. They say, 'There but for the grace of God, go I.'"

One of the most vocal persons now was former trial

juror Norman Patterson, of Mayhill, New Mexico. He told reporters, "I sincerely believe that we twelve jurors, indeed the entire system, failed young Cody Posey. While three or four of us on that jury fought hard for less stringent verdicts on the several counts, we were successful only in defeating more than the first-degree murder verdict. We were nevertheless unhappy with the final outcome that we helped to engineer."

Patterson went before television cameras and said that the final verdicts about guilt had been a compromise between jurors who wanted manslaughter on all counts, and those who wanted first-degree murder on all counts. He also spoke of learning new details about the way Cody had been treated, after jury duty, and he felt that these details only strengthened his position. Patterson said, "No one seriously doubted the abuse. There was just too much testimony by too many credible witnesses. But other jurors felt that no matter how much abuse, it did not justify murder, especially of Marilea."

By this time Rosemarie Ferrara had sent more than seven hundred e-mails to Alamogordo area residents in support of Cody. She said, "I just hope there is something good that will come for his life, and that he can live somewhat normally. It's like a bad movie, what happened to him. You couldn't write a worse script."

The Reverend Bruce Hausfeld, pastor of the Immaculate Conception Catholic Church, also was seeking signatures on a petition he intended to pass on to Judge Counts. Hausfeld said that he understood that Sandra Grisham had uttered the biblical passage during trial: "Thou shalt not kill." To this, Reverend Hausfeld said, "God tells us to respect all human life, and most people do unless they've been so abused or their life has been so horrendous they lose the freedom to think straight.

And at fourteen years old, who knows what any one of us would do if we were in his shoes?"

Gloria Garcia, of Alamogordo, planned a candlelight vigil in front of the courthouse for Cody on Sunday, February 19, 2006, on the evening before the sentencing phase began on Monday, February 20. She invited everyone in the area to come, hold a candle, and support Cody. Garcia told reporters, "I'm not saying that it's okay to kill anybody. I'm saying Cody has had such a sad first sixteen years of his life and that I would like him to start rebuilding his life with our love and support. If we can give Cody one little stick in building his life back up, it's worth it."

When the sun went down on New York Avenue, near the courthouse, on February 19, ordinary citizens of the area gathered with candles in their hands in front of the courthouse. They came from all walks of life—clerks, housewives, ranch hands, farmers, schoolteachers, children. There was no shouting or profanity, no picketing and yelling. It was all very still, serene, and otherworldly—hundreds of small candles burning in the darkness in Otero County.

Chapter 22

Killer or Victim?

The gallery was filled to capacity as the sentencing phase hearings began for Cody Posey on February 20, 2006. Among the gathered public, sitting on the left side of the court gallery, were Pat and Leona Basham, Tryone's dad and mom, and Verlin Posey and his family. On the right side of the gallery, sitting behind Cody and Gary Mitchell, were Corliss Clees, Rosemarie Ferrara, and even former juror Norman Patterson.

Before arguments for and against Cody being sentenced to a life in prison, Gary Mitchell brought forth a motion to Judge Counts saying that the Children's Code of New Mexico was illegal, because it did not give a defendant due process. Mitchell said that an adult standard was applied to children in New Mexico, and it created an impossible task for jurors and judges in the dispensing of justice. Jurors had to take certain steps, because they had been instructed by the judge to do so, and this created an "insurmountable task" for a defense attorney, in his opinion. As case law, Mitchell cited *Apprendi* v. *United States Supreme Court,* which dealt with the issues he was talking about.

Mitchell said, "We are still a state within the Union, and the New Mexico Children's Code is in violation of the Fourteenth Amendment. How can I have defended him when I don't know what standard to use? The whole system is a bizarre way to treat children. Because there is a lack of resources to treat children in New Mexico, children are treated poorly in the judicial system. Cody Posey was deprived of due process because the state legislature has denied adequate funding for children's facilities."

Mitchell contended it was a catch-22 situation for his client. Because the legislature would not fund adequate children's facilities, Sandra Grisham was arguing there was not a place to send Cody, except to prison, because there was no place for him to go to receive adequate supervision and psychiatric help as a child.

Grisham, on the other hand, argued that accountability—not competency—was now the issue. She said that only once before in her years of practice had she asked that a child be sentenced as an adult. The seriousness of three murders put Cody into that category in her line of reasoning, and she said that Cody should not be placed in a facility with other children—for their own safety. "State facilities for children cannot hold cases like Cody's. He is a danger to those around him."

Judge Counts took these arguments into his decision, and said, "The appellate court's guidance is that *Apprendi* does not apply here. My obligation as district judge is to comply with the appeals court guidelines. This is not a due process issue." He denied Mitchell's motion to have the jurors' decision thrown out. Sentencing arguments would proceed, and everyone who had testified would now have the job of trying to sway Judge Counts's final decision to their point of view.

Grisham started out by noting the seriousness of the crimes and said that if Cody were an adult, he would be facing the death penalty for the murder of Marilea alone. Grisham said, "I have rarely seen so much evidence in a case showing guilt." She noted that Cody did have a mitigating factor of not having done previous crimes, but the murder of three people far outweighed that factor. She said that a key factor in sentencing should be about Cody's psychopathic traits, as pointed out by Dr. Myers. She noted, "No one knows how to treat psychopathic traits. Cody has shown over and over that he is not treatable. There is no place on this planet where they treat psychopathy. Giving Cody Posey freedom would be a risk to public safety."

Grisham told the jurors that Cody took the snake shot cartridges out of Marilea's pistol and replaced them with regular ammunition. All of his actions showed premeditation, including lying in wait, shooting them all in the head to make sure they were dead, and shooting Tryone and Marilea twice. Grisham also noted that Cody reloaded the weapon at some point and she asked, "Do we have any doubt what would have happened if the Donaldsons had returned to the scene?"

Grisham added that Cody had stolen a pickup truck and drove some distance before throwing away the murder weapon. He also turned off an irrigation pump so that water wouldn't flood a field and show that something was wrong with the Posey family. After that he played basketball with his friends, smoked dope, and showed no remorse for his actions. She even said that after eighteen months of treatment at Sequoyah, he still got into fights and pretended to cock a pistol and shoot another boy there. Grisham ended her comments by saying, "There are just some kids we can't fix. Our only alternative is to keep society safe."

Mitchell on the other hand told the jury, "Thank God most people don't agree with Ms. Grisham." He noted that Sequoyah said that Cody was doing well in their facility and they would welcome him back. Then he added that everyone knew what would happen to Cody if he was sentenced to an adult prison. Mitchell said that Cody had only gotten into fights when picked on by others at the juvenile facility in Springer, New Mexico. He would not allow himself to be bullied or raped.

Mitchell explained that the Springer facility was not able to protect children, but that Sequoyah was. It specialized in helping violent and disruptive children. And once again Mitchell reiterated that a host of witnesses had agreed that Cody had been abused as a child, and "you cannot take the abuse factor out of this case. He suffers from post-traumatic stress disorder, and not psychopathy. There is no public outcry that they are in danger from Cody. I've received hundreds of letters from people who say they would adopt Cody. How much more has to go on in his life before he gets the rights of other children?"

As a first witness in the sentencing phase, Grisham called Verlin Posey. Verlin looked directly at Cody and proclaimed that his father, Paul Posey, was a good man. He was a man who spoke the truth, a man who kept his promises. He was a man who fought for what he believed, and did what he thought was right. Paul was a man who only wanted what was best for his son, who believed that Cody could achieve a great deal, and hoped that he would find success and prosperity. Instead, Verlin noted, Cody failed to live up to his father's standards and expectations, engaging in drug use. If Paul had punished Cody for his behavior, it was only in an attempt to shake off his bad habits. She couldn't accept Cody's justifications for his crimes, and suggested that it was Cody's weakness, and not Paul's severity, that was responsible for Cody's characterization of Paul's discipline as "abuse." Verlin also pointed out that she suspected the motivation behind Cody's murder of Marilea was to remove a potential witness who could refute Cody's tales of abuse. She said she wished to be able to forgive him one day, but still asked the judge to impose the maximum sentence on her nephew.

Shanda Posey was next, and she was just as adamant in her disgust at what Cody had done. Although she granted that Cody's father was not a perfect man, he was not a monster. He did not deserve to be a victim of his son's perceived sense of vigilante justice. Cody had a large and loving support system available to him, and she wondered why he had not gone to them first, before resorting to his horrible crime. Shanda told Cody that he lived in a family full of love, and that she would have helped her nephew if she believed he had been abused, but that she just did not believe that defense. She called him a liar, then told Cody's lawyer that Paul and Tryone were within their rights to punish their son when he strayed from the correct path. Underage sex and drug use were offenses that good parents could simply not permit. She concluded by telling Cody that he had committed a terrible crime, and robbed the world of good people. Paul Posey was more than just Cody's father—he was a brother, a veteran, a Christian, and a host of other things. He was a noble man who would have sacrificed everything for his family. Tryone was a woman who went to great lengths to connect with Cody, though her efforts were in vain. Marilea was a girl just beginning her life, a young woman who should have been out in the world, experiencing the same joys and challenges her friends still had to look forward to. Now, she would never have those opportunities. She implored the judge to give Cody the maximum sentence.

Chris Clements, who was a friend of Paul Posey, testified that the fact that the murders occurred on Sam Donaldson's ranch made the case more sensationalistic. He spoke of a case in 1986 where a boy had killed his entire family on a ranch, and it did not garner national attention. Clements said the fact that Court TV had been covering Cody's case live every day had added to its sensational nature.

Clements claimed that the most damaging evidence during the trial was Cody's own confession in the days after the murders. Clements made the point that he and Paul Posey had grown up together, that both their parents had worked on ranches when they were growing up, that they had been raised in similar ways, and that they had been disciplined in their upbringing, but not abused. Clements said that any measures Paul used to discipline Cody were done to prevent his son from ending up like some kids he had known growing up, kids who got into a lot of trouble. He concluded that American culture had developed to the point where people were more likely to blame bad actions, not on those who had committed them, but on the forces that had contributed to that person's development, and that as a result, "people are not held accountable for their actions."

Leona Basham said "On July 15, 2004, Cody Posey murdered three people, not in self-defense, but in a cold-blooded murder. Not a single one of them threatened his life. He had not sought help from anyone. My life will never be the same again.

"Cody Posey will commit murder again. Cody deserves no less than the maximum sentence."

Pat Basham had to use an oxygen mask throughout much of the trial, and the sentencing phrase was no exception. He started out by saying "Today I will not speak of the hurt, anguish, sadness, despair, and anger I feel at the loss of my only daughter, son-in-law, or my only granddaughter. Those are emotions that should not be imposed on anyone, ever." He went on to say that he would not speak about why Cody was the person he became, nor would he discuss the things he had done. According to Basham, those things had been "itemized, contested, analyzed, debated, and recorded."

Basham added that they weren't there to speak of Cody's guilt, because that had already been decided on by a jury. The jurors had found him to be a "liar, thief, drug user and murderer." They also, according to Basham, found that Cody could not control his actions when he was upset. Basham declared that Cody lied to family members, law enforcement personnel, school teachers, and possibly even to his own defense counsel.

As far as abuse went, Basham said that it was Cody who inflicted that upon Marilea when he killed her loved ones on the ranch, and then "committed the ultimate physical abuse, he deliberately killed her." Basham said Cody had done that to keep Marilea from recounting what she saw on the morning of July 5, 2004 and to keep her from telling the truth about his living conditions and the way he was treated fairly by Paul and Tryone.

Basham claimed that Cody would kill again if it suited his purpose, and his violent outbursts while incarcerated were proof. Basham said that both inmates and guards could testify to Cody lashing out if he did not get his way. Cody's predilection to violence had been seen numerous times during his altercations while in custody, suggesting that Cody's problems were not with his parents, but with his own violent nature. At times Cody had to be restrained in separate quarters from the other inmates because he couldn't control his actions.

Basham noted that Cody was trying to hide behind a smoke screen of his young age to conceal his true nature. To some degree that had worked, according to Basham, especially with the media. And Basham declared, "Cody Posey is a time bomb, waiting to go off." Basham asked if society wanted their sons working next to Cody, their children and grandchildren exposed to him, or even the possibility of one of their daughters marrying him. Basham said that if Cody decided one day that he'd had enough of a certain situation, he would kill again. In fact, Basham used one of Cody's own sentences to the investigators when he was interviewed in August 2004—"When I had all I could take, I thought, I might as well just kill them all."

Basham ended his comments by stating "Cody Posey did the unthinkable. He took the lives of three people, deliberately, brutally, and then celebrated his actions by proclaiming them 'the happiest three days of my life.' I beseech this court, do not turn this man loose on the world. Impose imprisonment for the maximum length of time the law allows."

Cody's cousin Clayton Posey was no more sympathetic of Cody's plea for leniency than Pat Basham was. He stated that he didn't believe Cody was abused, and that almost everything Cody had said was fabricated. He pointed out that both he and Cody were punished for doing wrong, and praised when they performed well. Cody's father provided him with every game or toy he could possibly have wanted—he was not deprived of anything. He concluded by telling the court that he wouldn't want to live down the street from Cody Posey.

Charlene Cooper had been Marilea's teacher at one time, and she mostly spoke about her. Cooper spoke very positively about Marilea, that she was a kind, considerate, and compassionate person who went out of her way for other people. She was a special person. Marilea was proud to be able to contribute to her family, and to earn her own keep. She wasn't afraid of hard work, and was tremendously proud that she was able to purchase her own boots with the money she earned through her labors. She said that Marilea had defended and stuck up for Cody. When Marilea saw that Cody was struggling in school, she didn't abandon him or take joy in his difficulty, but instead attempted to see if he could have benefited from a tutor and some help. She concluded by saying, "Cody, you can't seem to accept your own mistakes."

After family members and Charlene Cooper, Dr. Juan Sosa had his say once more, and once again he banged home the point that he believed Cody had psychopathic tendencies. Dr. Sosa said, "We don't know how to treat psychopathy. It is not like a mental disorder. There are no drugs for it, and it doesn't happen overnight. Cody shows those signs—lying, exaggeration, lack of emotion, use of drugs, and casual impersonal sex."

As far as lying and exaggeration went, Sosa claimed that Cody said he had been a member of the West Side Gang. Cody had told that to others at the Sequoyah facility, but it wasn't true.

"Cody has a lack of empathy. He has attempted to manipulate the staff at Sequoyah. If left there, he might taint the other children. Normally, abused children don't kill numerous people." Then Sosa told of an incident where he had treated a boy who had been abused by his father. The boy killed his father, but did not kill his mother or the rest of the family. The boy had said, "I was protecting them from my father. I can't believe I did it now." Sosa claimed that Cody, on the other hand, had no remorse about what he had done. He still blamed the others for what had happened.

Sosa spoke about a book, *Without Conscience,* and said that Cody displayed many of the traits portrayed in the book. "Cody fails to show emotion, even though he's quite verbal. For children like this, there can be a perfect parent, but it doesn't matter because it is the makeup of the child. I think Cody's chances of changing are slim to none. Kids with psychopathy are four times more likely to commit a crime once again."

Sosa was not just making a statement, he was on the stand testifying, and Mitchell had his chance with a cross-examination. If Mitchell had been skeptical of Dr. Sosa's statements before, it was nothing compared to his contempt now. Sosa had spoken of psychopathic traits showing up in some children as early as five years old.

Mitchell said with disdain, "Doctor, should we just lock up five-year-olds and throw away the key?"

Sosa seemed to dance around on this and answered, "We're not sure about if there is psychopathy by the age of five."

"So when do you give up on these kids?"

"We never give up."

"Oh, that's what we're doing here today!"

On other questions Sosa said that some kids were diagnosed incorrectly initially. He may have been thinking of Dr. Johnson's evaluation, but Mitchell jumped on this. "You have seen the reports about Sequoyah. Do you think the psyches there are doing well?"

Sosa agreed that they were.

"Would you be surprised to learn that they would like to have him back?"

It was more of a rhetorical question than one that called for an answer.

Then Mitchell slammed Dr. Sosa's ethics, saying that psychiatrists did not diagnose anyone as a psychopath before the age of eighteen. "Even the New Mexico codes say that no tests on that score should be done and used in court. Children have many different traits, because they are children."

Sosa replied, "We look at Cody with three murders, and the future for him does not look good. Psychopaths know how to play the game and look normal. My clinical impression is, he is not amenable to treatment."

During a break Mitchell handed four notebooks of letters to the judge. These were e-mails in support of Cody from around the world. Grisham said these letters were of no value, because they were like letters to the editor, but Judge Counts said he would read them, anyway.

* * *

As soon as Jim Forrester began speaking, Grisham objected that he was going to bring up the topic of the murder/suicide of Paul and Verlin's parents. Judge Counts had Grisham and Mitchell approach, and there was a long discussion on this matter. Finally it was agreed upon that Forrester would not just speak, but had to be sworn in as a regular witness who could be cross-examined by Grisham.

Forrester admitted that he was a friend of Sandy Posey Schmid's, and he had known Paul and Verlin for many years. According to Forrester, he and another man had gone to see Paul and Carla one morning when Cody was around two years old. Cody was fooling around, and Forrester claimed Paul had gotten so angry at him, that he threw Cody ten feet across the room onto a couch.

"Cody was screaming and crying, and urine and feces were coming out of his diapers. Me and the other guy got the kid out of the house. Months later, Paul and Sandy got together and lived in East Grand Plains. I used to go over on Sunday mornings just to check up on Cody. I saw hundreds of instances of abuse by Paul on Cody. He dumped hay all over him, hit him with bailing wire, and threw him up against a fence. I'd say, 'Hey, knock that crap off!' And Paul would say, 'Shut up, that's my kid!'

"I believe a person shouldn't be spoken of badly when he's dead—but Paul was an awful person. I used to be a counselor. Cody fought to preserve his life."

* * *

Grisham on cross said, "You were a counselor, but didn't report any of the alleged abuse?"

Forrester answered, "Sandy talked me out of it."

"You know you should have done something about it, if it happened, but you didn't tell the police. You saw the child up to the age of eleven years old, and you let Paul do these things hundreds of times?"

"I'd say, 'Paul, come on.' And get between him and Cody."

"You never called the authorities, did you?"

"No, ma'am," Forrester replied.

The next witness on the stand was Dr. Henry Gardner, an Albuquerque psychologist. Gardner had worked at the Sequoyah facility for fourteen years and now was a director there. He had a Ph.D. from Penn State, had worked at a children's psychiatric hospital, and the New Mexico Department of Health. Gardner said that the purpose of Sequoyah Adolescent Treatment Center was to treat mentally disturbed children who were too violent for a regular hospital. Sequoyah was constantly in contact with the juvenile justice system and was a place that served the protection of the community, as well as protection of the boys.

Gardner stated "When a kid first goes in, each child gets a unique assessment, and then we develop a treatment plan. Release factor for a child from Sequoyah depends upon the progress of the child and guidelines from the juvenile criminal system. CYFD gets reports from Sequoyah on a regular basis, and there is special education there for the boys and group services."

Mitchell wanted to know what the success rate was for Sequoyah in returning boys to the community. Gardner said that it was 92 percent. Asked if Cody Posey could be treated and returned to society, Gardner said yes.

Grisham on cross wanted to know how much Sequoyah received in compensation for having Cody there. Gardner said that it was $540 a day. Grisham asked if Cody showed psychopathic traits, and Gardner said that Cody didn't.

Grisham: But an area of concern is antisocial personality disorder?
Gardner: Yes, that can be.
Grisham: Can a probation officer see all the records on a child?
Gardner: Not if the child doesn't sign a consent form.

The next witness, also from Sequoyah, was Dr. Robert Buser. He was the head psychiatrist there and had a case load of eighteen to thirty-six boys at Sequoyah, depending on the fluctuation of the amount of boys in the facility. Sequoyah never took in more than thirty-six boys at a time, Buser had worked there for ten years by 2006, and had studied at the University of New Mexico School of Medicine.

Buser said, "We treat kids at Sequoyah who have a mental illness and a propensity for a history of violence. We thoroughly review their cases, and sometimes we even have to teach boys to brush their teeth, eat properly, et cetera. I've treated vets from World War One,

World War Two, Korea, Vietnam, and Kuwait for post-traumatic stress disorder.

"I read the reports and met Cody. It was not hard to see that he was suffering from PTSD. One of the main factors was surviving the death of his mother in the car accident. He actually witnessed his mom's death. Cody has described the wreck in very graphic terms. His nerves were already on edge, and the wreck exacerbated them."

Buser said that Cody showed no signs of psychopathic traits at Sequoyah, and he had no record of anti-social behavior. "Cody did not have an extensive history of lawbreaking. He didn't have a rap sheet, whereas some boys have pages of documents concerning criminality. His was a specific event. He had a single horrific event triggered by rage and adrenaline. Cody showed me the burn marks on his arm. That event pushed him over the edge.

"I've gotten to know Cody over five months. I took Cody off medication for PTSD, and noticed that there was then a problem. Cody would have a spooked look, a startled look about him. Like a deer in the headlights. That is consistent with PTSD. He was prone to hyper-vigilance and a psychic numbness. With PTSD it's like a false fire-alarm going off. He's spent his whole life looking over his shoulder. When he was off his PTSD meds, he became extremely anxious, had sleep problems, and irritability. Some boys when taken off meds become psychotic in four to five days. This did not happen with Cody."

Mitchell wanted to know if PTSD was treatable, and Gardner said that it was very treatable.

"I believe the murders were a brief psychotic episode. We deal with a rough bunch of guys at Sequoyah, and some are really violent. Cody has not been on my radar for that. He gets along fine with others, and is doing well in school. There is no bullying of the other kids. He is not a bully, though he may have been bullied."

Mitchell asked what Dr. Buser thought should happen to Cody, and Buser said, "I believe he should come back to Sequoyah."

Mitchell wanted to know if Buser thought Cody was amenable to treatment.

At that point someone in the gallery said, "Yes!"

Judge Counts was furious. He thundered, "I'm not going to have it! Who said that?"

A bailiff pointed at a woman in the gallery.

Judge Counts said, "I want her out of here now!"

The bailiff signaled to the woman to stand up, and he escorted her out of the courtroom.

After the outburst Mitchell asked, "Can we treat Cody in the state of New Mexico?"

Buser's answer was "Yes. Cody is very treatable in a facility like Sequoyah. I have a low expectation that Cody will ever reoffend. With a lot of boys, you wonder if they are going to still be alive by the age of twenty. I've found Cody to be engaging, and I never sensed that he was trying to con me. He's been very consistent in telling the same stories. He wasn't trying to pull a fast one on me. Sequoyah is a safe place for the boys. For many it is the safest place they've ever been in their lives."

Grisham on cross said, "It states in a report, 'Cody Posey has an inability to recognize reality.' What have you seen that possibly disrupts his judgment today?"

Buser said that PTSD clouded Cody's judgment.

Grisham stated that not one other psychiatrist wrote

that Cody was suffering at present from PTSD, not even Johnson or Cave. Buser seemed to tap-dance around this issue and never answered yes or no as to whether he was the only one who diagnosed Cody with PTSD.

The arguments went back and forth and were contentious and lengthy. There was even a disagreement about what the DSM-IV said about certain issues. Grisham got so fed up with Buser that she told Judge Counts, "The doctor will not answer my question directly!"

Judge Counts told Buser, "I want you to be responsive."

Grisham wanted to know why Cody was still so unemotional after all the months of therapy since 2004. She said, "Would Cody be expected to change his demeanor while listening to his grandfather, aunt, and uncle at court?"

Mitchell objected and said, "We tell Cody to be quiet in here."

Judge Counts replied, "It goes to relevance. Overruled."

Even on this, Buser remained evasive at best, and the question was not quite addressed.

Grisham wanted to know how long it could be expected that Cody would retain his unemotional aspect, and Buser said that couldn't be answered with certainty.

"So how long would we need to keep Cody in Sequoyah to get rid of his problems and make him safe for society?"

"I don't know," Buser answered.

Grisham got into Cody's penchant for lying, at least according to her. She said that Cody had claimed he was a bareback-riding champ in the Texas Hall of Fame, but no one could be inducted into that Hall of Fame until they were fifteen years old, and by that time Cody was already incarcerated. Cody said he was a member of the West Side Gang, which wasn't true, and he had been in a gifted program at school, which was not the case.

Mitchell on redirect asked, "If Cody remains in Sequoyah, can he improve?"

Buser said, "It is important that he continue at Sequoyah. Cody has hopes for something better in life. He wants to make changes in his life."

On recross Grisham had more of a statement than a question. She said, "Cody made changes in his life on July 5, 2004!" There was no response to that.

The next witness was Phyllis Denton, who was director of social services at Sequoyah. She spoke of activities for the boys throughout most of the day at the Sequoyah facility and some quiet time as well. It was a very structured day and had little space for them to get into trouble. Denton knew Cody and said, "He needs to deal with the death of his mother. The enormity of what happened there. He needs to deal with that on an emotional level.

"Cody is intelligent, eager to work, and has good feedback in group discussions. I believe that going through the process will bring out a lot of issues that he hasn't confronted, and he is willing to do so. He was in a family issues group where the boys have to talk about their experiences. Cody did very well at Sequoyah and was obviously relieved to be out of detention center. He is polite, completes tasks, works well with the staff, and gets along well with the other boys. He's a good role model for the other boys.

"If he stays in Sequoyah, his family members (such as Corliss Clees) can visit him there. It's a secure facility and the facility staff make sure the boys don't leave. Sequoyah has really been a blessing for the children of New Mexico."

Grisham said, "Sequoyah is not a place where kids go to live?"

Denton admitted that most boys were there for about five months, and Cody had already been there for eighteen months.

It was time for another family member to take the stand—Marilea's father, Jacob Schmid. Interestingly enough, Jake was sympathetic to Cody's cause, even though Cody had killed Marilea. Jake said, "I'm thoroughly convinced, and have seen with my own eyes, that Paul and Tryone abused Cody. I believe Paul had sexual relations with my daughter, and Tryone was aware of it. If I had known it at the time, I would have killed Paul and Tryone myself.

"If you give us a chance, we will help this boy. I give you my word on that. He will never be a threat to society."

Right after Jake Schmid, Dr. Johnson was back on the stand, and in some respects she was the most important person who would take the stand during the sentencing phase. Much of what the other psychiatrists—both for the defense and prosecution—based their initial findings on were Dr. Johnson's reports. Johnson also did one very important thing the others had not done. She didn't address Cody or the family members in the gallery; instead, she addressed her answers to Judge

Waylon Counts, who sat only a few feet away from her. She realized very well that it was Judge Counts, and no one else, who now held Cody Posey's fate within his hands.

Mitchell, right off the bat, asked, "Is Cody amenable to treatment in the state of New Mexico?"

Johnson answered, "Cody is mature and there is little likelihood that the public will need protection from him. His risk level is low to moderate. Sequoyah is the best place in New Mexico for Cody. He doesn't have a conduct disorder and he is not antisocial."

Asked about how kids who had killed their parents did in a national study, Johnson said they did much better than kids who had killed nonfamily. The reoffending rate was much lower for the former category of children. "I think Cody is much more prepared now, than he was, for whatever may come his way. He desires to deal with these issues."

Mitchell wanted to know about Cody's flat aspect, and Johnson said, "He's emotionally controlled still. And he has to sit here in court and be controlled. I have seen remorse from Cody."

During a break the question came up to Judge Counts about all the letters from people he was going to have to read as to their input about Cody Posey. Counts told Mitchell and Grisham in an only half-joking manner, "My cardiologist is probably going to be concerned about how much salt I'm going to have to take with those letters."

When court resumed, Mary Harrington said, "Years of abuse by his father and stepmother drove Cody to do this. I sometimes had Marilea over, and when she was

there, Cody would hardly speak. At other times Paul
would give Cody dirty looks and Cody would drop his
head. At one point Tryone told me that my daughter
should never call Marilea again. Cody never had a time
to grieve for his mother. Paul wouldn't let him."

Harrington turned directly toward Judge Counts and
said, "Find it in your heart to sentence Cody as a juvenile. I don't think he planned to shoot Marilea. I don't
think it was first-degree murder. I think he didn't know
what he was doing when he shot them."

Clayton Schmid, Marilea's cousin, said, "I grew up
with Marilea and we were like brother and sister. Way
back when I was young, Cody and I played basketball,
and he told me about how his father slapped him. Please
help him as a child. Give him the help he needs as a
child."

Sherry Gensler spoke directly to Cody. She said, "We
made some bad choices in your family. I asked about
you every chance I got. I called Hondo School and we
tried everything to be able to see you. I looked for you
in Capitan School and in Ruidoso. No one should say
you weren't abused. You were an abused young boy.
Tryone made some bad choices. She should not have
used you as a laborer and a sex toy.

"The DA is sending out a statement to our children
that they cannot be helped. I love you Cody, and my
family loves you. You are welcome at our door anytime.
I am not afraid of you."

Corliss Clees told Judge Counts, "You have the ability to hold life in your hands. I took and raised Cody as

a mother. This boy has been through so much. They want to crucify him as an adult. I respect my state and love my state, but I'm ashamed by what I've seen in this courtroom. I will stand by Cody step by step. Paul was a coward as a father and a man.

"When Cody lost Carla, it tore him apart. He never got to grieve for Carla. Cody is not a throwaway boy. He has my blood in him. I am his family. He is salvageable and he needs to be helped. If he goes to prison, you will only hand him over to monsters, [after] the monstrous parents he had. I will use my every breath to save that child. He doesn't deserve any more prison time, and he doesn't deserve any more hell."

After the lunch break Grisham had Dr. Myers on the stand once again. Myers said, "Cody is aggressive to people and has a long history of lying." Then Myers spoke of all the steps Cody had taken to shoot Tryone first so she couldn't call 911, and then the attempted cover-up after the murders. Myers said, "He didn't just snap. Snapping is nonthinking behavior. Cody has had a lack of remorse. He still blames others and talks of unfair treatment by the guards where he was incarcerated. There was the incident at Sequoyah, where someone didn't want to be on Cody's team, so he pretended to cock a pistol and shoot it at him. I don't see humor in that, after what he did. Psychopathy is a process and can grow over time. All we can do now is look at the risk factors."

Mitchell was not a fan of Dr. Myers, and once again referred to him as "Doc." When Myers spoke about

Cody fighting while incarcerated, Mitchell said that Cody had been a target for other boys as soon as he walked through the doors. "Others would pick on him to gain status, especially gang members." Even Myers had to admit that Cody never had any problems at Capitan High School, nor had he ever been arrested for anything during his childhood—besides the murders. And Mitchell was fed up with Dr. Myers saying Cody had "psychopathic" traits.

Myers replied, "I've never called him a psychopath."

Mitchell sneered, "Well, if I went outside and it was raining, I might not call it a 'thunderstorm,' but whatever you call it, it *is* a thunderstorm." Mitchell was getting at the fact that even though Dr. Myers wouldn't call Cody a "psychopath" directly, he implied that he was, on numerous occasions.

Dr. Myers was batted back and forth between Mitchell and Grisham once again. Grisham asked him, "Say Cody behaves perfectly at Sequoyah—would that make him safe?"

Myers answered, "Cody told me that he was on his best behavior at Sequoyah because it would reflect well at his trial."

Myers also said that Cody suffered from narcissism and that "he thinks he's the answer man at Sequoyah. There was a note by a staff member, 'Cody tries to be manipulative of the entire staff.'"

Myers quoted from a book that dealt with psychopathy and said, "There could be fifteen psychiatrists standing by, and it wouldn't make a difference. The chances of changing a budding psychopathic individual are slim."

Grisham asked, "Do people with psychopathic traits often fool professionals?"

Myers responded, "Yes, they represent themselves as charming and behave within the rules for months."

Once again one of the most anticipated and observed persons at trial was Cody Posey himself. In a neatly pressed green shirt and tan pants, he sat beside Gary Mitchell and smiled briefly at his lawyer. Then he began in a low, regular voice, "Before I start, I'd like to give thanks to all who have stood by me. Thank you to the Lincoln County Sheriff's Office, and the staff at Sequoyah and Bernalillo. Love, to my friends and family who have stood by me. Thanks to people—I never knew there were so many out there.

"I have been haunted by the actions I took. I know it wasn't right. I try to think of my family and the good times. I have never known emotions. I don't know how to express them, but I do have treatment plans and goals. One of my goals is anger management. At Sequoyah they've taught me how to handle my anger.

"I need to work on problem solving. I can tell you right now, I will never kill again. I am confident I can become a model citizen. I now know that children can go to teachers or friends in times of need. I want to be an advocate for abused children. I want to help people. I've got people from around the world—people that want to adopt me. I'm not as smart as I want to be. I want to get a high-school diploma. I have college goals. I'd like to study computer science and get a law degree. I would like to send out an apology to everyone I have hurt. I'd like to say I'm sorry."

Two things were quite evident as Cody spoke. One

was that he was right on one score, he didn't know how to express emotions. Even as he spoke about emotional events, there were no tears in his eyes, no raising and lowering of his voice. It was all very flat and featureless. And for those who were there, depending on how they felt about him, it seemed to them that he either was a psychopath devoid of empathy, or that his emotions had been beaten out of him by a monstrous pair of abusers long ago.

The second thing that came as a shock to many was that this person, Cody A. Posey, was still only a boy. He was sixteen years old as he stood by his lawyer. He should have been thinking about the junior prom or basketball games. Instead, he was thinking about the possibility of life behind bars.

Both Sandra Grisham and Gary Mitchell had their last words, and this time they were not trying to convince a jury, they were trying to convince Judge Waylon Counts. Two questions were paramount now: Was Cody Posey amenable to treatment? And if so, was there an adequate juvenile facility in New Mexico where he could receive such treatment? It was not a moot point that Cody could be amenable for treatment—but if Judge Counts decided there was no such place in New Mexico, then by law Cody would have to be sent to an adult place of incarceration. Public safety was paramount.

Grisham began by saying, "On July 5, 2004, Cody Posey thought he could get away with murder." She added that he reloaded the gun to make sure he'd take care of anyone else who unexpectedly arrived on the scene. Grisham touched upon the politics of the outpouring of sympathy for Cody in the press, and quoted

Thomas Jefferson, "Nothing is politically right, that is morally wrong."

Grisham said that the guidelines of the children's law code and not public opinion had to be the defining guide in this matter. She reiterated that Cody knew no one else would be on the ranch that day and chose it as the time and place to murder his family. She said his actions were "cold, calculated and deliberate."

Then she claimed, "We can't fix everybody. The best predictor of future history is past history. Cody had no right to be judge, jury, and executioner." Grisham said that she had been before the court many times asking a judge to give a child one more chance. But in this case Grisham said, "Cody does not have a treatable disorder. Cody Posey is a cold-hearted killer. The state is asking that you impose the maximum sentence for Cody Posey as an adult."

Gary Mitchell on the other hand said to Judge Counts, "A child came before this court at the age of fourteen. The question here is amenability to treatment." Mitchell emphasized that there was no public outcry to put Cody behind bars for life. In fact, just the opposite was true. He said the overwhelming response in the area was to have Cody treated as a child and sent to a safe place where he could be treated fairly. "Cody is amenable to treatment. Sequoyah wants him back. Sequoyah knows they can cure him."

Mitchell said that he was embarrassed as a New Mexican to hear some say that Cody had to be imprisoned just because the legislature had not given enough money to children's facilities to make them safe. He noted that Cody was still a child, and that society never gave up on children. "Children need our love and compassion. I ask